DOCUMENTS OF MODERN HISTORY

General Editor:

A.G. Dickens

Octobrists to Bolsheviks Imperial Russia 1905–1917

Martin McCauley

Assisted by Peter Waldron

EDWARD ARNOLD

© Martin McCauley 1984

First published in Great Britain 1984 by
Edward Arnold (Publishers) Ltd, 41 Bedford Square, London WC1B 3DQ

Edward Arnold (Australia) Pty Ltd, 80 Waverley Road, Caulfield East,
Victoria 3145, Australia

Edward Arnold, 300 North Charles Street, Baltimore, Maryland 21201,
U.S.A.

British Library Cataloguing in Publication Data

McCauley, Martin
 Octobrists to Bolsheviks.—(Documents of modern history)
 1. Soviet Union—Politics and government—1894–1917
 I. Title   II. Waldron, Peter   III. Series
 320.947   JN6524

ISBN 0–7131–6403–4

Text set in 10/11 pt Baskerville Compugraphic by Colset Private Limited,
Singapore
Printed and bound in Great Britain by Richard Clay (The Chaucer Press) Ltd,
Bungay, Suffolk

Contents

Acknowledgements

A number of friends and colleagues have suggested documentary material for inclusion in this selection. I am grateful to Chai Lieven for his help and advice about documents to be included in the section on foreign policy. My greatest debt of gratitude is to Olga Crisp whose incomparable knowledge of Russian social and economic development was generously shared and the sections on the economy and social development have benefited from her valuable suggestions. Peter Waldron was of enormous assistance as well as translating extracts from Russian, French and German. The shortcomings of this volume are entirely my responsibility.

Every effort has been made to trace the owners of copyright and if copyright has been infringed it has been done unintentionally. My thanks, and those of the Publishers, are due to the following for permission to reproduce copyright material:

Martin McCauley

The publishers would like to thank the following for permission to include copyright material:

The Athlone Press and Charles Scribner's Sons for R.F. Christian (ed.) © 1978 R.F. Christian; E.J. Brill for E. Amburger; Cambridge University Press for P. Mathias and M.M. Pastan (eds.); Carnegie Endowment for International Peace for Polner *et al.*; Gronsky and Astrov; Kayden and Antsiferov; and Antsiferov *et al.*; Armond Colin Editeur for R. Girault; Columbia University Press for J.S. Curtiss; the Harvester Press Ltd, and Indiana University Press for A. Bely, translated by R.A. Maguire and J.E. Malmstad; Harvill Press for Boris Pasternak and M. Buljakov; Indiana University Press for H.O. Mehlinger and J.M. Thompson; Macmillan, London and Basingstoke for Olga Crisp; A.D. Peters Ltd for N. Khrushchev; Prentice-Hall Inc. for Michael Cherniavsky © 1967 pp. 226–7, reprinted by permission, and F.A. Golder; Princeton University Press for Allan K. Wildman © 1980; *Slavic Review* for Leopold Haimson; *The Slavonic and East European Review* vol. 39 no. 93, 1961, pp. 509–10 for Olga Crisp, translated from the original French 'The Russian Liberals and the 1906 Anglo-French loan to Russia', © University of London, reprinted by permission; Stanford University Press for Alexander Vucinich © 1970 reprinted by permission of the Board of Trustees of the Leland Stanford Junior University; University of Toronto Press for R.C. Elwood © 1974 reprinted by permission and VAAP for the numerous works published in Russian and not previously translated.

The Russian Empire

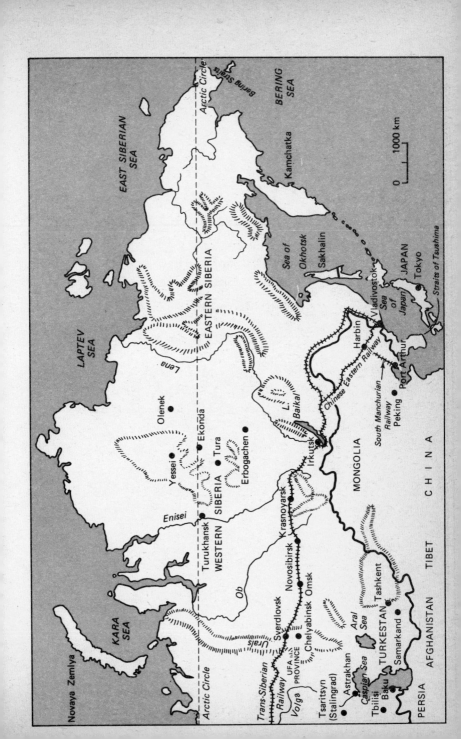

Glossary

desyatina	Measure of land; 1.09 ha or 2.7 acres
guberniya	Administrative province
pood (pud)	36.1 lb or 16.38 kilograms
ty	The familiar form of address; second person singular; thou
verst	0.7 mile or 1.06 km
uezd	Administrative area, subdivision of *guberniya* or province
volost	Administrative area, subdivision of uezd
zemstvo	Pre-revolutionary *uezd* or *guberniya* assembly and organ of local government

Unless otherwise stated all dates are Old Style (Julian Calendar). To obtain New Style dates (Gregorian Calendar) add 13 days.

Introduction

The sheer size of Imperial Russia impressed friend and foe alike. The largest country in the world from the sixteenth century onwards, although it was backward by West European standards, it was always regarded as one of the countries of the future. Russophobia surfaced in Britain about the middle of the nineteenth century and in July 1914 the German Chancellor, Bethmann Hollweg, saw the growing power of Russia as a 'nightmare'. However Russia's weaknesses outweighed her strengths. The system of government was autocratic. Power was centralized in St Petersburg (Petrograd–Leningrad) – on the periphery of the state. Communications were always a problem with such a vast terrain but no less so than communication between Russians and non-Russians. The authorities were dismayed to discover that only just under 45 per cent of the population declared themselves Russian in the 1897 census. Afterwards Russification was attempted in order to try to hold in check the growing national consciousness of the many non-Russian peoples. Baltic Germans and Finns played an important role in the government administration and the army; Jews – restricted to certain areas – were keen to deploy their commercial and other skills; Muslims had a well-knit social system; most Ukrainians saw themselves as different from Russians, and so on. How was St Petersburg to keep such an empire together on a shoestring budget? If any power was devolved would it not lead to local autonomy and even eventually to federalism? Russians could lose their dominating role in their own empire.

Given the size of the country and the population the bureaucracy was small and this meant that it could not deal very efficiently with the enormous burden of work placed upon it. There were enlightened bureaucrats but the dead hand of tradition and inertia worked against them. War turned out to be the midwife of change and the modern Russian state emerged after the shock of defeat in the Crimean War. Russia had to become more like the advanced countries of Europe or risk becoming subservient to them. It was a police state but too poor to realize all the objectives of such a state.

Economic development got under way in the 1880s and 1890s with railway construction playing a special role. Sergei Witte, Minister of Finance from 1892 to 1903, put Russia on the gold standard in 1897 and this helped to increase the inflow of foreign investment. With foreign money came foreign ideas and mores. The Tsar, Nicholas II, found himself in a quandary. The modernization of Russia would undermine his power but repression would slow down the growth of the economy, thus weakening Russia internationally.

The economic boom in Russia tailed off at the turn of the century as it did in Europe as a whole. Strikes hit the oil industry in Baku and other industries in the south in 1902-3. Textile workers also struck in large numbers in 1903. The quiescence of the peasantry after Emancipation was broken by events in Poltava province and in other localities in 1902. The slump seems to have affected consumer goods industries which supplied the peasant market to a much lesser extent than heavy industry which was financed by state and foreign investment.

Political parties made their appearance too – all illegal, of course, before 1905. The first to form was the All-Russian Social Democratic Workers' Party (RSDRP) in 1898 at Minsk. The delegates to the founding congress were soon arrested, so it was the second congress, in Brussels and London, in 1903 which had the greater impact. The party split into Bolsheviks (majoritarians) and Mensheviks (minoritarians). Liberation, the forerunner of the Constitutional Democratic Party, the Kadets, the main liberal party, came into being in Stuttgart in 1902. The social revolutionaries (SRs) emerged at the turn of the century and attempted to speak for the peasants. Since peasants made up about 80 per cent of the population and many of them were subsistence farmers there was enormous scope for political action. However the SRs could not agree among themselves on a programme of agrarian socialism and Viktor Chernov, their leader, was more given to theoretical writing than to political activism. The spiritual forefathers were the Populists and just as they divided over the use of terror for political ends, so did the SRs. The main Marxist party, the RSDRP, also had within its ranks some who viewed terrorism as a political weapon.

Intellectuals dominated the leadership of most political parties and this was most striking in the RSDRP. One of the reasons for this latter phenomenon was that a Marxist party, speaking for the working class, came into being before trades unions in Russia. The latter provided many of the leaders of social democratic parties in the rest of Europe.

Provocative Russian behaviour in the Far East led to Japan attacking Port Arthur in early 1904. War with Japan had not been consciously planned in St Petersburg. It was a direct result of the behaviour of the governor general and the army on the spot. Instead of winning easily, Russia was humiliated. Not only was the army beaten but the Russian navy was sunk in the Straits of Tsushima. Witte skilfully negotiated an advantageous peace (1) given the nature of the defeat and the usual custom of exacting indemnity.

The Russian defeats had a tremendous effect on the population at a time when the economic situation was becoming critical. On Sunday 9 January 1905 a crowd of workmen and their families, led by the Orthodox priest Father Gapon, converged on the Winter Palace in St Petersburg to petition the Tsar to provide aid to survive the harsh winter. The soldiers fired and 'Bloody Sunday' made an indelible mark on Mother Russia (2). The myth of the benevolent Tsar was exploded.

With political and social upheaval at home and the Russian army suffering defeat in the Far East, the Tsar had to give way and issued the October Manifesto (3). A Duma was promised, political parties and trades unions became legal and the survival of the monarchy was in doubt. A constitution emerged – the October Manifesto (3) and the Fundamental Laws (9) – and gradually the situation stabilized. The army on the whole stayed loyal and was used to crush unrest. The Kadets decided that they had more to lose than to gain from revolution since they feared that if the monarchy were swept away primitive anarchy would prevail.

The government was weakened during the last months of 1905 and the beginning of 1906 when soviets appeared in several cities and there was an uprising in Moscow.

The authority of the Duma was undermined before it met. A State Council, a second chamber, was set up (8) with half its members state officials. Also Witte negotiated a French loan which saved Russia from insolvency and the suspension of the gold standard. It also afforded the regime flexibility vis-à-vis the Duma though the Kadets probably exaggerated the importance of the loan in this respect (112). Witte referred to the parliamentary system as the 'great illusion of our century' but as a pragmatist he was willing to accept it if it made the country more manageable. However he was dropped as Prime Minister before he had a chance to oppose the Duma.

Elections to the First Duma (**4**) were held in April 1906 and produced a liberal parliament (**5**), quite unacceptable to the government (**20**). The government dissolved the Duma (**22**), called fresh elections but the Second Duma turned out to be just as unpalatable (**5**). The new Prime Minister, Stolypin, was determined to confront terrorism (**24, 25**). The only way to secure a docile Duma was to change the electoral law and this was done on 3 June 1907 (**27**). This duly produced a conservative Duma (**5**). Stolypin's *coup d'etat* ushered in the 'monarchy of 3 June' and signalled the desire of the government to claw back every concession it had been forced to disgorge. Like Witte, Stolypin was no believer in constitutional government and saw the Duma as a barrier to strong and effective rule if not kept under control. The coup of 3 June was staged by misapplying article 87 of the Fundamental Laws (**9**). By then the revolution of 1905–7 had subsided with the periodic waves of strikes and peasant uprisings never lasting long enough to undermine the state. The railwaymen did not strike and obligingly transported the army back to European Russia to quell trouble there. The Kadets feared anarchy more than monarchy and anyway faced with a resolute Stolypin – who refused to make concessions – there was little they could do. They did call for civil disobedience and a tax strike after the dissolution of the First Duma but all who signed the Vyborg Manifesto (**23**), if arrested and imprisoned were banned from subsequent Dumas.

The Third and Fourth Dumas had fewer members than the First and Second (**5**). Whereas the former had been elected by almost universal suffrage, the latter was heavily weighted in favour of men of property. With a few social democrats on the left, the Third and Fourth Dumas had a natural centre-right majority. The extreme right was well represented and varied from nationalists (**18**) to the Union of the Russian People (**19**), an openly anti-Semitic party. Extreme nationalists were referred to as Black Hundreds. Many of the anti-Semitic pogroms were instituted by this grouping (**149**). The Octobrists, led by the Moscow industrialist Aleksandr Guchkov, were moderate conservatives (**17**).

Stolypin, as befits someone who wanted to break the mould of incompetent, effete ministers, was found to be abrasive and his dynamism was ill-received. Since the government was neither appointed by nor responsible to the Duma but the Tsar, Stolypin had to maintain his contacts with the court and the establishment. There were constant intrigues against him and he was never popular with the Tsar. He might have worked with the liberals in the Duma but they could not overcome their suspicions about his motives. Anyway they were very concerned about their contacts with the left. Stolypin was assassinated, in circumstances which have still to be clarified, in September 1911 and was succeeded by the able bureaucrat Kokovtsov (**30**). He was likewise unable to put most of his ideas into effect. He suffered from the fact that the business community consistently compared him unfavourably with Stolypin. Nevertheless Russia was gradually moving towards a cabinet-style government.

One of Stolypin's many critics put his strictures down on paper (**28**). The reason why so little legislation was passed had more to do with the right-wing majority in the State Council than with Stolypin's lack of drive. Nevertheless he did attempt to solve the almost insoluble, the agrarian question. The population explosion in Russia had undermined still further the provisions of the Emancipation Act of 1861. It doubled during the second half of the nineteenth century and had reached 132.9 millions in 1900. By 1910 it had risen to 160.7 millions (**87**). Russian cereal production kept ahead of population growth but yields were poor by international standards. Whereas wheat yields were 45 poods per desyatina, they were 146 in Great Britain and Germany. Rye, the staple grain in the north, recorded 54 poods per desyatina but in France and the USA yields were 68 poods (**95**). An added problem was that north and northwest Russia were food deficit zones. At Emancipation the peasants were tied to the commune or *obshchina* and there was collective responsibility for redemption payments and taxes. Stolypin's legislation in November 1906 (**96**) and supplementary legislation in 1910 and 1911 permitted the peasant to leave the commune and consolidate his holdings in a single farm. He could continue to live in the village or move out to his farm. Redemption payments were officially abolished as of 1 January 1907 but in reality had long ceased to be paid in full. Stolypin's land reform was motivated by political as well as economic considerations. Lenin saw the danger (**97**) but Octobrists and Kadets considered it a move in the right direction (**98**, **99**). Stolypin's legislation also permitted migration (**102**, **103**). He once asked for 20 years of peace to effect his policy but this was denied him. By May 1915 only 14 per cent of communal allotment land had passed into private consolidated ownership (**100**). During the war these farmers tended to come back into the village or be dragged back in. Peasant landholding, however, expanded rapidly at the expense of noble estates. Violence or the threat of violence helped this process. In some provinces peasants owned practically all the arable land. By 1916, about 90 per cent of the sown area in Russia was in peasant hands. There was vigorous buying and selling of land in Voronezh province, for example (**117, 118**). It is instructive that 37 per cent of the land bought was purchased by landless peasants whereas farmers with 20 desyatinas and more only acquired about 4 per cent (**118**). This would tend to support the conclusions of those scholars, such as Shanin, who point out that there is no evidence for the tendency to concentrate land in fewer and fewer hands, rather there was cyclical change tied to the biological rhythm of the family. The big or well-to-do peasant was simply one with a large family while a middle farmer was one with a smaller family. Over time they could change places but even at one and the same time there was no clear dividing line between rich and poor peasants. A rich peasant's son could hire himself out to a poor peasant while another poor peasant might let his land and work in a factory. This reveals the enormous difficulty facing any policy trying to solve the agrarian conundrum. Stolypin's policy of fostering prosperous peasant farming was likely to have only moderate success in Russia in the short term. There was every likelihood that it would succeed in the long term though it is very doubtful if 20 years would have been sufficient. It required fast growth in the rest of the economy to siphon off surplus rural labour as well as changed attitudes and a higher cultural level among the peasantry.

Was Russia heading for revolution by 1914? The booming economy of 1909–13 inevitably favoured some segments of society rather than others. Economic expansion permitted the government to increase army and navy expenditure rapidly and it had no difficulties with the Duma on this score since it was also of the view that it was in the national interest. The gulf between the autocracy and the educated widened. A parallel phenomenon was also observable, the gap between the working class and the privileged and educated (**35**). In this climate a mystique of revolution, especially in the world of culture, developed. Only the Vekhi group doubted whether revolution was good *per se* (**147**). Post-revolutionary Russia might be even more frightful than under the Tsar, they hinted. The Vekhi group touched a raw nerve since every self-respecting *intelligent* had to support revolution and oppose the Imperial system. There was no half-way house. Among the industrialists there were those, like Guchkov, who scented danger (**33**). Moderate conservatives were taken aback by the refusal of the government to take even their wishes into consideration. Hence the support base of the autocratic regime was very narrow in 1914. Had war not intervened the confrontation between the authorities and the rest of the population would possibly have come sooner than 1917. The Tsar had a choice, respond to the aspirations of educated society, and thereby gradually introduce constitutional government, or continue to sail against the winds of change. The latter course would almost certainly produce a violent confrontation sooner or later. Modernization and economic development simply demanded a more efficient government. A democratic government was not preordained, however, since this century had revealed several examples of undemocratic regimes industrializing successfully. Given the fact that the Tsar had dropped Witte and Stolypin, men who could have spearheaded modernization without democratization, it was highly unlikely that the monarch would create and efficient administration. On the other hand a form of military dictatorship was possible. Revolution meant different things to different people. Artists and writers wanted the freedom to do their own thing, for example. If revolution is taken to mean that the Tsar would have to concede much of his power to an elected parliament and educated society then revolution was inevitable by 1914. If revolution means the Bolshevik seizure of power then revolution was not inevitable by 1914.

Was Nicholas II aware of the grave weaknesses of autocracy in 1914? It would not appear so. He was determined to follow the European trend of building up military power and planned a huge army and navy, irrespective of the burden on the economy. Given Russia's alliance with Britain and France this could only mean contemplating war with Imperial Germany. Durnovo regarded such a policy as folly and saw Germany as a natural ally (**86**). Witte, who had opposed military adventurism in the Far East in 1904, was also opposed to the Tsar's policy since he was well aware of the enormous strains such a policy imposed on the nation's economy. The Russian Minister of War and the Chief of the General Staff had an exaggerated opinion of Russia's military power, even believing that Russia could defeat Germany on her own (**79**).

Russia's war began with an advance into East Prussia, in response to French calls for help in their battle to save Paris. On 15 August 1914 two Russian armies moved forward but on 30 August disaster struck at Tannenberg (**37**, **38**). Progress against the Austro-Hungarians was more encouraging (**37**). When confronted only by them the Russians coped quite well but when the Germans came up as reinforcements, as in May 1915, the tables were turned. In this instance the Russians were simply driven out of central Poland. The Minister of War was changed and the new man, General Polivanov, painted a gloomy picture (**40**), with the German army having an 'inexhaustible' supply of shells. Russia was able to produce only one million rounds a month in September 1915 but increased this to four million a month later – against the Germans' seven million and the Austro-Hungarians' one million a month. The Russian situation was not improved by Nicholas taking over as Commander-in-Chief (**41**, **42**).

Defeats at the front had repercussions at home. A Progressive Bloc was set up in the Duma and it advocated a government of national salvation, one which would be efficient and enjoy wide public support. This would involve introducing many concessions (**43**). The Tsar was uninterested and had no desire to surrender any of his prerogatives. Since some of his ministers were in sympathy with the goals of the Progressive Bloc he adjourned the Duma in September 1915. The Tsar's decision caused consternation in the Council of Ministers (**44**). With the monarch at Staff Headquarters at Mogilev, the Tsarina attempted to fill the gap in Petrograd. Rasputin added to her unpopularity (**45**).

Government bureaucracy was quite unable to cope with the added burden of war so other agencies sprang into being to fill the gap – the Union of Towns (**46**) and Zemgor (**47**) – and they performed very creditably. Russian industry took it upon itself to establish a War Industries Committee in June 1915 (**48**). The regime's reaction to all this initiative was one of reserve since it was aware that its critics had considerable administrative skills and their organizations could develop into an alternative government.

Russia's military situation improved in June 1916 when General Brusilov launched a successful attack against the Austro-Hungarians (**50**, **51**) and Romania entered the war on the Allied side in August. However the Germans came to the rescue and drove the Russians back and had occupied most of Romania by the end of 1916. The production of war matériel improved and it was quite respectable in 1916 but still insufficient to meet demand. One solution proffered was to appoint a military dictator who would act as a master coordinator (**53**).

As difficulties mounted the Tsar dismissed his more competent ministers and chose very conservative men to replace them – they could be guaranteed not to disagree with him and the Tsarina. This made the new Prime Minister, Sturmer – a Russian with a German name was a politically and psychologically ill-advised choice – even more suspicious of the Progressive Bloc (**52**). The latter, in turn, became very frustrated with the government's refusal to treat it seriously. Milyukov, the Kadet leader, treated the government with contempt in his startling speech on 1 November 1916 (**54**). Police reports confirm how critical the internal situation was at that time (**55**).

The February Revolution came as a surprise to everyone but the collapse of the autocracy surprised very few. Whereas the army had stayed loyal in 1905 and saved the regime, this time it changed sides and doomed the Romanov dynasty to oblivion. The regime enjoyed practically no support among educated society and in the country at large. The Provisional Government, so called since it was filling in until the Constituent Assembly met, enjoyed widespread support, from the left to the right (**56, 57, 58, 59, 60**). The effect on the army was summed up by a perceptive junior officer (**62**). Had men like him been in command the situation would have been different but the old mentality lived on in most officers. Tension mounted (**65, 66**).

The Provisional Government represented the educated, the soviets the masses. This was how the average man and woman in the street viewed things and they were not far wrong. The moderate socialists who dominated the leadership of the soviets did not want to seize power. The SRs because the Constituent Assembly would confirm them as the leading party and the Mensheviks because as Marxists they regarded Russia as underdeveloped and hence in need of more capitalism. This situation would have continued until the convocation of the Constituent Assembly had it not been for Lenin. He launched the slogan 'All Power to the Soviets' and thereby advocated a proletarian revolution in the near future (**67**). Lenin knew that if the Provisional Government could not rely on the instruments of coercion, the police and the military, it would only take a small armed force to topple it. The Bolshevik policy of peace and land promised to lead to the disintegration of the army – soldiers in uniform – and sweep the remaining gentry landowners off the map.

Although the army was in no condition to fight, Kerensky launched an offensive in June 1917 with predictable consequences (**68**). The Bolsheviks benefited most from the débâcle but the Petrograd soviet was still strong enough to ban a Bolshevik march (**69**). The government accused Lenin of being a German agent to boot and neatly turned the tables on the Bolsheviks. The latter saw their fortunes changed dramatically in August when General Kornilov, the Supreme Commander-in-Chief, attempted to move troops to Petrograd. He believed he had a mandate from Kerensky, the Prime

Minister, but the latter denied all knowledge of it (**70**). This erased any legitimacy the Provisional Government possessed and Russia went into a period of limbo until the Constituent Assembly was elected and convened. It was during this period that the Bolsheviks staged their insurrection. It was carried out in the name of the soviets since the Bolsheviks had a majority in the Petrograd soviet and in many other cities. The army was also decidedly pro-Bolshevik. The October Revolution was a Soviet Revolution (**72**).

I   Politics between the Revolution of 1905–1907 and the Outbreak of War in 1914

1   Peace Treaty between Russia and Japan, concluded at Portsmouth (New Hampshire) on 23 August 1905

1905 was a traumatic year for Russia. The Russo-Japanese war had broken out in February 1904 and had gone badly. Port Arthur surrendered in December 1904 and the Russian navy was destroyed at Tsushima in May 1905. Given the magnitude of Russia's defeat the peace treaty was quite lenient. Japan wished to improve relations with Russia.

I   Henceforth peace will prevail between Their Majesties the Emperors of Russia and Japan, and between their respective states and subjects.

II   The Russian Imperial government, recognizing that Japan has predominant political, military and economic interests in Korea, commits itself not to interfere in those measures of guidance, protection and supervision which the Japanese government considers necessary to take in Korea.

. . . .

V   The Russian Imperial government cedes to Japan, with the agreement of the Chinese government, the lease of Port Arthur, its surrounding area and territorial waters, as well as all rights, privileges and concessions attached to the lease.

. . . .

IX   The Russian Imperial government cedes to Japan in perpetuity the southern part of the island of Sakhalin.

> B.A. Romanov, *Ocherki diplomaticheskoy istorii Russko-Yaponskoy voyny, 1895–1907*, Moscow-Leningrad, 1947, p. 464.

2   Report of the head of the St Petersburg secret police, L.N. Kremenetsky, to A.A. Lopukhin, Director of the Department of Police, 9 January 1905

At home there was revolution. The events of Bloody Sunday (9 January 1905) led to a general strike in the capital, and the whole year was one of mutinies in the armed forces, strikes in the towns and peasant disturbances in the countryside.

Today, at about 10 a.m., workers began to gather at the Narva Gates, in the Vyborg and Petersburg districts, and also on Vasilievsky Island at the premises of the Assembly of Factory Workers, with the aim, as announced by Father Georgy Gapon, of marching to Palace Square to present a petition to the Emperor. When a crowd of several thousand had assembled in the Narva district, Father Gapon said prayers and then together with the crowd, which had at its head banners and icons stolen from a Narva chapel as well as portraits of Their Majesties, moved off towards the Narva Gates where they were confronted by troops. Despite pleas by local police officers and cavalry charges, the crowd did not disperse but continued to advance. . . . Two companies then opened fire, killing ten and wounding twenty. . . .

A little later about 4,000 workers who had come from the Petersburg and Vyborg districts approached the Trinity Bridge: Father Gapon was also with them. A volley was fired into the crowd, killing five and seriously injuring ten. . . .

Towards 1 p.m. people began to gather in the Alexander Garden, over-flowing out of the garden itself into the adjoining part of Palace Square. The cavalry made a series of charges to disperse the crowd, but as this had no effect a number of volleys were fired into the crowd. The numbers of dead and wounded from these volleys is not known as the crowd carried off the victims.

The crowd then engulfed Nevsky Prospect and refused to disperse: a number of shots were fired, killing sixteen people, including one woman. . . .

In the evening a large crowd assembled on Vasilievsky Island and began to build barricades in the streets. . . . It was fired on . . . and two people were killed.

. . .In all some seventy-five people were killed and 200 wounded. It appears that among the dead are numbered women and children.

N.S. Trusova (ed.), *Nachalo pervoy Russkoy revolyutsii*. Moscow, 1935, p. 52

(On 23 January 1905 *Pravitelstvenny Vestnik* (Government Courier) reported 130 dead and an estimated 450 wounded as a result of the events of Bloody Sunday.)

3   Manifesto of 17 October 1905

In August 1905 the government conceded the establishment of a Consultative Legislative Assembly: the Duma. However unrest continued: most of the 3,300 peasant disturbances in 1905 took place during the last quarter of the year and in October 1905 the government was forced to agree to the establishment of a Duma with real legislative powers.

On the improvement of order in the state

The disturbances and unrest in St Petersburg, Moscow and in many other parts of our Empire have filled Our heart with great and profound sorrow. The welfare of the Russian Sovereign and His people is inseparable and national sorrow is His too. The present disturbances could give rise to national instability and present a threat to the unity of Our State.

The oath which We took as Tsar compels Us to use all Our strength, intelligence and power to put a speedy end to this unrest which is so dangerous for the State. The relevant authorities have been ordered to take measures to deal with direct outbreaks of disorder and violence and to protect people who only want to go about their daily business in peace. However, in view of the need to speedily implement earlier measures to pacify the country, we have decided that the work of the government must be unified.

We have therefore ordered the government to take the following measures in fulfilment of our unbending will:

1   Fundamental civil freedoms will be granted to the population, including real personal inviolability, freedom of conscience, speech, assembly and association.
2   Participation in the Duma will be granted to those classes of the population which are at present deprived of voting powers, insofar as is possible in the short period before the convocation of the Duma, and this will lead to the development of a universal

franchise. There will be no delay to the Duma elections which have already been organized.

3 It is established as an unshakeable rule that no law can come into force without its approval by the State Duma and that the elected representatives of the people will be given the opportunity to play a real part in the supervision of the legality of the activities of government bodies.

We call on all true sons of Russia to remember their duty to their homeland, to help put a stop to this unprecedented unrest and, together with this, to devote all their strength to the restoration of peace to their native land.

Nicholas

Polnoe Sobranie Zakonov Ros-siyskoy Imperii, 3rd ed., vol. XXV/I, no. 26803.

4   The Electoral System for the First Duma

H.D. Mehlinger and J.M. Thompson, *Count Witte and the Tsarist Government in the 1905 Revolution*. Blooming-ton, Ind., 1972, p. 244.

5   Duma Deputies by Party 1906–1912

These lists were drawn up at the first session of the Duma and were based on the declarations of Duma members. However during the life of the Duma many members crossed the floor so that there was constant flux as regards party affiliation. The nature of the parties themselves could change just as easily. The Nationalist Party emerged as a force during 1909; whilst the Progressists were born out of the Party of Peaceful Renewal at the beginning of the Third Duma. The Bolsheviks boycotted the First and Second Dumas but took part in the elections to the Third Duma. Technically the SRs boy-cotted the First Duma but 34 members declared themselves to be SRs. The number of deputies in the First Duma increased to 486. In the Second Duma some of the members of the National parties were Mensheviks; if these are added, the number of Social Democrats increases to 65.

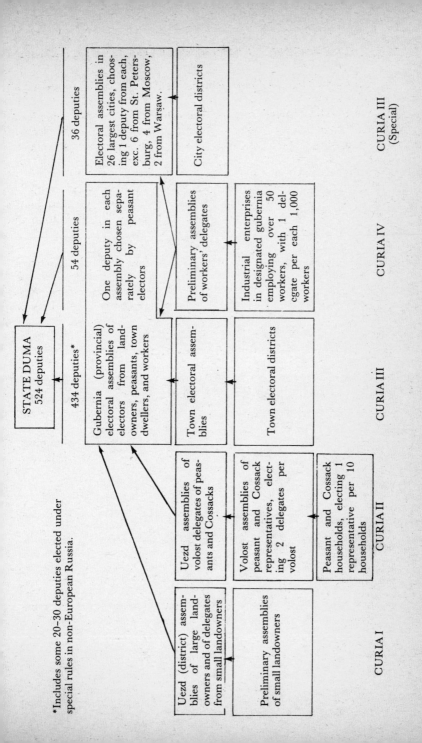

STATE DUMA
524 deputies

*Includes some 20–30 deputies elected under special rules in non-European Russia.

36 deputies

Electoral assemblies in 26 largest cities, choosing 1 deputy from each, exc. 6 from St. Petersburg, 4 from Moscow, 2 from Warsaw.

City electoral districts

CURIA III
(Special)

54 deputies

One deputy in each assembly chosen separately by peasant electors

Preliminary assemblies of workers' delegates

Industrial enterprises in designated gubernia employing over 50 workers, with 1 delegate per each 1,000 workers

CURIA IV

434 deputies*

Gubernia (provincial) electoral assemblies of electors from landowners, peasants, town dwellers, and workers

Town electoral assemblies

Town electoral districts

CURIA III

Uezd assemblies of volost delegates of peasants and Cossacks

Volost assemblies of peasant and Cossack representatives, electing 2 delegates per volost

Peasant and Cossack households, electing 1 representative per 10 households

CURIA II

Uezd (district) assemblies of large landowners and of delegates from small landowners

Preliminary assemblies of small landowners

CURIA I

First Duma 27 April 1906–8 July 1906

Social Democrats – Mensheviks	18
Social Revolutionaries (SRs)	34
Trudoviki	102
Kadets	182
Peaceful Renewal party	26
Octobrists	17
Trade and Industry group	1
Rightists	8
National parties	60
	448

Second Duma 20 Feburary 1907–2 June 1907

Social Democrats – Mensheviks	47
Social Revolutionaries (SRs)	37
Popular Socialists	16
Trudoviki	104
Peaceful Renewal party	28
Kadets	91
Octobrists	42
Rightists	10
National parties	93
Non-party	50
	518

Third Duma 1 November 1907–9 June 1912

Social Democrats – Bolsheviks	19
Trudoviki	13
Kadets	54
Octobrists	154
Progressists	28
Moderate Right & Nationalists	97
Extreme Right	50
National parties	26
	441

Fourth Duma 15 November 1912–25 February 1917

Social Democrats – Bolsheviks	15
Trudoviki	10
Kadets	53
Octobrists	95
Progressists	41
Centre	31
Nationalists (Nationalist Party)	91
Right	63
National parties	22
Non-party	11
	432

Gosudarstvennaya Duma,
*Ukazateli k stenograficheskim
otchetam*. St Petersburg,
1906–12, *passim*.

(A Progressive Bloc was formed in August 1914 and comprised an estimated 300 of the 432 deputies in the Fourth Duma. R. Pearson, *The Moderates in the Russian Revolution*, London, p. 53.)

6   Manifesto of 19 October 1905

Before 1905 Russia lacked any sort of cabinet institution: although both a Committee of Ministers and a Council of Ministers existed, they met infrequently, and together with the State Council, could only tender advice to the Tsar. Following the establishment of a legislative Duma, major changes were made to this structure: the State Council was reformed as a second legislative chamber, intended to provide a conservative counterweight to the expected critical Duma, whilst the Council of Ministers was established as a government coordinating body, but as individual ministers still retained their independence, the Council could not function as a Western-style cabinet.

Measures to strengthen the unified activity of the government

 . . .in view of the necessity to increase the unity of the ministerial structure, bearing in mind the new duties which will fall upon ministries with the creation of the State Duma, We have recognized the need for the following measures. . . .
1   The Council of Ministers is to direct and coordinate the work of the ministries, both in terms of legislation and of administration.
. . . .
3   The council of Ministers is to be under the chairmanship of a minister selected by the Tsar, or of any individual whom the Tsar appoints.
. . . .
8   The Chairman of the Council of Ministers is empowered to request necessary information and explanations from individual ministers.
. . . .
13   No decision of general significance may be taken by an individual minister without the knowledge of the Council of Ministers. . . . The Chairman of the Council of Ministers obtains information

from ministers about all prominent events, measures and regulations relevant to national life. If the Chairman considers it necessary, such measures are referred to the Council of Ministers for discussion.

. . . .

16 If the Council of Ministers does not come to unanimous agreement on a matter, it is to be referred to the Tsar for his decision.

. . . .

17 Ministers are to inform the Chairman of the Council of Ministers of the content of all their reports to the Tsar which are of general significance or concern other ministries. These reports are to be examined by the Council of Ministers . . . or may be made direct to the Tsar in the presence of the Chairman of the Council of Ministers.

Nicholas

Polnoe   Sobranie   Zakonov Rossiyskoy Imperii, 3rd ed., vol. XXV/I, no. 26820.

7   Government Ministers 1905–1917

Government ministers could be appointed and dismissed by the Tsar at will; the post of Chairman of the Council of Ministers gave its occupant few of the powers of a British Prime Minister. The position of Ober-Procurator of the Holy Synod was akin to that of 'Minister for the Church'. The Holy Synod had been established by Peter the Great as a government department to administer the Orthodox Church.

Chairman of the Council of Ministers

17.10.05–24.4.06	S. Yu. Witte
24.4.06–8.7.06	I.L. Goremykin
10.7.06–5.9.11	P.A. Stolypin
11.9.11–30.1.14	V.N. Kokovtsov
30.1.14–20.1.16	I.L. Goremykin
20.1.16–10.11.16	B.V. Sturmer
19.11.16–27.12.16	A.F. Trepov
27.12.16–27.2.17	N.D. Golytsin

Minister of the Interior

20.1.05–22.10.05	A.G. Bulygin
23.10.05–22.4.06	P.N. Durnovo
25.4.06–5.9.11	P.A. Stolypin
20.9.11–16.12.12	A.A. Makarov
26.12.12–5.7.15	N.A. Maklakov
5.7.15–26.9.15	N.B. Shcherbatov
27.9.15–3.3.16	A.N. Khvostov
3.3.16–7.7.16	B.V. Sturmer
7.7.16–16.9.16	A.N. Khvostov
18.9.16–27.2.17	A.D. Protopopov

Minister of Finance

28.3.04–24.10.05	V.N. Kokovtsov
24.10.05–22.4.06	I.P. Shipov
26.4.06–30.1.14	V.N. Kokovtsov
30.1.14–27.2.17	P.L. Bark

Minister of Justice

14.1.05–16.12.05	S.S. Manukhin
16.12.05–24.4.06	M.G. Akimov
24.4.06–6.7.15	I.G. Shcheglovitov
6.7.15–7.7.16	A.A. Khvostov
7.7.16–19.12.16	A.A. Makarov
20.12.16–27.2.17	N.A. Dobrovolsky

Minister of Foreign Affairs

25.7.00–28.4.06	V.N. Lambsdorf
28.4.06–14.9.10	A.P. Izvolsky
14.9.10–7.7.16	S.D. Sazonov
7.7.16–10.11.16	B.V. Sturmer
30.11.16–27.2.17	N.N. Pokrovsky

Minister of War

21.6.05–11.3.09	A.F. Rediger
11.3.09–13.6.15	V.A. Sukhomlinov
13.6.15–15.3.16	A.A. Polivanov
15.3.16–3.1.17	D.S. Shuvaev
31.1.17–27.2.17	M.A. Belyaev

Minister of Education

17.10.05–22.4.06	I.I. Tolstoy
24.4.06–1.1.08	P.M. Kaufman
1.1.08–25.9.10	A.N. Shvarts
25.9.10–26.11.14	L.A. Kasso
19.8.14–9.1.15	V.O. Kazmin-Karavaev
9.1.15–27.12.16	P.N. Ignatev
28.12.16–27.2.17	N.K. Kulchisky

Minister of Trade and Industry

27.10.05–18.2.06	V.I. Timiryazev
18.2.06–24.4.06	M.M. Fedorov
25.4.06–10.7.06	A.A. Stoff
10.7.06–26.1.08	D.A. Filosofov
26.1.08–14.1.09	I.P. Shipov
14.1.09–5.11.09	V.I. Timiryazev
5.11.09–18.2.15	S.I. Timashev
18.2.15–27.2.17	V.N. Shakhovsky

Ober-Procurator of the Holy Synod

20.10.05–14.4.06	A.D. Obolensky
26.4.06–9.7.06	A.A. Shirinsky-Shikhmatov
27.6.06–5.2.09	P.P. Izvolsky
5.2.09–2.5.11	S.M. Lukyanov
2.5.11–4.7.15	V.K. Sabler
5.7.15–26.9.15	A.D. Samarin
1.10.15–7.8.16	A.N. Volzin
7.8.16–3.3.17	N.P. Raev

E. Amburger, *Geschichte der
Behördenorganisation Russlands
von Peter dem Grossen bis 1917.*
Leiden, 1966, *passim.*

8   The Statutes of the State Council, 23 February 1906

The Council had 196 members in its reformed composition.

1   The State Council is a state institution in which legislative
proposals are discussed. . . .

2   The State Council is composed of elected members and members
appointed by the Tsar.

3   The Chairman and Vice-Chairman of the State Council are

appointed annually by the Tsar from amongst the appointed members of the Council. . . .

6   Deputations to the State Council are prohibited, as are oral or written petitions.

9   The number of appointed members of the State Council should not exceed that of the elected members. . . .

12   Members of the State Council are to be elected: 1. from the clergy of the Russian Orthodox Church; 2. from provincial zemstvo assemblies; 3. from assemblies of the nobility; 4. from the Imperial Academy of Sciences and from the Imperial Russian Universities; 5. from the Moscow Council of Trade and Industry, local committees of trade and industry, Stock Exchange committees and merchants' guilds.

13   Six members are to be elected from the Orthodox clergy by the Holy Synod: three from the monastic and three from the parish clergy.

14   Each provincial zemstvo assembly will elect one State Council member.

15   Each elected provincial noble assembly will elect two electors. A conference of these electors will convene in St Petersburg and will elect eighteen of their number as State Council members.

16   The Academy of Sciences and each Imperial Russian University will elect three electors; the Academy from amongst the full academicians, and each university council from the full professors. These electors will then meet in St Petersburg and elect six of their number as State Council members.

17   The Council of Trade and Industry will elect four electors, two from trade and two from industry. Two electors will be elected from each of the Moscow, Ivanovo-Voznesensk, Kostroma and Lvov committees of trade and industry; four electors from each of the St Petersburg and Moscow Stock Exchange Committees and two from each of the seventeen local stock exchange committees. The Merchants' Guilds will each elect one elector. These electors will meet in St Petersburg to choose twelve of their number as State Council members.

18   The elected members of the State Council will serve for a term of nine years, with one third of them being re-elected every three years. . . .

20   Members of the State Council must: 1. be aged over forty; 2. have completed a course of secondary education or similar. . . .

36   The State Council may ask Ministers for explanations of matters

directly concerned with business under its consideration. Ministers may refuse to give such explanations for reasons of state security. . . .

44 The State Council may interpellate Ministers. . . .

47 Bills which have been approved by the Duma are passed to the State Council. . . .

48 Bills which are approved neither by the Duma nor the State Council are considered rejected.

49 In cases where the State Council does not reject a bill approved by the Duma, but feels it necessary to make amendments to it, the bill may either, by decision of the Council, be returned to the Duma, or else be passed to a special commission, made up of an equal number of members elected from the State Council and Duma.

N.I. Lazarevsky, *Zakono-datelnye akty perekhodnogo vremeni*. Moscow, 1909, pp. 958–69.

9   The Fundamental Laws of 23 April 1906

1 The Russian State is one and indivisible. . . .

3 The Russian language is the general language of the state, and its use is compulsory in the army, the navy and state and public institutions. . . .

4 Supreme Autocratic Power belongs to the emperor of all Russia. . . .

7 The sovereign emperor exercises power in conjunction with the State Council and the State Duma.

8 The sovereign emperor possesses the initiative in all legislative matters. The Fundamental Laws may be subject to revision in the State Council and State Duma only on His initiative.

9 The sovereign emperor ratifies the laws. No law can come into force without his approval. . . .

12 The sovereign emperor takes charge of all the external relations of the Russian State. He determines the direction of Russia's foreign policy. . . .

14 The sovereign emperor is the Commander-in-Chief of the Russian army and navy.

15 The sovereign emperor appoints and dismisses the Chairman of the Council of Ministers and individual Ministers. . . .

63 The emperor who holds the throne of all Russia cannot profess any religion save the Orthodox. . . .

65 In the administration of the church, the autocratic power acts through the intermediary of the Holy Governing Synod which it has institued.

66 All subjects of the Russian state who do not belong to the established church . . . as well as foreigners . . . residing in Russia, shall everywhere be free to profess their religion, and to worship in accordance with its ritual.

67 Freedom of religion is accorded, not only to Christians of foreign denominations, but also to Jews, Muslims and heathens. . . .

72 No one can be prosecuted for criminal offences except in the manner prescribed by law.

73 No one can be held under arrest except in cases prescribed by law. . . .

75 All dwellings are inviolable. No search or seizure may take place in a dwelling without the consent of the head of the household, except in cases and in a manner prescribed by law.

76 Every Russian subject has the right freely to choose his place of residence and occupation, to acquire and dispose of property, and to travel abroad without hindrance. Limitations of these rights are regulated by special laws.

77 Property is inviolable. Compulsory alienation of property, when such is necessary for the welfare of the state or the public, is permissible only on the basis of just and adequate compensation.

78 Russian subjects have the right to organize meetings for purposes that are not contrary to the laws, peacefully, and without weapons. . . .

79 Everyone may, within the limits of the law, express his ideas orally and in writing and may also disseminate them by means of the press or by other methods.

80 Russian subjects have the right to form societies and associations for purposes that are not in contravention of the laws. . . .

86 No new law can come into force without the approval of the State Council and State Duma and the ratification of the sovereign emperor.

87 If extraordinary circumstances require legislative action whilst the State Duma is in recess, the Council of Ministers may make recommendations direct to the sovereign emperor. Such a

measure may not, however, introduce changes in the Fundamental Laws, in the statutes of the State Council and State Duma or in the regulations governing elections to the Council and the Duma. Should such a measure not be introduced into the Duma as a bill within two months from the date of its next meeting . . . it loses force. . . .

98 The State Council and State Duma are summoned annually by edict of the sovereign emperor. . . .

106 The State Council and the State Duma possess equal legislative powers. . . .

108 The State Council and State Duma may . . . interpellate ministers . . . concerning actions taken by them, or by persons or agencies under their jurisdiction that are held to be illegal. . . .

123 The Chairman of the Council of Ministers and the Ministers . . . are responsible to the sovereign emperor for the general operation of the state administration. Each of them is individually responsible for his own actions and orders.

> *Svod Zakonov Rossiyskoy Imperii*, 3rd ed., vol. 1, pt. 1. St Petersburg, 1912, pp. 5–26

10 Official Petersburg

In this extract from Andrei Bely's famous novel about St Petersburg he paints a sardonic picture of bureaucratic life in the capital.

. . .the little old man was already ascending the staircase which was carpeted in red. As they ascended, his legs formed angles, which soothed his spirit: he loved symmetry.

Little old men came up to him: sidewhiskers, beards, bald spots, chins, and chests adorned with decorations. They guided the movements of our wheel of state. Standing grandly at the balustrade was a small gold-chested cluster who were discussing the fateful rotation of that wheel, until the Master of Ceremonies, staff in hand, requested them to line up.

Immediately after the levee, the little old men once more swarmed together by the columns of the balustrade. One sparkling swarm suddenly took form, and from it came a velvety beelike droning . . . When Count Witte, heroically proportioned, a shining blue ribbon across his chest, his hand passing through his grey hair, came up with studied casualness and squinted, he saw that it was Apollon Apollonovich who was droning on. Apollon Apollonovich interrupted his speech and with vague cordiality, but with cordiality all the same, extended his hand to the hand which had just signed the terms of a certain treaty. Count Witte bent over toward the head which came up to his shoulder, and cracked a joke. But his joke evoked no smile. The little old men did not smile at the joke either. And the small cluster melted away. Apollon Apollonovich descended the staircase with Witte. Above them descended the little old men; below them, a hook-nosed ambassador, a red-lipped little old man, oriental; amidst them, all gold, ramrod straight, descended the senator against the fiery background of the carpet that covered the staircase.

> A. Bely, *Petersburg*, trans-lated by R.A. Maguire and J.E. Malmstad. Brighton, 1978, p. 72.

11   Party Programmes: The Social Democratic Party

Political parties were only legalized by the manifesto of October 1905 although some had existed illegally before that (such as the Social Democratic Party) and others existed in embryo in the Union of Liberation and in the zemstvo movement. A full spectrum of political views developed, but only the Octobrist Party was committed to the new system as it stood; all other parties wanted to see further changes in the structure of government.

This document was agreed before the party split into Bolsheviks (majoritarians) and Mensheviks (minoritarians) and is mainly agitational: i.e. it is not a blueprint for action. It looks forward to the bourgeois revolution (when the middle classes would take power from the autocracy) and lists minimal demands which are to be made then. Lenin succeeded in having inserted some modest peasant demands. Nevertheless this represented the first incorporation of peasant demands in a European social democratic programme. The RSDRP was a Marxist party, as were all European social democratic parties before 1917.

Programme of the All-Russian Social Democratic Labour Party (RSDRP), 1 August 1903

. . .The Russian Social Democratic Labour Party sets as its immediate political task the overthrow of the tsarist autocracy and its replacement by a democratic republic whose constitution would guarantee:

1 The sovereignty of the people; i.e., the concentration of the

supreme power of the state in a unicameral legislative assembly composed of representatives of the people.

2 Universal, equal and direct suffrage for all citizens, male and female, who have reached the age of twenty; . . . a secret ballot in these elections. . . .

3 Broad local self-government; regional self-government for localities with special conditions of life or a particular make-up of the population.

4 Inviolability of person and dwelling.

5 Unrestricted freedom of conscience, speech, press and assembly; the right to strike and to form trade unions.

6 Freedom of movement and occupation.

7 Elimination of class privileges and the complete equality of all regardless of sex, religion, race or nationality.

8 The right of any person to obtain an education in their native language. . .; the use of the native language together with the state language in all local, public and state institutions.

9 National self-determination for all nations forming part of the state.

10 The right of every person through normal channels to prosecute before a jury any official.

11 The popular election of judges.

12 The replacement of the standing army by the general arming of the population (i.e. the formation of a people's militia).

13 Separation of church and state, and of school and church.

14 Free and compulsory general or vocational education for all children of both sexes up to the age of sixteen; provision by the state of food, clothes, and school supplies for poor children.

As a fundamental condition for the democratization of our national economy, the RSDRP demands *the abolition of all indirect taxation and the introduction of a graduated tax on incomes and inheritances*.

To protect the working class from physical and moral degradation, and also to develop its capacity for the liberation struggle, the party demands:

1 Limitation of the working day to eight hours for all hired workers. . . .

3 A complete ban on overtime work.

4 A ban on night work . . . with the exception of those (industries) which absolutely require it for technical reasons. . . .

5 The prohibition of the employment of children of school age. . . .

6   A ban on the use of female labour in occupations which are harmful to the health of women; maternity leave from four weeks prior to childbirth until six weeks after birth. . . .

7   The provision of nurseries for infants and young children in all . . . enterprises employing women.

8   State insurance for workers against old age and partial or complete disability through a special fund supported by a tax on capitalists. . . .

11   The appointment of an adequate number of factory inspectors in all branches of the economy. . . .

12   The supervision by organs of local self-government, together with elected workers' representatives, of sanitary conditions in factory housing. . . .

13   The establishment of properly organized health inspection in all enterprises . . . free medical services for workers at the employer's expense, with wages to be paid during time of illness.

14   Establishment of criminal responsibility of employers for violations of laws intended to protect workers.

15   The establishment in all branches of the economy of industrial tribunals made up equally of representatives of the workers and of management. . . .

In order to eliminate the remnants of serfdom, which lie as an oppressive burden on the peasantry, and to further the free development of the class struggle in the countryside, the party demands above all: . . .

2   The repeal of all laws hampering the peasant's disposal of his own land.

3   The return to the peasants of all monies taken from them in the form of redemption payments and quitrents; the confiscation, for this purpose, of monastic and church property as well as of lands owned by the emperor, government agencies and members of the tsar's family; the imposition of a special tax on estates of the landowning nobility who have availed themselves of the redemption loans; the deposit of sums obtained in this way into a special fund for the cultural and charitable needs of the village communities.

4   The institution of peasant committees:

    a   for the return to village communities (through expropriation or, if the lands have passed into other hands, through purchase by the state at the expense of the large holdings of the nobility) of lands cut off from peasant

ownership at the time of the abolition of serfdom and which are now used by the landowners as a means of keeping the peasants in bondage. . . .
5 The granting to the courts of the right to reduce excessively high rents and to declare null and void all transactions reflecting relations of servitude.

In striving to achieve its immediate goals, the RSDRP will support any oppositional or revolutionary movement directed against the existing social and political order in Russia. At the same time, it resolutely rejects all reformist projects involving any broadening or strengthening of police or bureaucratic tutelage over the toiling classes.

The RSDRP, for its part, is firmly convinced that the complete, consistent and lasting realization of these political and social changes can only be achieved *through the overthrow of the autocracy* and the convocation of *a constituent assembly* freely elected by the entire nation.

> *Resolutions and Decisions of the Communist Party of the Soviet Union*, general ed. R.H. McNeal, vol. 1: *The Russian Social Democratic Labour Party, 1898–October 1917*, ed. R.C. Elwood. Toronto, 1974, pp. 42–5.

12   Party Programmes: Bolsheviks

Revolution had broken out in Russia in January 1905. At the III Party Congress, which had a Bolshevik majority, delegates had to decide on their response. If the revolution succeeded, a democratic or bourgeois government would come into being. Should social democrats participate in such a government? Lenin and the Bolsheviks proposed that they should.

On a Provisional Revolutionary Government: 19 April 1905

Considering:
1 that both the immediate interests of the proletariat and the interests of its struggle for the ultimate goals of socialism require . . . the replacement of the autocratic form of government by a democratic republic;
2 that a democratic republic can be established in Russia only as the

result of a victorious popular uprising whose agency will be a provisional revolutionary government. . . .

The III Congress of the RSDRP therefore resolves that: . . .

a   it is necessary to disseminate among the working class a concrete idea of the most probable course the revolution will take and of the necessity for the emergence at a given moment in the revolution of a provisional revolutionary government from which the proletariat will demand the implementation of all the immediate political and economic demands of our Programme;

b   depending upon the alignment of forces and other factors which cannot be precisely defined in advance, representatives of our party may be allowed to take part in the provisional revolutionary government so as to conduct a relentless struggle against all counter-revolutionary attempts and to uphold the independent interests of the working class;

c   as an essential condition of such participation, our party will maintain strict control over its representatives. . . .

d   regardless of whether or not the Social Democrats will be able to participate in the provisional revolutionary government, we must propagandize amongst the broadest sections of the proletariat the idea that the proletariat, armed and led by the Social Democratic Party, must keep constant pressure on the provisional government with the aim of preserving, consolidating and extending the gains of the revolution.

Ibid pp. 60–1.

13   Party Programmes: Mensheviks

The Mensheviks, in contrast to the Bolsheviks, did not advocate any participation in a provisional revolutionary government. They preferred to remain the 'party of extreme revolutionary opposition' unless the proletarian revolution should prove victorious in the industrially advanced countries of Western Europe. As Marxists they expected the liberal bourgeoisie to be the main agent of change. The Bolsheviks perceived that the middle and poorer strata of the peasantry could prove important allies of the proletariat in the democratic and proletarian revolutions. The Mensheviks proposed that the land question be left to a subsequent Constituent Assembly – not a policy likely to attract much peasant support. On the other hand the Mensheviks perceived more clearly than the Bolsheviks the possibilities which were opening up for Social Democratic activity in the trade unions and other legal working-class organizations.

On the Seizure of Power and Participation in a Provisional Government, April 1905

The decisive victory of the revolution over tsarism may be marked either by the establishment of a provisional government – issuing from the victorious popular uprising – or by the revolutionary initiative of one or another representative institution which will decide, under the direct revolutionary pressure of the people, to organize a national constituent assembly.

In either case, such a victory will inaugurate a new phase in the revolutionary epoch. . . .

Social democracy must strive to retain for itself, throughout the entire (bourgeois) revolution, a position which would best afford it the opportunity of furthering the revolution, which would not bind its hands in the struggle against the inconsistent and self-seeking policies of the bourgeois parties, and which would prevent it from losing its identity in bourgeois democracy.

Therefore, social democracy should not set itself the goal of seizing or sharing power in the provisional government but must remain the party of the extreme revolutionary opposition. . . .

In only one case should social democracy take the initiative and direct its efforts towards seizing power and holding it as long as possible – and that is if the revolution should spread to the advanced countries of western Europe where conditions for the realization of socialism have already attained a certain degree of maturity. In such a case, the limited historical scope of the Russian revolution may be considerably broadened and it may become possible to set out on the path of socialist reforms.

By basing its tactics on the expectation that throughout the entire revolutionary period the Social Democratic Party will maintain a position of extreme revolutionary opposition to all the governments which may succeed one another during the course of the revolution, social democracy can best prepare itself for wielding governmental power if it should fall into its hands.

Ibid pp. 72–3.

14   Party Programmes: Social Democrats

This is Lenin's biting critique of Menshevik views of the democratic revolution.

Lenin on Menshevism, July 1905

. . .the new-Iskrists [Mensheviks] are actually betraying to the bourgeoisie the interests of the proletariat in the democratic revolution, i.e., are leading the Party along a path whose objective significance is exactly such. . . . The new-Iskrists think that the active conduct of the democratic revolution is no concern of the Social-Democrats, but properly speaking, that of the democratic bourgeoisie, for, they argue, the proletariat's guidance and pre-eminent part will 'diminish the sweep' of the revolution.

. . .In its social and economic sense, the democratic revolution in Russia is a bourgeois revolution. It is, however, not enough merely to repeat this correct Marxist proposition. It has to be properly understood and properly applied to political slogans. In general, all political liberty founded on present-day, i.e., capitalist relations of production is bourgeois liberty. . . .

But only rebel Narodniks, anarchists and Economists could conclude therefrom that the struggle for liberty should be negated or disparaged. These intellectual-philistine doctrines could be foisted on the proletariat only for a time and against its will. The proletariat has always realized instinctively that it needs political liberty, needs it more than anyone else, although the immediate effect of that liberty will be to strengthen and organize the bourgeoisie. It is not by evading the class struggle that the proletariat expects to find its salvation, but by developing it, by extending its scope, its consciousness, organization, and resoluteness. . . .

Social-Democracy has fought, and is quite rightly fighting, against the bourgeois democratic abuse of the word 'people'. It demands that this word shall not be used to cover up failure to understand class antagonisms within the people. It insists categorically on the need for complete class independence for the party of the proletariat. . . .

The democratic revolution is bourgeois in nature . . . But we Marxists should know that there is not, nor can there be, any other path to real freedom for the proletariat and the peasantry, than the path of bourgeois freedom and bourgeois progress. We must not forget that there is not, not can there be at the present time, any other means of bringing socialism nearer, than complete political liberty, than a democratic republic, than the revolutionary-democratic dictatorship of the proletariat and the peasantry. As representatives of the advanced and only revolutionary class, revolutionary without any reservations, doubts, or looking back, we must confront the whole of the people with the tasks of the democratic revolution as extensively and boldly as possible and with the utmost initiative. . . . The difficulties that lie on the road to complete victory of the revolution are very great. No one will be able to blame the proletariat's representatives if, when they have done everything in their power, their efforts are defeated by the resistance of reaction, the treachery of the bourgeoisie, and the ignorance of the masses. But everybody, and, above all the class-conscious proletariat will condemn Social-Democracy if it curtails the revolutionary energy of the democratic revolution and dampens revolutionary ardour because it is afraid to win, because it is actuated by the consideration: lest the bourgeois recoil.

> V.I. Lenin, 'Two Tactics of Social-Democracy in the Democratic Revolution', in *Collected Works*, vol. IX. Moscow, 1962, pp. 110–13.

15   Party Programmes: The Social Revolutionary Party (PSR), November 1905

The PSR was an agrarian socialist party and therefore spoke for the peasants.

The PSR will . . . defend and support the following reforms or else extort them through its revolutionary struggle:

A. *Political and Legal*

The establishment of a democratic republic with wide autonomy for regions and both rural and urban settlements; the widest possible application of the federal principle to relations between the separate nationalities; the recognition of their undoubted right to self-determination; a direct, secret, equal and universal ballot for all citizens aged over twenty; proportional representation; direct popular legislation (referendum and initiative); the appointment by election, removal at any time and legal responsibility of all officials; complete freedom of conscience, speech, the press, meetings, strikes and trades unions; complete and universal civil equality; the inviolability of individuals and their residences; the total separation of church and state. . .; the establishment of compulsory free secular education for all; equality of languages. . .; the abolition of the standing army and its replacement by a people's militia.

B. Economic

1   . . .the establishment of a legal maximum to working hours. . .; the setting out of minimum wages. . .; a state insurance scheme.
2   . . .the party stands for the socialisation of all privately owned land, that is its removal from the private ownership of individuals and its transfer to public ownership, with it being placed at the disposal of democratically organized communes. . . . Should this fundamental measure not be implemented immediately the party . . . will support the following transitional measures: the extension of the rights of communes to expropriate private land; the confiscation of monastery, crown and government land. . . .
3   The party will press for the introduction of a progressive income tax.

. . .In beginning a direct revolutionary struggle with autocracy, the PSR calls for the summoning of a Constituent Assembly to abolish the autocratic regime and to replace it by a modern system. The Party will defend its programme in a Constituent Assembly, as well as trying to implement it directly during the revolutionary period.

> V.V. Vodovozov (ed.), *Sbornik programm politicheskikh partiy v Rossii*, edition 1. St Petersburg, 1905 pp. 20–1.

16 Party Programmes: The Constitutional Democratic Party (Kadets), 1905

The Kadets were the main liberal party.

I. Fundamental Civil Rights

1   All Russian citizens, irrespective of sex, religion or nationality, are equal before the law. . . .
2   Each citizen shall have freedom of conscience and religious belief. . . .
3   Each individual is free to express himself orally, in writing and in published works . . . censorship will be abolished. . . .

11   All peoples of the Russian Empire shall be guaranteed, through complete civil and political equality, the right to cultural self-determination.

II. The State Structure

..14   Popular representatives shall be elected by universal, direct, equal and secret ballot . . . The Party contains differing views about whether there should be a bicameral legislature, with the second chamber consisting of representatives from local self-government. . . .

15   The representatives will take part in the work of legislating, in discussions on the state budget and in checking on the legality and appropriateness of the activities of the administration.

16   No resolution, regulation, edict or order or similar act can become law without the approval of the representatives. . . .

19   Ministers are responsible to the assembly of popular representatives. . . .

III. Local Self-Government and Autonomy

20   Local self-government should be extended throughout the entire empire. . . .

22   The responsibilities of local self-government should extend to all areas of local administration, including the police. . . .

24   . . .local autonomy should be increased by the establishment of regional representative assemblies.

25   . . .Poland should be granted autonomy, with the preservation of the unity of the state, and it should be represented in the central institutions on the same basis as other parts of the empire.

IV. Justice

27   All measures which depart from the law of 20 November 1864, which separated legal power from administrative, should be repealed. . . .

28   . . .the death penalty should be abolished.

V. Financial and Economic Policy

..31   Redemption payments shall be abolished.

32   Direct taxation should be increased, in place of indirect taxes. . . .

VI. Agrarian Legislation

..36   There should be an increase in the area of land available to
       those who themselves work on the land. This should be
       provided from state, crown and monastery lands, and also by
       the purchase by the state, at a fair price, of private land. . . .

38   The state should provide extensive help for resettlement and
       migration.

VII. Workers' Legislation

..41   Freedom of trades unions.

42   The right to strike. . . .

44   The introduction of an eight-hour working day. . . .

47   Compulsory state insurance against sickness and
       accidents. . . .

48   State insurance for old age.

VIII. Educational Questions

..53   Complete autonomy and freedom of teaching in universities
       and other institutions of higher education. . . .

54   The number of secondary schools should be increased. . . .

55   Universal, free and compulsory primary education should be
       introduced.

Ibid pp. 40–9.

17   Party Programmes: The Union of 17 October, November 1905

The Union of 17 October or the Octobrists were a moderate conservative
party.

The Union of 17 October saw its main task as being to contribute
fundamentally to the rapid establishment of a constitutional
monarchy, on the basis of the manifesto of 17 October, insofar as was
possible in our state system, and to the rapid convocation of the State
Duma. It called for unity amongst those who sincerely wanted the
peaceful renewal of Russia and the triumph of law and order in the
country, who rejected both stagnation and revolution and who
recognized the need for the establishment of a strong and authoritative
regime, which, together with the representatives of the people, could
bring peace to the country through constructive legislative work.
. . .The basis of the Unions's programme [was]: (1) The

preservation of the unity and indivisibility of the Russian state, whilst allowing individual nationalities significant rights in the cultural field; (2) The development and strengthening of the foundations of a constitutional monarchy with a representative assembly elected on a broad franchise. . . . (3) The guaranteeing of civil rights, and the inviolability of the individual, his residence, correspondence and property. (4) The urgent summoning of the State Duma to put through political reforms . . . to deal with such matters as (a) the peasant question – the peasantry should be granted the same civil rights as the rest of the population; peasant land-holding should be extended and regulated (b) workers' insurance, a limitation of the working day and the freedom to form trades unions and to strike (c) the development of local self-government . . . (d) measures on education (e) judicial and administrative reforms (f) economic and financial measures to achieve a more rational and just tax system.

> D.N. Shipov, *Vospominaniya i dumy o perezhitom*. Moscow, 1918, pp. 404–6.

18   Party Programmes: The Nationalist Party

The Nationalist Party was on the right politically.

1   The unity of the Empire, the protection of Russians in all parts of the Empire and Russia for the Russians.
2   Loyalty to both autocracy and representative institutions.
3   Development of the Orthodox church, especially in the villages.
4   Improvement of the peasants' economic situation and support for private peasant landowning.
5   The inviolability of private property.
6   The right to work.
7   Development of local government in Russia to protect Russians in areas in which they are a minority.
8   Opposition to equal rights for Jews.
9   National agricultural and industrial planning.
10 Development of Russian national self-consciousness in the schools.

> 25 October 1909

> R. Edelman, *Gentry Politics on the Eve of the Russian*

Revolution. New Brunswick, 1980, p. 94.

19   Party Programmes: The Union of the Russian People

A conservative, openly anti-semitic party.

. . .The UNION OF THE RUSSIAN PEOPLE aims to unite all true Russians, loyal to their sworn oath in the name of Faith, TSAR and Fatherland.

The UNION openly declares that it does not desire a return to the bureaucratic ways of past years, when many illegalities were perpetrated in the name of the Tsar. . . .

The UNION will support the following proposals both inside and outside the Duma:

1. Orthodoxy

The UNION recognizes the Orthodox faith, held by the indigenous Russian population, as THE FOUNDATION OF RUSSIAN LIFE, AND ESTABLISHED in Russia. . . .

The UNION is completely tolerant of other religions. . . .

2. Autocracy

The AUTOCRACY of the Russian TSARS . . . has remained unchanged . . . after 17 October and should always remain so for the good and enlightenment o Russia.

The autocratic sovereign is THE SUPREME TRUTH, LAW AND STRENGTH . . . and he has decided that participation in the Duma and State Council, in full consultation with his people, is the best way to decide the immediate problems about the welfare of the Russian People and the peaceful development of our HOMELAND.

3. Nationality

The UNION OF THE RUSSIAN PEOPLE believes that the Russian nation as the consolidator of the Russian land and the founder of the Russian State is the SOVEREIGN NATION; other nationalities, with the exception of the Jews, have equal civil rights.

4. The Unity and Indivisibility of Russia

The UNION OF THE RUSSIAN PEOPLE strongly proclaims and holds a public belief in the INDIVISIBILITY OF THE RUSSIAN EMPIRE in its present frontiers. . . .

5. The Jewish Question

The Jews have, over many years, declared their uncompromising hatred for Russia and all things Russian, their incredible detestation for humanity, their complete alienation from other nationalities and their unique Jewish outlook. . . .

As is well known, and as the Jews themselves have announced . . . the unrest which we are experiencing and the general revolutionary movement in Russia . . . is almost exclusively the work of Jews and is conducted with the help of Jewish money.

. . . Taking into account that in recent years the Jews have been striving by all possible means to emigrate to Palestine and to create a separate state, and realizing that their emigration from the countries in which they live at present is the only sure way to save humanity from the evil which the Jews represent, the UNION OF THE RUSSIAN PEOPLE will press . . . for its representatives in the STATE DUMA to raise before all else the question of the creation of a Jewish state and of co-operation in Jewish emigration. . . .

. . . the UNION OF THE RUSSIAN PEOPLE realizes that the fact that the fulfilment of this dream is close will undoubtably be reflected in the performance of the Jews' civil duties in the countries which are giving them hospitality, to the detriment of the peoples amongst whom they live.

Therefore the UNION OF THE RUSSIAN PEOPLE . . . proposes that all Jews resident in Russia should immediately be declared foreigners, but without any of the rights and privileges which apply to other foreigners. Such a move, in conjunction with other restrictive measures, would undoubtably increase the efforts of the Jews to emigrate quickly. . . .

6. The Land Question

The UNION OF THE RUSSIAN PEOPLE will press for the extension of peasant landholding. . . .

It will support:

1 Equality of property and family rights for the peasantry, excluding any forcible measures against the commune. . . .

2 The transfer to 'land-shortage' peasants of crown lands on advantageous terms for them. . . .

3 As the quantity of crown lands is not sufficient for this purpose, . . . land should be bought by the State from private landowners.

4 Such land should be sold to the peasantry at prices which it can

afford . . . and any difference between the price at which it was bought and sold should be met by the state.

7. *The Workers' Question*

. . .The UNION will work for a reduction in the working day. . ., and state insurance against death, sickness and old age.

8. *Education*

The UNION OF THE RUSSIAN PEOPLE will demand free universal primary education, in the main agricultural and craft-orientated. . . . The UNION is also concerned that a Russian school . . . should bring up its youth in the spirit of Orthodox beliefs; love for the Tsar and for the fatherland.

9. *Trade, Industry and Finance*

. . .the UNION considers it its duty to aim to remove Russian finances from their control by foreign markets.

The UNION will . . . summon Russian capitalists to the struggle with Jewish and foreign capital. . . .

10. *Justice*

. . .crimes against the state, against life, robbery, arson, the preparation, transporting, carrying and use of explosive substances by ANARCHISTS AND REVOLUTIONARIES. . ., the sabotage of bridges, communications and machinery with the aim of preventing work taking place, armed opposition to the authorities, revolutionary propaganda in the army and the incitement of women and children to such crimes shall all be punished by the DEATH PENALTY.

2 September 1906.

V.V. Vodovozov (ed.), *Sbornik programm politicheskikh partiy v Rossii*, edition 6, St Petersburg, 1906, pp. 17–30.

20   Goremykin, the Chairman of the Council of Ministers, responds to the aspirations of the First Duma, 13 May 1906

The First Duma was a radical body since the expected peasant conservatism had not materialised. The Duma pressed for far reaching constitutional changes and insisted on the right to present proposals to the government.

The government declares, firstly, its readiness to cooperate fully in the discussion of those questions which have been raised by the Duma and which do not exceed the jurisdictional limits set down by law for it. . . .

The Council of Ministers will pay special attention to the questions raised by the State Duma of the immediate satisfaction of the pressing needs of the rural population,. . . The preparation of a law on the universal primary education, the imposition of taxation on the more prosperous sections of society and the reform of local administration and self-government. . . .

Equal significance is attached . . . to the issuing of a new law providing for personal inviolability, and the freedoms of conscience, speech, the press, assembly and association . . . The Council of Ministers declares that . . . the administration must provide it with sufficient means . . . to prevent abuse of these freedoms. . . .

The Council of Ministers regards the solution of the peasant-land question proposed by the Duma through the use of crown, cabinet and church lands and the compulsory expropriation of private land . . . as completely unacceptable.

Other suggestions made . . . by the Duma dealt with the introduction of a government responsible to, and having the confidence of, the majority of the Duma, the abolition of the State Council and the removal of the limits placed on the Duma's legislative competence. The Council of Ministers does not feel that it has the right to consider these proposals: they imply a huge change in the Fundamental Laws, which cannot be dealt with at the instigation of the Duma.

Turning to the Duma's . . . suggestions to repeal the exceptional laws and to prevent arbitrary action by officials, the Council of Ministers finds that these matters are completely within the sphere of government administration. The powers of the Duma in this respect are confined to interpellating ministers. . . .

The Council of Ministers wishes to give, in general terms, its immediate legislative plans. . . . The peasant question demands . . . special attention and caution in its solution. Caution is vital to avoid any sudden upheaval in the historically unique development of the peasant way of life. . . .

The government is preparing a proposal on universal primary education . . . and on the reform of the secondary school. . . .

The Council of Ministers sees the question of the establishment of the local court on lines which would make it easily accessible to the people as of first importance, together with the simplification of legal organization, speeding up and a reduction in the cost of the legal process. . . .

The Council of Ministers hopes that the Duma will be convinced that the peaceful flourishing of the Russian state depends on a rational combination of freedom and order and will, through peaceful and creative work, help [the government] to bring to Russia the calm which is so needed by all sections of the population.

> Gosudarstvennaya Duma,
> *Stenograficheskie Otchety*, I
> Duma Vol. 1, cols. 321–4.

21 Reaction of the First Duma to the Declaration of the Chairman of the Council of Ministers, Goremykin, 13 May 1906

The declaration of the Chairman of the Council of Ministers clearly indicated that the government had absolutely no desire to satisfy the demands of the people and their expectations of land, rights and freedom, which were set out by the State Duma is its reply to the speech from the throne. Peace in the country and fruitful work by the people's representatives are impossible without the satisfaction of these demands. By its refusal to fulfil the people's demands, the government is displaying obvious contempt for the true interests of the people and is clearly willing to countenance new upheavals in the country, already rent by poverty, a lack of basic rights and the continued rule of arbitrary power, left unpunished.

[The Duma] declares to the country its complete distrust of a ministry without responsibility to the people's representatives, and it believes that a necessary condition of peace being brought to the country and of fruitful work by the people's representatives is that the present ministry should resign immediately and be replaced by a government enjoying the trust of the State Duma.

. . .the resolution was passed by a majority.

> Ibid pp. 352–3

22   Manifesto Dissolving the First Duma, 8 July 1906

The Goremykin government and the First Duma could not coexist: after two months it was obvious to both sides that stalemate had been reached. Neither the government nor the Duma was willing to compromise.

. . .by Our will, people selected from the population were summoned to legislative work.

Trusting in God's mercy and believing in a great and glowing future for Our people, We expected benefits for the country from their work.

We had intended to make great changes in all areas of the life of the people. In first place has always been the important task of dispelling darkness from Our peoples' lives through the light of education, and of easing the conditions of work on the land. Instead of embarking on constructive legislative work, the elected members moved into areas outside their jurisdiction and turned to investigate actions carried out by Our local authorities, to indicate the incompleteness of the Fundamental Laws, the initiative for amendment to which can only be undertaken by Us, and to clearly illegal actions, such as an address from the Duma as a body to the population.

The peasantry was confused by these irregularities, and as it saw no likelihood of an improvement in its conditions through law, in a series of provinces it turned to open robbery, seized other people's property and disobeyed the law and legal authority.

Our subjects should remember, however, that any improvement in the life of Our peoples is possible only in conditions of complete order and calm. It should be known that We will not permit any form of wilfulness or lawlessness and will use the full force of the state to bring lawbreakers to submit to Our will. We call on all right-thinking Russian people to unite in support of legal authority and the establishment of peace in Our dear fatherland.

May peace be established across Russia and may the Almighty aid Us in fulfilling the most important of Our tasks as Tsar – an improvement in peasant welfare. Our will is unshakeable on this point, and in those areas where land is short the Russian ploughman will be given a legal and honourable way of increasing his land-holding, without any sacrifice from other landowners. We appeal to people of all classes to devote all their efforts to the completion of this great task: its final solution in legislative form will be dealt with by the new Duma.

In dissolving the present Duma, we affirm our unshakeable intention of keeping in force the law which set up this institution, and in accordance with that law. . . . We have fixed the date for the assembly of a new Duma to be 20 February 1907.

It is with a constant faith in God's mercy and in the intelligence of the Russian people that We expect that the new Duma will fulfil our expectations and will legislate in accordance with the needs of a renewed Russia.

Faithful sons of Russia!

Your Tsar calls on you, as the father of His children, to join with Him in renewing and resurrecting Our holy motherland.

We believe that heroes of thought and deed will appear and that the glory of Russia will shine from their selfless work.

Nicholas.

*Polnoe Sobranie Zakonov Rossiy-
skoy Imperii*, 3rd ed., vol.
XXV/I, no. 28105.

23 The Vyborg Manifesto, 10 July 1906

The First Duma's dissolution provoked a strong reaction from the Kadets. Their call for civil disobedience in the Vyborg Manifesto severely reduced their credibility as a responsible party in the eyes of the government. Their overreaction affected their representation in subsequent Dumas since many of those who had signed the Vyborg Manifesto were imprisoned and thus became ineligible for Duma membership.

To the people, from the people's representatives.

Citizens throughout Russia! The decree of 8 July dissolved the State Duma. When you elected us as your representatives, you entrusted us with the task of securing land and freedom. Fulfilling your charge and our duty, we drafted laws to assure the people's freedom and demanded the removal of irresponsible ministers who suppressed freedom with impunity, in violation of the law. But above all we wished to promulgate a law concerning the allotment of land to the working peasantry by drawing for this purpose on state lands, appanage lands, cabinet lands, monastery lands and church lands and by the compulsory expropriation of privately owned lands. The government declared such a law inadmissable and replied to the Duma's insistent reaffirmation of its resolution concerning compulsory   expropriation   by   dismissing   the   people's representatives. . . .

Citizens, stand firmly for the trampled rights of the people's representatives, stand firmly for the State Duma. Russia must not remain a single day without popular representatives. We have the means of achieving this: the government has no right either to collect taxes from the people or to mobilize men for military service without the consent of the people's representatives. Now, therefore, when the government has dismissed the State Duma, you have the right not to give it either soldiers or money. And if, in order to obtain funds, the government begins to resort to borrowing, then such loans, made without the consent of the people's representatives, are henceforth invalid, and the Russian people will never recognize them or repay them. And so, until the convocation of the people's representatives, do not give a single kopek to the Treasury or a single soldier to the army. Be firm in your refusal. Defend your rights together. No force can prevail before the united and unbending will of the people. Citizens, in this forced and unavoidable struggle your elected representatives will be with you.

> G. Vernadsky, *A Source Book for Russian History from Early Times to 1917*, vol. 3. New Haven, 1972, p. 779.

24   Stolypin's Policy: Government Declaration of 24 August 1906

The dissolution of the First Duma was accompanied by the appointment of the Minister of Internal Affairs, P.A Stolypin, as Chairman of the Council of Ministers in place of the aged Goremykin. Stolypin believed that reform was necessary in Russia, but at the same time he was determined to deal firmly with terrorism. The first statement of the new Prime Minister's policy was on 24 August 1906, only two weeks after he had survived a bomb attack on his house.

In the last two years the revolutionary movement has manifested itself with extreme intensity. Since this spring it has increased extraordinarily. Hardly a day goes by without some new crime. Mutinies at Sebastopol, at Sveaborg, in Reval harbour and in Kronstadt, murders of government and police officials, attacks and robberies follow one after the other. . . .

After the dissolution of the State Duma, the speedy suppression of the Kronstadt and Sveaborg mutinies, the failure of the projected general strike, and the initiation of decisive measures against the agrarian disorders, the revolutionary extremists, hoping to counteract the impression made by the failure of their plots and to impede the constructive work of the government, decided to create an impression on the country and to induce panic in government circles by the murder of high state officials. . . .

But it would be a great mistake to believe that the sole task of the government is to protect the state from criminal attacks, forgetting the profound causes that have given birth to such monstrous manifestations.

The government cannot, as some groups in society demand, call a halt to all reforms, and direct the entire power of the state towards the struggle with sedition, concentrating on the symptoms of the evil without penetrating to its essence. How would the circumstances and the interests of Russia be served by the other solution proposed by the opponents of the first opinion: to concentrate exclusively on the implementation of liberating reforms, in the belief that in this case sedition will cease of itself, having lost its whole meaning. This latter opinion is unacceptable if for no other reason than that the revolution is fighting, not for reforms, which the government also considers it its duty to enact, but rather to achieve the destruction of the political order itself, the destruction of the monarchy and the introduction of a socialist system. Hence it is clear what the path of the government must be: to preserve order and, by decisive measures, to protect the population from revolutionary disturbances, while, at the same time, it employs all its political power to follow a constructive path, so as to re-establish an abiding order of things based on legitimacy and a genuine, intelligently conceived liberty. . . .

At present the government is at work on a whole series of problems of the greatest political importance. The most important of these are the following:

1 Freedom of conscience.
2 Personal inviolability and civil equality, in the sense of the removal of the limitations and checks placed on separate groups of the population.
3 The improvement of peasant land tenure.
4 The improvement of the way of life of the workers and, in particular, the introduction of a system of state insurance.
5 The reform of local administration, which it is proposed to organize in such a fashion that the provincial and county administrative institutions should be placed in direct contact with

reformed organs of self-government. . . .

6 The introduction of zemstvo self-government into the Baltic region and also into the northern and south-western regions.

7 The introduction of zemstvo and municipal self-government into the provinces of the Kingdom of Poland.

8 The reform of the local courts.

9 The reform of secondary and higher education.

10 An income tax.

11 A reform of the police, directed, in part, towards a merger of the general police force with the gendarmerie.

12 Means for the special protection of the political order and of public tranquility, with the consolidation of the various kinds of emergency legislation now used into a single law.

Finally, along with this, preparatory work is continuing for the impending summons, by imperial command, of an all-Russian church council.

Ibid p. 784.

25 Terrorism 1905–1909

Despite government measures, terrorism continued to be a significant feature of Russian life. Fields court-martial were temporarily introduced by the government under Article 87 of the Fundamental Laws (see document 9), but they were allowed to lapse because it was obvious that they would never gain the approval of the Duma. The severity of the government's anti-terrorist campaign caused it great difficulties in its relations with the Octobrist and Kadet parties.

Numbers killed or wounded by terrorist attacks, and numbers sentenced to death

| Year | Victims of attacks | | | Sentenced to death | |
	Killed	Wounded	Total	Sentenced	Executed
1905	233	358	591	72	10
1906	768	820	1588	450	144
1907	1231	1312	2543	1056	456
And, by decision of fields court-martial, 19.8.06–20.4.07					
	–	–	–	683	683
1908	394	615	1009	1741	825
1909 (to 1.6.09)	202	227	429	567	237
Total	2828	3332	6160	4579	2365

Krasny Arkhiv, vol. 8 (1925), pp. 242–3.

(This information was originally included in telegrams sent by Sazonov, the Minister of Foreign Affairs, to Benkendorff, Ambassador to London, on 29 June and 10 August 1909)

26   Manifesto dissolving the Second Duma and changing the electoral law to the State Duma, 3 June 1907

Elected on the same franchise as the First Duma, the Second Duma convened in February 1907. It proved just as radical as the First Duma and the government could not find the 'common language' which Stolypin desired. When it appeared that members of the Social Democratic Party were implicated in attempts to provoke revolution amongst army units, the government seized upon this as an excuse to dissolve the Second Duma. The government was determined that the Third Duma should be more malleable and therefore decided to amend the electoral system.

. . .We summoned the second State Duma to cooperate, in accordance with Our will, in the pacification of Russia; firstly, through legislative work, without which the life of the State and improvements in its structure are impossible, secondly, by examining the budget which shows the condition of the state economy, and lastly by a sensible use of the right to interpellate the government with the aim of increasing truth and justice everywhere.

These duties, entrusted by Us to those elected from the population, laid upon them heavy responsibilities and the sacred duty of using their right for sensible work to benefit and strengthen the Russian state.

Such were Our thoughts and will when We gave to the population a new basis for government.

To Our great sorrow, a significant part of the second Duma did not live up to Our expectations.

Many of the deputies had neither a clear conscience, nor a desire to strengthen Russia and improve her administration, but instead aimed at increasing chaos and facilitating the destruction of the state.

The activity of these people in the Duma was an insuperable obstacle to fruitful work. A spirit of enmity was present in the Duma itself, preventing united work by those of its members who wanted to work to benefit their native land.

For this reason, the State Duma either did not consider the wide-ranging measures introduced by our government, delayed discussion of them, or else rejected them, even going so far as to reject a bill to punish open incitement to crime and setting out penalties for incitement to mutiny in the armed forces. The State Duma declined to discuss murders and violence and did not demonstrate proper cooperation with the government in the promotion of order, so that Russia continues to suffer the shame of criminal evil-doing.

The slow examination by the Duma of the state budget meant that difficulties were encountered in fulfilling many of the pressing demands of the people.

A significant section of the Duma transformed the right to interpellate the government into a method of attacking the government and of provoking mistrust of it amongst a wide section of the population.

Finally, this was capped by an event unparalleled in the annals of history. The authorities uncovered a conspiracy by a section of the State Duma directed against the state and Tsar. When Our government requested the temporary suspension from the Duma of the fifty five members accused of this crime until the conclusion of the trial and the detention in custody of the most guilty of them, the Duma rejected the authorities' lawful request, not allowing the urgency of the matter.

All this prompted Our . . . dissolution of the second State Duma and the summoning of a new Duma for 1 November 1907.

But, whilst believing in Our people's love for their homeland and their civic sense, We believe that the reason for the double failure of the State Duma is that, owing to the newness of the institution and the imperfectness of the electoral law, the legislative body has been filled with members who do not really express the needs and desires of the people.

Therefore, whilst We shall leave in force all the rights conferred on Our subjects by the manifesto of 17 October 1905 and the fundamental laws, We have taken the decision to alter only the actual method of electing representatives from the people, retaining for each section of the population the right to elect representatives.

The State Duma, created to strengthen the Russian state, should be Russian in spirit.

The other nationalities which are part of Our state should have sufficient representatives in the State Duma for their needs, but should not have so many that they have a deciding voice in questions of purely Russian concern.

Elections to the State Duma should be temporarily suspended in those areas where the population has not reached a sufficient level of civic development.

All these changes in the method of election cannot be enacted in the usual way by legislation through that same State Duma whose composition is seen by Us as unsatisfactory, because of imperfections in the way in which its members are chosen. Only the authority which gave the first electoral law, the historical authority of the Russian Tsar, has the right to amend and replace it.

The Lord God has given Us kingly authority over Our people. We will answer for the fate of the Russian state before His throne.

In recognition of this we are determined to carry on to the finish the work we have begun of reconstructing Russia and will provide it with a new electoral law. . . .

We expect from Our faithful subjects united and cheerful service, along the course We have indicated, to their homeland, the sons of which have always been firm supporters of its strength, greatness and glory.

Nicholas.

Polnoe Sobranie Zakonov Rossiy-skoy Imperii, 3rd ed., vol. XXVII/I, no. 29240.

27   The Electoral Law of 3 June 1907

S.E. Kryzhanovsky, the assistant Minister of Internal Affairs, was the person entrusted with the task of preparing a new electoral law.

A few weeks of work with the Second Duma convinced the government that it was impossible to live with it, as the aim of the majority of the Duma was struggle with government and not legislative work. . . . By April [1907] it was clear that the Duma would be dissolved and P.A. Stolypin decided to make alterations to the [electoral] law so that future elections would be dominated by the more cultured elements of the population.

. . . He [Stolypin] instructed me to prepare a new draft of the law which would not destroy the general outline of the electoral process, but would allow the more well-to-do and, therefore, more cultured elements to be elected . . . also the change in the law was not to deprive any section of the population which was then represented in the Duma of participation in the elections. This was a task akin to squaring the circle, but there was no arguing.

. . . I drew up three possible variants. The first, based on elections by estate, pre-determined the number of Duma deputies from each section of the propulation.

The second variant was based fully on the existing system, but it gave a majority of votes in the provincial electoral assembly, and with it control over the elections, to the representatives of large property owners, whilst providing for the election of one member per province from each class of electors.

Its basic principle was, of course, that the number of electors was redistributed among different groups of voters, giving most weight to the ownership of extensive property, and among provinces, giving numerical advantage to the most cultured areas.

Finally, the third possibility based the elections on district zemstvo assemblies. . . . This variant, of course, could not satisfy the criterion of retaining represention from all groups, since the circle of participants in zemstvo elections was very much narrower than had been the case in Duma elections, and was put forward, so to say, for the sake of conscience.

Together with this were prepared draft changes in the Fundamental Laws, and in the statutes of the State Duma and State Council. The projected changes would have given the government the power to regulate legislative business in the Duma and State Council by setting out the order in which bills should be examined and by establishing a period of time for discussion; after this had elapsed the government would be able to introduce these measures without the need for the Duma's approval. It was also proposed that the government should have the right to demand that the Duma look again at matters which had only been approved or rejected by a small majority.

To begin with, Stolypin was full of determination to implement a fundamental change in the relationship of the government to the Duma by giving the government a more powerful part in the administration of the country. Later, as often happened, he hesitated, got cold feet, and these proposals came to nothing. . . .

The Council [of Ministers] after much hesitation, decided on the second scheme. . . .

This scheme was called 'shameless' by some, as it was too easy to see its underlying principle – to filter the elections through the medium of large property ownership. When Stolypin told the Tsar of this and laughingly repeated this description, the Tsar smiled and said 'I too am shameless'.

S.E. Kryzhanovsky, *Vospominaniya*, Berlin, 1925, pp.
107–11.

28   Stolypin's Failure

Although the composition of the Third Duma was more amenable to the
government's wishes, it was still not prepared to pass bills without giving them
a thorough examination. Delay allowed time for right-wing opposition to
develop, especially in the State Council, which, with its extreme conservative
majority, was able to block reform projects approved by the Third Duma.
Stolypin was assassinated on 1 September 1911. Izgoev, a leading Kadet,
compares Stolypin's pronouncements in 1906 and 1907 with his
government's actual achievements by the time of his death.

1   The granting to the peasantry of state, crown and cabinet lands.
      Up to 1 January 1911, only 281,000 desyatinas out of more
   than 9m. had been sold to the peasantry.
2   'A series of bills, to lay down rules concerning transfer from one
   religion to another, unrestricted worship, the building of
   churches, the formation of religious societies and the removal of
   restrictions imposed solely because of one's religion.'
      Nothing has been accomplished. Most of the bills got bogged
   down in the State Council, and will meet their death there. . . .
3   Personal inviolability, by which 'detention, searches and the
   perlustration of correspondence can only be carried out by a
   decision of the relevant legal authority, which would also be
   responsible for the confirmation of the legality of any detention
   within 24 hours. . . .'
      Administrative arbitrariness rules right across Russia. An
   attempt by Petersburg judges to rule on the legality of detention
   met with substantial opposition from the government. . . .
6   The establishment of an 'all-estate' self-governing village council,
   as the lowest level of zemstvo.
      This has not yet been implemented and it is not known when it
   will be. . . .
11   Representation in the zemstva is to be based on the principle of a
   tax qualification. This will widen the circle of people taking part
   in local life. The jurisdiction of self-governing bodies is to be
   increased by the transfer to them of a whole range of new
   responsibilities, and the relation of government to them will
   consist in supervising the legality of their actions.
      Everything is still as before, and the attitude of the government

to even 'right-wing' zemstva under Stolypin is no better than under Plehve, when the zemstva were treated as opposition bodies. . . .

13   Laws about provincial and district administration.
Everything is still as before.

14   Complaints about administrative and elected officials and institutions are to be examined by an administrative-judicial body . . . .
Everything is still as before.

15   The office of land captain is to be abolished.
They thankfully exist. . . .

19   The establishment of village courts.
Stolypin's government withdrew this proposal after it had reached the State Council.

20   A local court of elected JPs.
The bill passed the Duma but was then bogged down, seemingly inextricably, in the State Council. . . .

32   Insurance of workers in case of sickness, disability, invalidity and old age and the organization of medical care.
In reality, nothing was achieved under Stolypin.

33   A limitation of the working day for children and the prohibition of nighttime and underground work by women and children.
Still all as before.

34   A reduction in the working day for adults.
Still all as before. . . .

38   Compulsory and universal primary education.
Two government bills – one about the provision of funds for this and one on the organization of primary schools – were approved by the Duma, but met their end in the State Council. . . .

41   Examination of the budget.
This is the only area where government and Duma have been able to co-operate, perhaps as a result of a limitation of the Duma's rights.

42   Income tax.
Stuck in the Financial Commission of the Duma, from where it is unlikely to emerge.

43   The transfer of some of the revenue of central government to local self-government.
Nothing substantive has been done.

A.S. Izgoev, *P.A. Stolypin: ocherk zhizni i deyatelnosti.* Moscow, 1912 pp. 117–23.

29 The Position of the Tsar

Nicholas II believed that he should play an active role in government. He relied largely on his conscience when making decisions, and in the case of the naval general staffs' affair the Tsar rejected the bill because he believed that the legislative institutions were usurping prerogatives which rightfully belonged to him as Tsar.

10 December 1906

Petr Arkadevich!

I am returning the [Council of Ministers'] minutes on the Jewish question unapproved.

Even before the minutes were sent to me, I pondered on the matter day and night.

Despite the most convincing arguments in favour of my approving the matter, my inner voice tells me more and more insistently that I should not take the decision myself. Up to now my conscience has never deceived me. Therefore in this case I intend to follow its guidance.

I know that you also believe that 'the Tsar's heart is in God's hands'.

Let it be so.

I bear a fearful responsibility to God for all the powers granted to me and I am ready at any time to give account of them to Him.

Nicholas
25 April 1909

Petr Arkadevich!

After our last conversation I have constantly thought about the question of the Naval General Staffs.

Weighing up everything, I have finally decided not to approve the bill.

. . . There can be no talk of confidence or lack of it. Remember that we live in Russia . . . and therefore I will not allow any thought of resignation.

. . . I warn you that I will categorically refuse to consider a request to resign from you or anybody else.

Nicholas

'Perepiska N.A. Romanova i P.A. Stolypina', *Krasny Arkhiv*, vol. 5 (1926), pp. 105, 120.

30   Kokovtsov as Prime Minister

On Stolypin's assassination Kokovtsov, the Minister of Finance, was appointed Chairman of the Council of Ministers. But he was too inflexible and was uninterested in continuing Stolypin's reform programme. His main achievements were in the economic field. Here one of his colleagues, the Minister of Foreign Affairs, sums him up.

Kokovtsov had a number of enemies, for with all his fine qualities as a statesman, he was a man lacking in subtlety and accustomed through his long experience as a bureaucratic official to act according to his own ideas without taking into consideration the opinion of his opponents. These failings had an immediate effect upon his relations with the Duma. Being a young institution, it had an exaggerated idea of its own importance, and Kokovtsov did not always know how to spare its vanity. He had no supporters at Court, although the Tsar recognized his merit. His extreme dislike of Rasputin set the Empress against him, for she had grown accustomed of late years to show favour only to persons who were friendly to Rasputin and his clique. Under these circumstances, the effects of one or two influential members of the Council [of Ministers] hostile to Kokovtsov were sufficient to make it impossible for him to remain at the helm of government.

S.D. Sazonov, *Fateful Years*. London, 1928, p. 279.

31   Kokovtsov's dismissal: Nicholas II's letter

Kokovtsov was dismissed in January 1914. Whilst Stolypin and Kokovtsov had combined respectively the office of Minister of Internal Affairs and Minister of Finance with that of the chairmanship of the Council of Ministers, this practice came to an end with Kokovtsov's dismissal. A Chairman of the Council of Ministers without specific departmental responsibilities posed less of a threat to the Tsar's authority.

Vladimir Nikolaevich!

It is not a feeling of enmity, but rather my deep and long-felt recognition of the needs of the state, that forces me to tell you that it is necessary for me to part with you.

I am doing this in writing because it is easier for me to find the right words than during an unsettling interview.

The experience of the last eight years has completely convinced me that the combination in one person of the posts of Chairman of the Council of Ministers and Minister of Finance or Minister of Internal Affairs is incorrect and inconvenient in such a country as Russia.

Besides this, the rapid progress of domestic affairs and the striking increase in our economic strength requires a series of serious and decisive measures, and only a new man will be equal to this task.

Over the past two years I have, regrettably, not always approved of the activities of the Ministry of Finance, and I recognize that such a state of affairs cannot continue.

I greatly value your devotion to me and your enormous services in improving Russia's state credit, and am deeply grateful to you for this. You may rest assured that I am sorry to part with you, after all your work over the last ten years, and that I will not forget to look after you and your family. I will expect you, as always, on Friday at 11 o'clock for your final report, as ever as a friend.

With sincere regards,
Nicholas.

V.N. Kokovtsov, *Iz moego proshlego*, vol. 2. Paris, 1933, pp. 278–9.

32   Kokovtsov's reaction to dismissal

. . .This letter was written by the Tsar under the influence of those forces which had long been trying to remove me from power. The Tsar evidently did not trust himself in a face-to-face interview with me, feeling that I might put forward arguments to make him change his mind. The persistent pressure exerted on the Tsar by those whom he trusted had continued and he had decided on this method of doing things so that his decision was irreversible.

. . .My first impression of the letter was that it was very strange for the Tsar to say that he had for eight years been convinced of the inappropriateness of combining the offices of Chairman of the Council of Ministers and Minister of Finance or Minister of Internal

Affairs. On Stolypin's death, three years earlier, he appointed me as Chairman of the Council, adding the words, 'You will, of course, remain as Minister of Finance,' and not once over all those years had I heard the slightest hint from the Tsar that he considered it wrong to combine the two posts. Indeed the Tsar had more than once remarked on the fact that in my time as Prime Minister, disagreements in the Council of Ministers had become far fewer, and he had heard from various sources that I was extremely impartial in my chairing of cabinet meetings, often to the detriment of the interests of the Ministry of Finance.

I was also hurt by the part of the letter which referred to Russia's enormous economic growth and the whole series of new tasks which this brought with it – tasks which only new people could deal with. . . .

Involuntarily, I thought – who had created this huge economic growth, who had succeeded in protecting Russia's finances during the war with Japan and even more in the years of internal disturbance, and had thus laid the foundation for Russia's economic development? This sentence obviously did not represent the true thoughts of the writer and was merely an excuse. Even less understandable was the next sentence, that 'over the last two years, the Tsar had not always approved of the activities of the Ministry of Finance, and that this state of affairs could not be allowed to continue'. Not once in my ten years as Minister of Finance had I heard such disapproval; not once had I heard from the Tsar in writing or by word of mouth that he was in the slightest way unhappy with the way the Ministry of Finance was being run. All my reports had been approved in the kindest way. A whole range of written reports, right up to the most recent, had been annotated in the most complimentary terms by the Tsar. . . .

The last sentence of the letter also made a great impression on me. Whilst he wrote that he expected me on Friday at the usual time for my last report, the Tsar was at the same time saying that I should not try to alter his decision – it was irreversible. Even after ten years, the Tsar did not know me well enough to know that I would never ask to stay on against his will.

Ibid pp. 279–81.

33   Guchkov's Presentiment of Catastrophe, 1913

Guchkov was the leader of the Octobrist Party, and a prominent figure in industrial and commercial circles. His speech demonstrates the gulf which existed between the government and even moderate opinion in Russia. The years after 1905 did nothing to remove the distrust which existed between government and society.

Speech by A.I. Guchkov to the Conference of the Octobrist Party, 8 November 1913

What is to be the issue of the grave crisis through which we are now passing? What does the encroachment of reaction bring with it? Whither is the government policy, or rather lack of policy, carrying us?

Towards an inevitable and grave catastrophe! In this general forecast all are agreed; people of the most sharply opposed political views, of the most varied social groups, all agree with a rare, an unprecedented unanimity. Even representatives of the government, of that government which is the chief offender against the Russian people, are prepared to agree to this forecast, and their official and obligatory optimism ill conceals their inward alarm.

When will the catastrophe take effect? What forms will it assume? Who can foretell? Some scan the horizon with joyful anticipation, others with dread. But greatly do those err who calculate that on the ruins of the demolished system will arise that order which corresponds to their particular political and social views. In those forces that seem likely to come to the top in the approaching struggle, I do not see stable elements that would guarantee any kind of permanent political order. Are we not rather in danger of being plunged into a period of protracted, chronic anarchy which will lead to the dissolution of the Empire? Shall we not again pass through a Time of Troubles, only under new and more dangerous international conditions?. . .

Will our voice be heard? Will our cry of warning reach the heights where the fate of Russia is decided? Shall we succeed in communicating our own alarm to the government? Shall we awaken it from the lethargy that envelops it? We should be glad to think so. In any case, this is our last opportunity of securing a peaceful issue from the crisis. Let those in power make no mistake about the temper of the people; let them not take outward indications of prosperity as a pretext for lulling themselves into security. Never were those revolutionary organizations which aim at a violent upheaval so broken and impotent as they are now, and never were the Russian public and the Russian people so profoundly revolutionized by the actions of the government, for day by day faith in the government is steadily waning, and with it is waning faith in the possibility of a peaceful issue from the crisis.

The danger at the present moment lies, in fact, not in the revolutionary parties, not in anti-monarchical propaganda, not in anti-religious teaching, not in the dissemination of the ideas of socialism and antimilitarism, not in the agitation of anarchists against the government. The historical drama through which we are now passing lies in the fact that we are compelled to uphold the monarchy against those who are the natural defenders of the monarchical principle, we are compelled to defend the Church against the ecclesiastical hierarchy, the army against its leaders, the authority of the government against the government itself. We seemed to have sunk into a state of public despondency and apathy, a passive condition. But thence it is only one step to depair, which is an active force of tremendously destructive quality. May God avert from our country the danger that overshadows it.

> 'The General Political Situa-
> tion and the Octobrist
> Party', *Russian Review*, vol.
> III (1914), no. 1, pp. 151–2,
> 157–8.

34   Goremykin as Prime Minister

Goremykin succeeded Kokovtsov as Prime Minister. Nicholas II was keen to have someone in the office who would cause him little trouble. Goremykin was aged 74 at the time of his appointment. Pavel Milyukov was a leading Kadet and became the Minister of Foreign Affairs in the first Provisional Government after the February Revolution of 1917.

If it was necessary to conceal the seething passion of prerevolutionary society behind a mask of peace and tranquility – with the sole aim of deceiving the supreme authority and of lengthening the time during which we waited for something to happen spontaneously – then a better choice than Goremykin could not have been made. Decrepit, not only in years but also in his senile indifference to everything, Goremykin was not looking for power. After his appointment, he himself told Kokovtsov: 'I completely fail to understand why I was needed; I ressemble an old racoon fur coat which was packed away in a trunk long ago and sprinkled with camphor. . . . Nevertheless, they will put the coat back in the trunk just as unexpectedly as they took it out.' It was Krivoshein, a very intelligent man who understood the situation better than the majority of those around him, who dreamed up the idea of Goremykin. Subsequently, I was able to convince myself personally of the breadth of his outlook. Kokovtsov was right in his description of Krivoshein, he did not want to bear the responsibility and deliberately remained in the background. Goremykin was convenient for him in that he was a vacuum, inert, and would not interfere in any future plans that might be needed. As I had occasion to find out later, it was absolutely impossible to surprise Goremykin with anything or to rouse him to action. He waved his hand at everything, called it 'nonsense', and then settled down on the road like some heavy stone. The greatest mistake in appointing him was that one could not make up the lost time. In the absence of any creative programme at all, an interregnum of chaos set in.

> P.N. Milyukov, *Political Memoirs, 1905–1917*, ed. A.P. Mendel. Ann Arbor, Mich., 1967, p. 284.

35 Was Revolution inevitable by 1914?

Haimson presents two fundamentally opposing views, the Soviet and the common Western response. His own point of view is more subtle. It amounts to seeing the crisis as operating at two levels: educated society against the unpopular and incompetent autocracy, and, as the war progressed, the mounting hatred and resentment of those living under harsh conditions against the educated and the privileged. Hence all established values were under attack.

. . . The first of these, which Soviet historians have advanced to demonstrate the *zakonomernost*, the historical logic (and therefore the historical legitimacy) of October, distinguishes in the years immediately preceding the First World War the shape of a new, rapidly mounting 'revolutionary upsurge'. According to the periodization that has become established for this stereotype, the first modest signs that the period of 'reaction' that had descended on Russian society with the Stolypin *coup d'état* had come to an end appeared as early as 1910–11 . . .
. . . the war is not viewed as contributing decisively to the unleashing of the revolutionary storm. . . .
Partly as a response to this Soviet stereotype and to the gross distortions of evidence that its presentation often involves, we have witnessed during the last quarter of a century the crystallization in many Western representations of the origins of 1917 of a diametrically

different, and equally sweeping, point of view. It is that between the Revolution of 1905 and the outbreak of the First World War a process of political and social stabilization was under way in every sphere of Russian life which, but for the extraneous stresses that the war imposed, would have saved the Russian body politic from revolution – or at least from the radical overturn that Russia eventually experienced with the Bolshevik conquest of power. . . .

If I might summarize my own . . . argument, it is that by 1914 a dangerous process of polarization appeared to be taking place in Russia's major urban centres between an *obshchestvo* [society] that had now reabsorbed the vast majority of the once alienated elements of the intelligentsia (and which was now beginning to draw to itself many of the workers' own intelligentsia) and a growing discontented and disaffected mass of industrial workers, now left largely exposed to the pleas of an embittered revolutionary minority. . . .

[B]y July 1914 along with the polarization between workers and educated, privileged society . . . a second process of polarization – this one between the vast bulk of privileged society and the tsarist regime – appeared almost equally advanced. . . .

Clearly . . . the crude representations to be found in recent Soviet writings of the 'revolutionary situation' already at hand in July 1914, can hardly be sustained. Yet when one views the political and social tensions evident in Russian society in 1914 in a wider framework and in broader perspective, any flat-footed statement of the case for stabilization appears equally shaky.

Leopold Haimson, 'The Problem of Social Stability in Urban Russia, 1905–1917', *Slavic Review*, vol. XXIII no. 4, December 1964, pp. 619–20, 639 and *Slavic Review*, vol. XXIV no. 1, March 1965, p. 2.

Strikes

(i) The compilations published by the Ministry of Trade and Industry provide the following statistical aggregates about strikes in factories covered by factory inspection for the period 1905–14:

Year	Strikes	Strikers	Number of strikes listed as political	Number of strikers listed as political
1905	13,995	2,863,173	6,024	1,082,576
1906	6,114	1,108,406	2,950	514,854
1907	3,573	740,074	2,558	521,573
1908	892	176,101	464	92,694
1909	340	64,166	50	8,863
1910	222	46,623	8	3,777
1911	466	105,110	24	8,380
1912	2,032	725,491	1,300	549,812
1913	2,404	887,096	1,034	502,442
1914	3,534	1,337,458	2,401	985,655

Haimson Ibid p. 627, originally published in Ministerstvo torgovli i promyshlennosti, *Svod otchetov fabrichnykh inspektorov za 1913 god* (St Petersburg, 1914).

There is considerable dispute about the accuracy of these figures and since the inspectors almost certainly erred on the conservative side, add 20 per cent to get a more realistic figure.

(ii)
Number   of   strikes   in   Petrograd,   1914–1917

	Political strikes			Economic strikes		
Month	No. of strikes	No. of strikers	No. of working days lost through strikes	No. of strikes	No. of strikers	No. of working days lost through strikes
1914						
July 1–18	–	160,099	–	–	580	–
July 19	26	27,400	48,540	16	10,942	76,914
August	–	–	–	–	–	–
September	1	1,400	280	3	905	1,180
October	–	–	–	2	160	42
November	2	3,150	1,260	3	785	785
December	–	–	–	2	1,020	1,240
1915						
January	14	2,595	2,488.5	2	115	565
February	6	340	183.5	2	120	85
March	–	–	–	6	461	311

continued

Month	Political strikes			Economic strikes		
	No. of strikes	No. of strikers	No. of working days lost through strikes	No. of strikes	No. of strikers	No. of working days lost through strikes
April	–	–	–	7	4,064	9,988
May	10	1,259	899	7	2,571	1,607
June	–	–	–	9	1,141	531
July	–	–	–	29	17,934	33,965.5
August	24	23,178	24,574.5	16	11,640	15,879
September	70	82,728	176,623.5	13	7,470	12,730.5
October	10	11,268	34,911.5	21	13,350	69,031.5
November	5	11,020	6,280	19	6,838	7,509.5
December	7	8,985	5,624.5	26	13,284	15,261
1916						
January	68	61,447	64,566	35	16,418	37,749.5
February	3	3,200	170	55	53,723	220,026.5
March	51	77,877	386,405.5	16	11,811	81,162.5
April	7	14,152	87,019	48	25,112	47,758
May	3	8,932	2,282	42	26,756	125,496
June	6	3,452	3,062.5	37	15,603	72,191.5
July	2	5,333	60,025	27	20,326	26,004
August	4	1,686	2,761	18	6,259	10,934.5
September	2	2,800	2,400	33	24,918	84,783.5
October	177	174,592	452,158.5	12	15,184	12,912
November	6	22,950	8,283	24	18,592	30,204.5
December	1	1,000	25	7	8,798	29,835
1917						
January	135	151,886	144,116	34	24,869	59,024.5
Feb. 1–17	85	123,953	137,508	14	19,809	62,647
TOTAL	1,044	826,593	1,652,446.5	585	380,978	1,148,354

I.P. Leiberov, 'Stachechnaya borba petrogradskogo proletariata v period pervoy mirovoy voyny (19 iyulya 1914g.–16 fevralya 1917g.)', *Istoriya rabochego klassa Leningrada*, issue 2 (Leningrad, 1963), pp. 166, 177, 183. S.A. Smith, *Red Petrograd*, Cambridge, 1983, p. 50.

II Politics and War 1914-1917

36 The Declaration of War, August 1914

The summer of 1914 brought war with Germany and Austria-Hungary. Politics became inextricably mixed with Russia's fortunes in battle and with the government's handling of the domestic war effort.

. . .Following her historical traditions, Russia, united in faith and blood with the Slav nations, has never regarded their fate with indifference. The unanimous fraternal sentiments of the Russian people for the Slavs have been aroused to special intensity in the past few days, when Austria-Hungary presented to Serbia demands which she foresaw would be unacceptable to a Sovereign state.

Having disregarded the conciliatory and peaceable reply of the Serbian government, and having declined Russia's well-intentioned mediation, Austria-Hungary hastened to launch an armed attack in a bombardment of unprotected Belgrade.

Compelled, by the force of circumstances thus created, to adopt the necessary means of protection, We commanded that the army and the navy be put on a war footing, but, at the same time, holding the blood and the treasure of Our subjects dear, we made every effort to obtain a peaceable issue of the negotiations that had been started.

In the middle of friendly communications, Austria's ally, Germany, contrary to our trust in century-old relations of neighbourliness, and paying no heed to Our assurances that the measures We had adopted implied no hostile aims whatever, insisted upon their immediate abandonment, and, meeting with a rejection of this demand, suddenly declared war on Russia.

We have now to intercede not only for a related country, unjustly attacked, but also to safeguard the honour, dignity and integrity of Russia and her position among the Great Powers. We firmly believe that all Our loyal subjects will rally self-sacrificingly and with one accord to the defence of the Russian soil.

At this hour of threatening danger, let domestic strife be forgotten. Let the union between the Tsar and His people be stronger than ever, and let Russia, rising like one man, repel the insolent assault of the enemy.

With a profound faith in the justice of Our cause, and trusting humbly in Almighty Providence, we invoke prayerfully the Divine blessing for Holy Russia and Our valiant troops.

Nicholas
2 August 1914 (NS)

F.A. Golder, *Documents of Russian History 1914–1917,* New York 1927, pp. 29–30.

37   Early Military Disasters, 1914

The Russian army advanced quickly into East Prussia but met with a severe defeat at the battle of Tannenberg.

On 4 and 5 August our armies on the north-western front, the 1st under the command of General Rennenkampf and the 2nd under Samsonov, . . . began their attack on East Prussia. This was done at the insistent request of the French, to draw off the Germans from their assault on Paris. Rennenkampf's army advanced swiftly into Prussia and moved triumphantly forward, around the northern Masurian marshes. To the south, Samsonov attacked, passing the marshes from the west. Good news began to come in. . . . But unpleasant rumours soon began to spread. It was said that all was not well with Samsonov's army. Headquarters kept silent, and this only increased the alarm. And then it eventually became known that Samsonov's army had suffered a defeat.

On 17 August the Germans surrounded our 13, 15 and part of the 23 Corps and took 90,000 men prisoner. General Samsonov himself vanished without trace. It was said that he had shot himself. . . .

But from the south, from Galicia, came better news. The armies of the south-western front had begun an offensive between 5 and 10 August and had successfully penetrated into Galicia. After a stubborn fight, the enemy began to retreat. On 20 August we took Lvov. By the 30th the Austro-German army had begun to retreat along the entire SW front. We had won a decisive victory.

General A.I. Spiridovich, *Velikaya Voyna i Fevralskaya Revolyutsiya 1914–1917,* vol. 2. New York, 1960, pp. 19–21.

38   Early Military Disasters, 1914

Knox, as the British military attaché in Russia during the war, left the Allied governments with no illusions about the effectiveness of the Russian army. The Russians did have some successes, however, on the south-western Front against Austria-Hungary: Lvov and parts of Galicia were taken.

Russians claim that the invasion of East Prussia . . . was a raid altruistically undertaken with the sole object of relieving pressure on Russia's allies in the West. . . .

On the other hand, of course, the Russian Command did not deliberately send to the sacrifice some nine corps and eight cavalry divisions – more than a quarter of the whole army.

The two armies were launched with the primary idea of a raid, but the Russians, with their sanguine temperament, underrated the difficulties and hoped for a permanent local success. They forget the miserable capacity of the Warsaw-Mlava railway and the alternate marsh and sand of Northern Poland, which had been purposely left without railways and roads to delay an enemy's advance. They forget the wonderful capacity of the East Prussian railway system. They sent the 2nd Army forward without field bakeries, imagining, if they thought of the soldiers' stomachs at all, that a large army could be fed in a region devoid of surplus supplies. They probably imagined that during the strain of the campaign in Western Europe the enemy's opposition would be less serious than it actually proved. They took no count of the inferiority of the Russian machine to the German in command and armament and in power of manoeuvre.

. . .In about three weeks they [the Germans] cleared East Prussia of the enemy. With an army that averaged little over 150,000 in strength, they inflicted losses of upwards of a quarter of a million men. They dealt a severe blow to Russian morale, and deprived the Russian army of a vast quantity of very necessary material.

Major-General A. Knox, *With the Russian Army,*

1914–1917, London, 1921, pp. 90–2.

39   The Atmosphere in Russia after the Outbreak of the First World War

The outbreak of the war was marked by considerable popular enthusiasm. Cheering crowds greeted the manifesto declaring war on Germany and Austria-Hungary and war credits were approved by the Fourth Duma in a single day. Despite the evidence of initial military reverses, some sections of the population remained optimistic about the outcome, and saw war as an uplifting force which would unite the country.

A letter from V.V. Musin-Pushkin, a wealthy Moscow landowner and member of the Centre group in the Fourth Duma

. . .I consider that with the atmosphere which I have seen to exist in the army, and with the mood of the people which is heard of on all sides, we cannot fail to be victorious. More difficult than the war will be peace and the resolution of the many questions which have accumulated over the centuries and which have, in the everyday business of the last few years, been approached only with 'the fear of God and faith'. But, there is no doubt that a miracle will occur. Two things educate the people in an instant: revolution and, especially, victorious wars like this one. The people reaches an unprecedented high point and immediately displays its genius, and its leaders, as if independent of themselves, flourish and perform miracles. Without a belief in a victorious war bringing this interval of clarity, one could only crawl away and hide from the list of 'questions' which need solving. But I already see clearly the forerunners of the future – this soberness, and general love and goodwill.

29 December 1914

Krasny Arkhiv, vol. 61 (1935), pp. 134–5.

40   Report of General A.A. Polivanov, Minister of War, to the Council of Ministers on the military situation, 16 July 1915

German and Austrian attacks in the early part of 1915 were intended to deal with Russia before the expected entry of Italy into the war on the Allied side. The Central Powers succeeded in recapturing all of Russian-held Austrian territory, Russian Poland and parts of the western borderlands. Sukhomlinov, the Minister of War, was replaced in June 1915 by Polivanov.

I consider it my duty as a citizen and a soldier to report to the Council of Ministers that our fatherland is in danger. . . . The Minister of War then gave a general picture of the front, but noted that his information was probably out of date as, firstly, our retreat was developing with growing speed and in many cases had assumed the character of almost a rout and, secondly, Headquarters was not giving the Ministry of War any information about the position at the front. The Minister of War had been compelled to make his report on the basis of information provided by our counter-intelligence services about [troop] movements in the enemy camp. In any case it was obvious to anyone with the slightest knowledge of military affairs that we were approaching a time which would be decisive to the outcome of the entire war. The Germans had forced us to retreat by artillery fire alone, using their enormous superiority in this field and their inexhaustible supplies of shells. As they were firing our batteries had to remain silent even during serious clashes. As the enemy did not need to use its infantry they suffered hardly any losses, whilst our soldiers were dying by the thousand. Naturally our resistance weakened daily, whilst the enemy onslaught intensified. Only God knows where the retreat will end. . . . The troops are undoubtably exhausted by the continual defeats and retreats. Their confidence in final victory and in their leaders is undermined. Threatening signs of growing demoralization are becoming more and more evident. Cases of desertion and of soldiers voluntarilly giving themselves up to the enemy are becoming more frequent. In is difficult to expect selflessness and enthusiasm from men sent into battle without weapons and ordered to take rifles from their dead comrades.

But on this gloomy background of an army disintegrating both morally and numerically, there is yet one other development fraught with danger and about which it is no longer possible to keep silent. There is growing confusion at Headquarters. It also is gripped by the fatal psychology of retreat and is preparing to move to a new location deep inside Russia. Retreat, retreat and retreat – that is all that is heard from HQ. No system, no plan is obvious from its orders and dispositions. Not one boldly conceived manoeuvre, not one attempt to make use of the mistakes of an over-confident enemy. At the same time, HQ continues to guard its prerogatives jealously. In the midst of a growing catastrophe it does not consider it necessary to consult with close colleagues. Neither army commanders nor commanders-in-chief of whole fronts have been summoned to HQ to confer about the situation, to suggest possible ways out of our difficulties and to discuss ways in which we can carry on the struggle. General Yanushkevich rules over everyone and everything. Everyone else must silently carry out orders issued by him in the name of the Grand Duke. No initiative is permitted. Silence, no discussion – this is HQ's favourite cry. But the blame for our present misfortunes falls not on HQ but on everyone else. . . . The generals, the regimental and company commanders are to blame, the fairy-tale knights of old are to blame, the Minister of War is to blame, the government is to blame both as a body and as individuals, the home front is to blame. In a word, everyone is to blame except for the one body which carries any direct responsibility.

> A.N. Yakhontov (compiler), 'Thyazhelye Dni. Sekretnye zasedaniya Soveta Ministrov 16 iyul-2 sentyabr 1915'. *Arkhiv Russkoy Revolyutsii*, vol. XVIII. Berlin 1926, pp. 15–16.

41   Nicholas II as Commander-in-Chief: Rodzyanko's Letter, 12 August 1915

In August 1915 Nicholas II decided to assume the role of Commander-in-Chief himself in place of Grand Duke Nikolai Nikolaevich. The Tsar was motivated by a sense of deep responsibility to Russia, but he failed to see the disadvantages of the move.

Your Imperial Majesty:
    . . .I make bold to beg Your Majesty again not to subject Your sacred person to the dangers in which You may be placed by the consequences of Your decision.
    Sire! You are the symbol and the standard around which all the nationalities of Russia rally. This standard cannot and must not be dragged into the stress and storm of the ordeals which have come to us. It must shine radiantly as the torch for all the strivings of the nation and serve as the invincible bulwark of all the sons of Russia and as the promise of security for their minds, alarmed by these events.
    Sire! You have no right, in the face of the nation, to allow anything

to happen that might possible cast the faintest shadow to fall upon this sacred standard.

At this dreadful hour of peril, unprecedented in the history of Russia, when the possibility arises of a heavy Teuton yoke over the Russian land, You, Sire, must be beyond and above those organs of government which shoulder the duty of immediately repulsing the enemy.

You cannot act as executive: You must be judge, a benign encourager or implacable punisher.

But if You, Sire, should take over the direct command of our glorious army – You, Sire, the last refuge of Your people – who will then pass judgement in the event of failure or defeat? Is it not really obvious, Sire, that You will then voluntarily have surrendered Your inviolable person to the judgment of the people? – and that is fatal to Russia.

Consider, Sire, what You are laying hands on – on Your own self, Sire!

Our native land is going through a painful crisis. General mistrust surrounds the present government, which has lost will power and confidence in itself. All idea of authority has been shattered by its disorderly measures, and yet, more than ever before, there has now grown up in the country a realization of the need for a firm, unshakeable faith in oneself and in the popular strength of the government. The minds of all the Russians have reached a state of an unprecedented strain, fearing for the fate of Russia.

The nation is impatiently longing for a power which will instil confidence and lead the country into the path of victory. Yet at such a time, Your Majesty, You decide to displace the Supreme Commander-in-Chief, whom the Russian people still trusts absolutely. The people will interpret Your step in no other way but as inspired by the Germans around You, who in the minds of the people are identified with our enemies and with treason to the Russian cause.

In the popular mind, the result of Your Majesty's decision will be a reaalization of the hoplessness of the situation and of the chaos which has invaded the administration.

Sire! The situation will be even worse if the army, deprived of a leader enjoying its absolute confidence, loses its courage.

In this event defeat is inevitable, and within the country revolution and anarchy will then break out, sweeping everything from their path.

Your Majesty! Before it is too late, revoke your decision, no matter how hard it may be for you.

Retain Grand Duke Nicholas Nicholaevich at the head of the army.

Reassure alarmed and agitated minds by forming a government of people who enjoy Your confidence and are known to the country by their public activities.

Sire, it is not yet too late! . .

Sire, give heed to this truthful word from the heart of Your loyal servant.

The President of the State Duma
Mikhail Rodzyanko
12 August 1915

F.A. Golder, *Documents of Russian History, 1914–1917.* New York 1927, pp. 208–10.

42   Nicholas II as Commander-in-Chief

The Ministers' Appeal to the Tsar, 21 August 1915.

Most Gracious Sovereign:

Do not count against us our bold and candid address. We are driven to this action by our duty as faithful subjects, our love for You and our native country, and our alarmed consciousness of the dire portent of the events now taking place.

Yesterday, at the meeting of the Council of Ministers under Your personal chairmanship, we laid before You our unanimous appeal that Grand Duke Nicholas Nicholaevich should not be removed from his part in the supreme command of the army. But we fear that Your Imperial Majesty did not deign to incline to our plea, which, in our opinion, is the plea of all loyal Russia.

Sire, we dare once more to tell You that, to the best of our understanding, Your decision threatens Russia, Yourself, and Your dynasty with evil consequences.

At the same meeting the radical difference between the view of the Chairman of the Council of Ministers and our own became manifest in estimating events within the country and considering the course of action to be followed by the Government. A situation such as this, intolerable at any time, is fatal in these days.

In these circumstances, we lose faith in the possibility of being of service to You and the country.

Your Imperial Majesty's loyal subjects:

Petr Kharitonov
Petr Bark
Count Pavel Ignatev
Aleksandr Krivosheyn

Prince N. Shcherbatov
Prince Vsevolod Shakhovskoy
Sergei Sazonov
Aleksandr Samarin

21 August 1915
Ibid pp. 210–11.

43   Programme of the Progressive Bloc, August 1915

Discontent with the conduct of the war affected a wide spectrum of political opinion. The Progressive Bloc had a majority in the Fourth Duma but the Tsar, with the strong support of the Empress, was utterly opposed to relinquishing any of his power.

The undersigned representatives of factions and groups in the State Duma and State Council, believing(1) that only a strong, firm and active government can lead our country to victory and(2) that such a government must be one which enjoys the confidence of the people and is capable of organizing real cooperation between all citizens, have come to the unanimous conclusion that such cooperation can only be achieved, and the government gain sufficient authority if the following [minimum] conditions are observed.

1 The formation of a unified government of individuals who have the confidence of the country and are in agreement with the legislative institutions about the need for the rapid implementation of a definite programme.

2 A radical change in the present methods of administration, which are based on a distrust of initiative by the public, in particular:

(a)   strict observation of the principles of legality in government.

(b)   the removal of the dual authority of the military and civil powers in questions which have no direct relevance to the execution of military operations.

(c)   the renewal of the system of local administration.

(d)   a rational and consistent policy to preserve internal peace, and the removal of discordances between nationalities and classes.

To implement this policy, the following administrative and legislative measures must be taken.

1   The Imperial prerogative of mercy must be used to release those who are imprisoned for purely political or religious crimes, without having committed any other offences, and improvements must be made to the conditions of others convicted of political or religious offences.

2   The release of those exiled by administrative order for political and religious offences.

3   A complete and definite halt to prosecutions undertaken, for whatever reason, on grounds of religion, and the withdrawal of circulars which have limited and altered the provisions of the edict of 17 April 1905.

4   The preparation of a bill to grant autonomy to Poland and its rapid introduction into the legislative institutions and, simultaneously, the removal of restrictions on the rights of Poles and a review of legislation on Polish landowning.

5   The process of repealing restrictive laws about the Jews must be begun. Steps must be taken to abolish the Pale of settlement and the restrictions on Jewish entry to educational institutions and to various professions. The Jewish press should be revived.

6   A conciliatory policy towards Finland, in particular including changes in the make-up of the administration and Senate, and the ending of legal action against officials.

7   The revival of the Ukrainian press, the release from imprisonment and exile of priests, convicted for belonging to the Uniate Church, and a review of the question of exiled Galician inhabitants.

8   The revival of the activity of trade unions and the ending of legal action against representatives of workers' sickness funds on suspicion of their belonging to an illegal [political] party. The revival of the workers' press.

9   Agreement of the government and legislative bodies on the rapid implementation of the following programme of bills, designed to organise the country to assist in victory and to maintain its internal peace: amendments to the zemstvo statute of 1890 and the municipal regulations of 1892, the introduction of a *volost* zemstvo, the introduction of zemstva into the borderlands. . . . A law on co-operatives. A bill on rest time for commercial employees. An improvement in the conditions of post and telegraph workers. The permanent introduction of prohibition. A bill on zemstvo and municipal unions. A bill on changing from one religion to another. Regulations about inspections. The introduction of a local court in those provinces where this had been prevented for financial

reasons. The implementation of legislative measures which are necessary to fulfil the above programme.

For the faction of the progressive group of Nationalists - V. Bobrinsky
Centre-V. Lvov
Zemstvo-Octobrists-I. Dmitriukhov
Union of 17 October-S. Shidlovsky
Progressists-I. Efremov
Kadets-P. Milyukov

Krasny Arkhiv, vol. 50-1 (1932), pp. 133-6.

44   Disunity in the Government, September 1915

Some of the government was in sympathy with the aims of the Progressive Bloc, but Goremykin and Nicholas II decided, without further consultation, to adjourn the Duma in September 1915. These notes on the meeting of the Council of Ministers reflect the Ministers' attitude to this decision.

The Notes of I.A. Yakhontov - a secretary - on the meeting of 2 September 1915

I.L. Goremykin returned from Headquarters on the 1st of September with an Imperial order to release the Duma for its autumn vacations not later than the 3rd of September, and for the present Council of Ministers to remain at its post in its present composition. When the situation at the front permits, His Majesty will personally summon the Council of Ministers and will decide everything.

By the beginning of the meeting, the Ministers had apparently already been informed of the decisions brought back by the Chairman, and this was reflected in their mood and in their discussions . . :

The crisis is at hand. Terrible nervousness. I have often seen the Council in an informal situation, but nothing like this has ever happened during meetings. S.D. Sazonov was particularly upset and virtually hysterical by the end of the meeting. When I.L. Goremykin was leaving the room, having adjourned the meeting, the Minister of Foreign Affairs [Sazonov] announced: 'I do not wish to say goodbye to this madman or to shake his hand.' Then he walked towards the exit, staggering, so that I followed him to try to catch him if he fainted. Sazonov noticed nothing and had the air of a man unconscious of his surroundings. In the anteroom he cried out hysterically, 'Il est fou, ce vieillard,'* and ran out of the building.

Polivanov was boiling over with bile, and looked ready to bite; he behaved quite indecently towards the Chairman. Krivoshein looked hopelessly sad and anxious. Ignatev, as he always does in difficult moments, was violently messing up his sparse hair. The sniper, Kharitonov, was silent most of the time, for some reason. The conversation was extraordinarily feverish, jumping from one point to another and inevitably returning to the adjournment and its consequences. It was most difficult, not only to catch characteristic sentences, but in some cases, to catch even the substance of the discussions.

> M. Cherniavsky (ed), *Prologue to Revolution*. Englewood Cliffs, NJ, 1967 pp. 226-7

45   Rasputin, the Empress and the Tsarevich Aleksey

Rumours about Rasputin proliferated in Russia: most of them were wildly exaggerated. However the existence of such tales was enough to produce a significant feeling against the Empress and Rasputin. Kokovtsov, not known for his feelings of friendship towards the Empress, explains the roots of Rasputin's influence over the royal family.

. . .Rasputin soon broached a subject near Her Majesty's heart. He began to tell her that she and the Tsar were surrounded with difficulties; that they would never learn the truth, surrounded as they were by flatterers and selfish climbers who would never show how to make the people's lot easier; only by searching their own hearts and by supporting each other could the Imperial couple learn the truth. When in doubt, they must pray and ask God to intruct and enlighten them. If they put faith in God, everything would be right, as God would never abandon those he had set to rule over the people. Here he struck another note, pleasing to the Tsarina's ears. He advised closer contact with and closer study of the people, who deserved to be trusted more. . . . The people would tell the real truth, the exact opposite of what was told by ministers and officials, who were not concerned over the tears and wants of the people.

. . .Now the fatal moment drew near. The little Tsarevich had for

---

* This old man is mad.

some time shown symtoms of the incurable disease, haemophilia. The Empress had tried to convince herself that it was not so, but in the end she had to accept reality. Physicians were helpless not only to cure but even to alleviate the sufferings of the patient. It is easy to understand the mother's state of mind. Having had her hopes for an heir fulfilled . . . and having lavished upon her son all her tenderness, she had finally learned that she herself had transmitted to him the dreaded disease.

. . . At that moment the Empress again heard from the *starets*, who could pray as no one else, who spoke a language different from everbody else, who had a faith different from the faith of those about her. She was told of cases where persons visited by great sorrow had asked the *starets* to pray for them and were given help in their trouble. She was even told of cases where his prayer had arrested mortal illness. Therefore he was summoned more and more frequently, taken more and more into the confidence of Their Majesties, and entered into the life of the court; he became an adviser on the most knotty problems and was generally referred to as 'friend'.

. . . one of the court ladies known for her hostility to Rasputin, which caused her to lose her position at court, told me that she had been witness to a consultation of doctors during one of the most severe attacks of haemophilia when they had been unable to stop the haemorrhage. Rasputin came, stayed at the child's side for some time, and the haemorrhage stopped.

> V. N. Kokovtsov, *Out of My Past*. Stanford, 1953, pp. 450–1.

46   The Union of Towns

War placed great strains on the already inefficient Russian economy. The government was slow to react to the demands of the army and of industry which had been cut off from many of its former sources of supply. Other agencies stepped in to deal with the situation: in September 1914 the Union of Towns was founded. Astrov, the author of this piece, was mayor of Moscow and Chairman of the Central Committee of the Union of Towns.

The amalgamation of Russian towns into an All-Russian Union was inevitable. It was dictated by the force of events. And the necessity for such an organization was further emphasized when the government announced its plan for supplying the army and evacuating the wounded. The districts directly affected by the war were to be cut off from the rest of the country. No organization, with the exception of the Red Cross, was to be allowed to cross the demarcation line. But public organizations were entrusted exclusively with the task of the relief and care of those sick and wounded soldiers who had been sent from the army to the clearing stations situated on this line. The military authorities had come to see that they would be unable to fulfil their task without such assistance. The carrying out of the plan naturally called for the creation of strong and, at the same time flexible, organizations, which would be able to fill all gaps, and prepare the whole country for the reception of the wounded. The Unions of Zemstvos and Towns undertook the work.

. . .The problems with which the Union was confronted were summed up in the following eight paragraphs:

(1) aiding the municipalities to establish and maintain the necessary number of hospital beds;

(2) arrangements for the distribution of the wounded among the districts appointed to receive them, and the creation for this purpose of special local committees and bureaus of enquiry;

(3) the equipment of hospital trains;

(4) the building and equipment of suitable premises for the reception and evacuation of the wounded;

(5) the organization of army canteens along the routes chosen for the evacuation of the wounded;

(6) the organization of central depots of medical goods, surgical instruments, underwear and winter clothing; the organization of similar depots attached to the clearing stations; and the establishment of a central workshop for the manufacture of surgical instruments;

(7) the provision of medical staffs for the various towns and cities concerned;

(8) the raising of funds for the work of the Union.

. . .Some idea of the scope and scale of the work of the Union of Towns may be gathered from the number of persons employed in its central administration, in local institutions and at the front.

On 1 September 1917 the figures were as follows:

	Men and women	Women	% of women
Local and district committees	30,000	16,000	53.2
Central committee and administration	2,636	876	33.2
Committees of the Front	21,500	5,420	25.2

Total number of persons employed by the Union	54,136
Number of non-commissioned soldiers attached to the Union	16,000
Total	70,136

. . .the representatives of the municipalities . . . found themselves compelled to acknowledge that the financial resources of the towns were quite inadequate to meet the new demands resulting from the outbreak of hostilities. They pointed out that they could not undertake to carry out their new obligations except on the understanding that only a small fraction of their modest revenues should be devoted to war purposes, and that the necessary funds should be provided by the State Treasury. Treasury grants were in fact the chief source of the money spent by the Union of Towns on the relief of sick and wounded soldiers, on the prevention of epidemics, on the organization of the relief of refugees and other charitable work.

. . . The ratio between the amount of the government grants and the revenue from other sources may be seen in the following data, taken from a report of 1 January 1915:

	Rubles
Government grants	32,099,000
Subscriptions by towns	1,282,543
Donations	1,846,619

A report, dated 1 August 1916, shows that during the first two years of the war, the Central Committee alone effected payments to the amount of 125 million rubles. Of this sum 117 million rubles represented government grants . . . and only 8 million came from donations, subscriptions or from other sources.

> P.P. Gronsky and N. J. Astrov, *The War and the Russian Government*. New Haven, 1929, pp. 171-3, 192-5.

47   The Union of Zemstva and Towns

In July 1915 a joint committee of the Union of Zemstva and the Union of Towns (Zemgor) was set up.

The evacuation of the industrial plants of Riga was naturally suggested immediately after the occupation of Libau by the Germans. The idea, however, found little support amongst the local manufacturers and among the highest military and civil authorities and . . . it was decided that such a measure would be 'simply impossible'. The Germans were expected to capture Riga about the middle of July [1915]; yet the officer commanding the city thought it necessary as late as June 17 to issue an order prohibiting the dispatch of any freights from Riga, with the exception of finished products and factory equipment not required for work then in progress. . . . As for Petrograd, the authorities there looked upon Riga and its industry as already doomed. . . . Owners of factories engaged on work for national defence were asked to send representatives to Riga in order to select equipment from local factories which they might use for their own plants. . . .

The Union of Zemstvos and Towns decided to intervene. Their representatives submitted to the Minister of Trade and Industry a memorandum in which his attention was drawn to the necessity of conducting the evacuation of Riga in an orderly and systematic fashion. The memorandum urged that the factories of Riga should be transferred to the interior of the country as integral units, together with their technical staffs and workers, in order that production might be resumed at the new places . . . the heads of the unions, Prince Lvov and M. Chelnokov, succeeded in obtaining the appointment of a special commission to supervise the speedy evacuation of Riga. This commission was vested with extraordinary powers. It consisted of three generals and five representatives of the unions, and on 6 July began its work. Although absolute unanimity prevailed among the members of the commission, the officer commanding the city placed many needless vexations and simply ridiculous obstacles in their way, while his petty bureaucratic methods greatly hampered its labours. Still worse were the difficulties in dealing with the Riga State Railway. Instead of cooperation and help, the commission found there an atmosphere of peevishness, in addition to the habitual carelessness and irregularity in the work of the officials of this railway. . . .

In Riga, one of the most important industrial centres of the Empire, an immense quantity of highly valuable materials and manufactured goods had accumulated. Many factories had in stock thousands of tons of copper, steel, lead, tin and other metals. The work of the commission was of a highly responsible and delicate nature, since, in spite of its intention to evacuate industrial plants as integral units, the commission found itself compelled to break them up to a considerable extent, lest materials of great value for the production of military equipment should fall into the hands of the enemy. Fortunately the German offensive was delayed, so that the commission was able to complete its work at the beginning of September, by which time most of the valuable equipment was evacuated.

. . .the executive functions of the evacuation of the city were performed chiefly by the officials of the two unions, for the army generals had at their disposal only a very small staff, not more than some three or four officers. The number of engineers, students, and other trained . . . workers despatched from Moscow to Riga to assist in the evacuation was about sixty.

> T.I. Polner, V.A. Obolensky, S.P. Turin, *Russian Local Government during the War and the Union of Zemstvos.* New Haven, 1930, pp. 277–8. Based on N.N. Kovalevsky, *Izvestiya glavnogo komiteta po snabzheniyu armii zemskogo i gorodskogo soyuza,* no. 2–3, 1915, pp. 58–64.

48 Formation of the War Industries Committee, June 1915

The regime was not overkeen to cooperate with the Union of Towns, the Union of Zemstva and the War Industries Committee since it saw them as an incipient alternative government.

Resolution of the Congress of the Association of Industry and Trade, 27 May 1915

Recognizing the inevitability of the application of all productive forces to the organization of work for defence, and in view of the extreme necessity for a better organization of the rear, the Association of Trade and Industry . . . unanimously resolves:

1 to organize all the unutilized power of Russian industry for the satisfaction of the needs of the state's defence;

   (a)   to instruct all commercial-industrial organizations to form regional committees for the unification of local commerce and industry with the aim of defining the capabilities of enterprises for producing all that is necessary for the army and navy, and, coordinating the activities of factories and mills, to draft a plan for the urgent fulfilment of present work, as well as to define the requirements in raw materials, fuel, transport and labour force;

(b)   for the coordination of all work of various regions and groups, and equally for the coordination of this work with the activities of the High Governmental Institutions, the congress resolves to establish in Petrograd a Central War-Industries Committee, assigning the organization of the Committee to the Council of the Association such that representatives of science and technology, from various commercial-industrial organizations, from the railway administrations and the All-Russian Unions of Zemstvos and Cities may participate;

2 to propose to the Central War-Industries Committee that it turn its attention to questions of communication and transportation, to ensure industry the necessary supplies, for which the congress considers advantageous the division of the Committee into sections. The elaboration of a plan of general activity, to be communicated to local organizations, must be the first order of business of the Committee as far as organizational work is concerned;

3 to cover the organizational expenses of the War-Industries Committee by preliminarily assigning 25,000 rubles, and directing the Council to work out a budget of expenses and ways of meeting them.

The activity of the War-Industries Committee must be directed towards the satisfaction of the requirements of the army's Supreme Command. The congress expresses its confidence that all Russian industry will whole-heartedly give itself to this matter and find within itself the strength to deal within the great historic tasks. The best and most capable people must be attracted to the business of administration to fulfil them.

In recognizing the need to carry the war to a victorious conclusion, of not being stopped by any sacrifice, by the length of the struggle, and in the firm conviction that our glorious army under the leadership of the Supreme Commander in close cooperation with the nation will fulfil this great historic task, the Association of Industry and Trade calls on the entire country, on employees and workers, to establish a plan of work for industry in a calm and systematic manner with the consciousness of full responsibility which this historic moment places upon Russian industry. The War Committee of Russian Industry, using the guidelines of previous experience, must devote itself to the realization of the tasks placed before it, making good all the deficiencies of supplies.

> L. Siegelbaum, *The War-Industries Committees and the Politics of Industrial Mobilization in Russia, 1915–17,* unpublished DPhil thesis, University of Oxford 1975, pp. 50–1. Originally in *Promyshlennost i torgovlya* , no. 11 (179) (Petrograd), 1 June 1915, pp. 543–4.

49   The Placing and Fulfilment of Orders by the Central War Industries Committee, September 1915–January1917

Date	Orders placed	Total placed	Orders fulfilled	Total fulfilled	% fulfilled
to Sep 1915	36.69	36.69	—	—	—
Sep 1915	81.71	118.40	—	—	—
Oct 1915	50.62	169.02	—	—	—
Nov 1915	30.87	199.89	—	—	—
Dec 1915	11.13	211.02	1.81	1.81	0.85
Jan 1916	21.42	232.44	0.49	2.30	0.98
Feb 1916	-3.05*	229.39	4.93	7.23	3.98
Mar 1916	18.64	248.03	6.79	14.02	5.64
Apr 1916	16.32	261.35	4.27	18.29	7.00
May 1916	19.49	280.84	4.78	23.07	8.21
Jun 1916	25.62	306.46	9.63	32.70	10.01
Jul 1916	13.94	320.40	n.a.	n.a.	n.a.
Jan 1917	69.60	390.00	99.30	132.00	33.74

* Indicates that number of orders cancelled was greater than number placed.
n.a. not available.
1   All figures are in millions of rubles.
2   The table includes only orders from the Artillery, Quartermasters' and Technical units.

Ibid p. 111.

50   The Brusilov Offensive

Only in 1916 did the military situation improve. The military supply situation was much better organized. The Brusilov offensive against Austria-Hungary was successful and was instrumental in persuading Romania to join the Allies. Against Germany, however, it was quite a different matter. Attacks in Lithuania and Latvia met with little success.

From dawn on 22 May heavy artillery fire began along the entire south-west front. The main obstacle to the advancing artillery was barbed wire and . . . therefore the light artillery was required to make gaps in it. The heavy artillery was given the task of destroying the trenches is the forward fortified zone, and part of the artillery also had the job of silencing the enemy's guns. . . .

Our artillery attack was marked by complete success in all areas. In most cases gaps in the wire were made in sufficient number and the forward fortified zone was completely destroyed along with its defenders, leaving only piles of wreckage and mutilated bodies. . . .

Between 22 May and 30 July my armies captured 8,255 officers and 370,153 other ranks, 496 guns, 144 machine guns and much other equipment. The south-western armies ceased operations for the winter having taken heavily fortified positions which the enemy had considered to be near-impregnable. On the northern part of the front we retook a substantial part of our own territory, and in the centre and on the left flank we took part of Eastern Galicia and the whole of the Bukovina. A direct result of these successes was Romania's departure from the neutral camp and her entry into the war on our side. The enemy's defeat was a grave disappointment for him: the Austrians and Germans had firmly believed that their eastern front, which had been reinforced over a period of ten months, was completely secure. . . . These impregnable strongholds, which in places had been fortified with reinforced concrete, collapsed under the irresistible attacks of our valiant troops.

Whatever has been said, it must be recognized that the preparation for this operation was exemplary, and that this involved the full co-operation of officers of all ranks. Everything was thought out beforehand and carried out at the right time. This operation also showed that the view, for some reason widespread in Russia, that the Russian army had collapsed after the setbacks of 1915, was incorrect. In 1916 the army was strong and ready for battle, for it defeated an army significantly superior in numbers and produced successes such as no single army had up to that time had.

A.A. Brusilov, *Moi Vospominaniya*. Riga, 1929, pp.
198, 206.

51   The Brusilov Offensive: A Western View

The preparation ordered by Brusilov's staff was thorough beyond
anything hitherto seen on the eastern front. The front-trenches were
sapped forward, in places to within fifty paces of the enemy lines – at
that, on more or less the entire front. Huge dug-outs for reserve-troops
were constructed, often with earth ramparts high enough to prevent
enemy gunners from seeing what was going on in the Russian rear.
Accurate models of the Austrian trenches were made, and troops
trained with them; aerial photography came into its own, and the
position of each Austrian battery noted – an innovation, since on the
other fronts pilots were not given any training in aerial photography at
all. The fact, too, that reserve-troops were under the same command
for a number of months also helped organization – another
comparative rarity.

. . .It took much pressure from Brusilov himself to make sure that
subordinates undertook novel work of the type he had in mind; and
Brusilov himself appears to have been the best type of commander –
striking the fear of God into his subordinates, but never to the point
where they became terrified of responsibility. He was himself a tireless
worker, but not one like Alexeyev – [Alekseev] for whom work
became an end in itself. He and his staff paid continual visits to the
very front lines, again a considerable rarity. . . . He had to deal with
innumerable objections from his subordinates. Kaledin, commanding
VIII Army, showed little stomach for action; Lechitsky, of IX Army,
complained continually of poor heavy artillery; Shcherbaev, one of
the cavalry-General Staff would-be imitators of French methods, also
had his own schemes and grumbled at Brusilov's challenge to French
supremacy. Only, perhaps, Sakharov of XI Army had much sympathy with what Brusilov was attempting. For Brusilov to force, not
only the three dissenting army commanders, but also the dissenting
Alexeyev, to accept his methods shows tactical skills of an unusually
high order.

N. Stone, *The Eastern Front,*

1914–1917. London, 1975, pp. 238–9.

52   The Government and the Progressive Bloc, June 1916

The Progressive Bloc continued to gain support. Distrust of the government was increased in 1916 by the dismissal of most of the more liberal and capable ministers, and their replacement by ultra-conservatives. The views of Sturmer (Goremykin's replacement as Chairman of the Council of Ministers) on the Progressive Bloc reveals the isolation of government from society: even from conservatives such as Kokovtsov.

Report of B.V. Sturmer to Nicholas II

. . .The aim of the so-called 'Progressive Bloc', supported by a majority in the Duma, is to implement during the summer session the main bills in the progressive programme. These include a bill to remove all legal restrictions from the peasantry, a zemstvo reform, alterations to the system of minicipal government, a new law about societies and unions, a bill to establish national zemstvo and munici-pal unions as bodies which would continue to function after the war, outside the supervision of the government.

Each of these bills interests the so-called 'Progressive Bloc' not so much for its content, as by the fact that they will allow the Duma tribune to be used to persuade society that the Duma is filled with the best intentions, but that it is unable to actually do anything practical since the government, which fears any sort of change, is engaged in a continuous struggle with progressive tendencies in society.

In reality, each of these bills is constructed on principles so incom-patible with history, practice and the spirit of Russian legislation, that if they became law by any method, the country would be plunged into an interminable situation.

If, on the basis of the Duma's bill, national zemstvo and municipal unions came into permanent existence, Russian society would find itself with two governments, in which the 'unofficial government', financed from the State Treasury, would be independent not only of the government proper, but also of the state in general. The changes in zemstvo organization proposed by the Duma would lead to the trans-formation of the Zemstvo from institutions dealing with the local economy under the supervision of the government, into organs of local government, independent of the authorities. The municipal reform which the Duma proposes would mean that life in the towns would be under the control of lawyers, journalists and other such less reliable elements of the urban population.

The Duma bill on the peasantry is of the same type. . . . At a time when the war demands that exceptional care should be used in questions which might increase class antagonisms, the Duma has begun to discuss an [old government] bill [on the peasantry] and speeches on the matter have been marked by a hardly permissible passion, at times becoming harsh slogans of the peasant masses against the gentry, the most important class in the country. . . .

The 'Progressive Bloc' is trying to use the bill on the peasantry as an excuse to put through Jewish equality, as well as to make changes to the Duma electoral law. This is being done by means of amendments to individual articles of the bill, in the belief that there will be no attempt to delay the bill as a whole as it is so closely in tune with the peasants' immediate needs.

Despite this, the position in the legislature would not give cause for concern if one could state with certainty that the State Council's present membership would protect the interests of the state. However, it is unfortunately not so, for the aims of the so-called 'Progressive Bloc' in the Duma have found definite support among some of the influential members of the State Council, including its appointed members. . . .

The leader of this movement in the State Council is Count Kokovtsov, officially a member of the non-party group, but his present mood and actions make him one of the especially uncompromising supporters of the 'Progressive Bloc'.

> V.P. Semennikov (ed),
> *Monarkhiya pered Krushe-*
> *niem 1914–1917*. Moscow–
> Leningrad, 1927, pp. 122–4.

53   Shortages and their effect on the army; proposal for a military dictator

Despite efforts from outside the government, the army was still experiencing difficulties in securing supplies. Alekseev, the Chief of Staff, proposes the appointment of a military dictator. In July 1916 Stumer was given extensive powers inside Russia but he was unable to assert his authority and by late August the experiment had failed.

Report of General Alekseev to Nicholas II, 15 June 1916

During our recent operations much of the fighting has been against heavily fortified positions.

. . .It is therefore vital that the army has a sufficient quantity of heavy artillery. The war has seen the formation of many heavy batteries . . . but unfortunately the supply of shells has not yet reached the necessary level. . . .

We must take exceptional measures and concentrate all our forces on providing the army with munitions.

The Minister of War and the head of the Artilley Corps have reported that they are taking all possible steps, but are far from achieving the desired results, due to a whole series of serious difficulties which are outside their control:

1. Transport

At the present time there is no area of life where the effects of inadequate transport are not felt.

Transport for factories working on defence materials is given special preference, at an undoubted cost to other areas. Despite this, even special state factories are not receiving everything they need . . . even though they have ordered it and materials are ready for dispatch, but sit for months waiting to be moved because 'there are no wagons available', 'there are wagons, but we've had no instructions' or 'that piece of line cannot take any more traffic'.

. . .On average, defence industries are only getting 50-60 per cent of their transport requirements; the Minister of Communications reports that instead of the 18.5 million poods which Petersburg needs, it will only be possible to transport 8 million.

In such conditions, it is not only inconceivable that production can be increased, but the present level of work will have to be reduced.

2. Metal

There has recently been a 'metal famine' on the world market. Without exception, all defence industries have a demand for metal, which is not being met by the available supply. Besides the general difficulty of getting metal on the world market, the exceptional problems of transporting it to Archangel and thence throughout Russia and the unsatisfactory arrangements for mining metals in Russia have a large part to play in the approaching crisis.

. . .The Minister of Trade and Industry reports that . . . defence industries are at present receiving at most 50 per cent of their requirements for metal. In such a dangerous, almost tragic position, no increase in the production of shells and cartridges can be envisaged.

3. The Work Force
The defence industries are suffering a severe crisis in relation to their workforce. The strike movement grows daily; criminal propaganda spreads its fatal message widely – in the main on fertile soil because of the shortages of food and the high prices of vital products.

The number of workers is decreasing, and this, together with propaganda, is the reason for impossibly high demands from the work force, as a result of which there is a never-ending series of strikes and any increase in production is impossible.

The opinion of the Minister of War is that a sure means of combatting strikes is the militarization of factories engaged on defence work. Besides this, it is absolutely vital to remove the basic cause of the discontent – to provide cheap food.

4. Foreign orders and currency
Many orders for artillery supplies have been placed abroad, but serious transport difficulties . . . have slowed down the arrival of our orders in Archangel, whilst some of them have been destroyed by mines. The non-arrival of factory equipment has has a serious effect on our output of shells.

Our lack of foreign currency makes it very difficult to increase the number of orders we can place abroad. Our representative in England . . . reports that our most important orders have not been placed because of our lack of credit.

. . . To prevent the coming crisis . . . the following measures must be taken immediately:

1   . . . Power in the interior of the empire must be concentrated in the hands of a single person, the Supreme Minister of Defence. This official must coordinate and direct the activity of all ministries, government and public institutions which are outside the combat area.

    All government institutions must, without exception, be subordinate to the orders of this official.

    The Supreme Minister of Defence must be responsible only to Your Majesty. . . .

2   Transport must be organized for fuel, materials and provisions for workers in defence industries.

3   The mining of coal, other fuels and metals must be increased. . . .

4   The militarization of factories in defence industries. . . .

5 Those nationalities which are not liable for military service should be conscripted to work in defence industries and in the mining of essential materials.

Ibid pp. 259-66.

54   Speech by P.N. Milyukov to the Fourth Duma, 1 November 1916

By late 1916 the regime was completely isolated. Milyukov's speech treats the government with derision, and outside Petrograd the mass of the population was alienated both from the government and from educated society. The only uniting factor was a belief in all sections of society that a catastrophe was imminent.

. . .There is an enormous difference between the meetings we had with Goremykin in July 1915 and February 1916 and the meeting we are having now. These meetings are as different as the general situation in the country. We were able then to discuss how to organize the country with the help of Duma legislation. If we had been given the opportunity to put through our proposed bills . . . Russia would now not be so helpless over her food supply. But this is in the past. The question of our legislation has moved into the background. We now see and know that we can no more legislate with this government than we can lead Russia to victory with it. (Voices from the left: true.) We tried earlier to prove that it was impossible to use all the country's strength to fight a war against an external enemy if a war was going on inside the country, for popular support is vital in achieving the nation's aims. . . . It now appears that it is useless to give proof: it is useless when fear of the people, of one's own country grips the government and when the fundamental task becomes to put an end to the war, at any cost, so that the government can distance itself as quickly as possibly from the need to find popular support. (Voices from the left: true.) On 10 February 1916 I finished my speech by saying that we had decided to pay no more attention to the 'wisdom of the authorities' and that I did not expect any answer from the cabinet in its present form to these alarming questions. My words sounded a little too gloomy then. We can now go further and perhaps these words will seem too optimistic. We say to this government, as the declaration of the [Progressive] Bloc stated: we will fight you, we will fight by all legal means until you go. (Voices from left: true.) It is said that one member of the Council of Ministers, . . . hearing that on that occasion the

Duma was going to talk about treason, excitably exclaimed, 'I may be a fool, but I'm no traitor'. (Laughter.) The predecessor of this Minister was undoubtably intelligent, just as the predecessor of the Minister of Foreign Affairs was honourable. But they are no longer in the cabinet. And surely it has no bearing on the actual result whether we are dealing with stupidity or with treason? . . .

When the Duma declares again and again that the home front must be organized for a succesful war and the government continues to insist that to organize the country means to organize a revolution, and consciously chooses chaos and disorganization – is this stupidity or treason? (Voices from left: treason.) Moreover, when on the basis of this general discontent the government deliberately busies itself with provoking popular outbursts – for the involvement of the police in the spring disturbances in the factories is proven – when provocation is used to incite disturbances, knowing that they could be a reason for shortening the war – is this done consciously or not? . . .

You must understand why we have no other task than to get rid of this government. You ask why we are carrying on this struggle in wartime. It is only in wartime that they are dangerous. They are dangerous to the war, and therefore in time of war, and in the name of the war, in the name of that which has united us, we now fight them. (Voices from left: bravo. Applause.)

. . .We have many different reasons for being discontented with this government . . . But all these reasons boil down to one general one: the incompetence and evil intentions of the present government. This is Russia's chief evil, and victory over it will be equal to winning an entire campaign. (Voices from left: true.) And therefore in the name of the millions of victims and of their spilled blood, in the name of our achieving our national interests . . . in the name of our responsibility to those people who elected us, we shall fight until we get a responsible government which is in agreement with the three general principles of our programme. Cabinet members must agree unanimously as to the most urgent tasks, they must agree and be prepared to implement the programme of the Duma majority and they must rely on this majority not just in the implementation of this programme, but in all their actions. A cabinet which does not satisfy these conditions does not deserve the confidence of the Duma and should go. (Voices: bravo; loud and prolonged applause from the left, centre and left wing of the right.)

Gosudarstvennaya Duma. *Stenograficheskie otchety.* Sozyv IV, session V, cols. 46-8.

55   The Political and Social Situation in Russia in October 1916: Police Reports

1. . . . .the mass of the population is at present in a very troubled mood. At the beginning of September this year an exceptional heightening of opposition and bitterness of mood became very obvious amongst wide sections of the population of Petrograd. There were more and more frequent complaints about the administration and fierce and relentless criticism of government policies.

Towards the end of the month this mood of opposition . . . reached such an extent among the masses as had not even been seen in 1905-6. Complaints were openly voiced about the venality of the government, the unbelievable burdens of the war, the unbearable conditions of everyday life. Calls from radical and left-wing elements on the need to 'first defeat the Germans here at home, and then deal with the enemy abroad' began to get a more and more sympathetic hearing.

The difficult material position of the ordinary people, living a half-starved existence and seeing no hope of improvement in the near future, made them look sympathetically and with a rare attention at any sort of plan based on a promise to improve the conditions of life. As a result, a situation was created which was highly favourable to any sort of revolutionary propaganda and actions and which was correctly evaluated by the active leaders of left-wing and other anti-government groups. It is difficult to discount the possibility that German secret agents were operating in such a conducive atmosphere – they have announced to the world many times that Russia is on the verge of revolution and that Petrograd is close to armed uprising, in order to get a rapid end to the war etc.

Without doubt, rumours of this type are greatly exaggerated in comparison with the real situation, but all the same, the position is so serious that attention should be paid to it without delay. In the capital, Kadet groups, always well acquainted with the economic position of the population, long ago predicted that Russia was near, if not to revolution, at least to serious disturbances which could break out everywhere unless preventive measures were taken.

Recently, in various committees dealing with refugees, in food commissions, in municipal organizations dealing with the poor, and in a whole range of institutions close to the people, aware of its needs and moods, the conviction has been expressed, without exception, that 'we are on the eve of great events' in comparison with which '1905 was but a toy'; that 'the government's system of keeping the population in ignorance has completely collapsed, the population has now woken up, and instead of giving the expected applause, is calling for help', etc.

In view of the fact that similar opinions are being heard at the moment in literally all sections of the population, including those which in previous years have never expressed discontent (for example, certain groups of Guards officers) one cannot but share the opinion of the Kadet leaders, who say, in the words of Shingarev, that 'we are very close to events of the greatest importance, in no way forseen by the government, and which will be tragic and terrible, but are at the same time inevitable. . . .'

2 . . .The Kadet delegates paint no less sorry a picture of food purchase in Russia. In the words of one of them, 'there is absolute ruin everywhere': the peasantry, cowed by requisitions, unhappy with interference in trading deals by provincial governors and the police, has no desire to sell its grain and other stocks, fearing that they will get only the statutory price. They refuse to believe all assurances that they will get paid at the going rate. As a result of this the provinces are almost devoid of food. The peasants, having learnt by experience what are the prices for 'city goods' (Sugar – R1.50 per pood, tea – R4 per pood, sausage – R2 per pood, etc) do not want to sell their goods as they are frightened of selling them too cheap. As a result, prices are rising everywhere, and goods are disappearing.

High prices affect the country no less than the towns: in the country as well they bring with them improbable rumours, even more fantastic than those heard in the towns. The peasants willingly believe rumours about the export of leather, grain, sugar, etc. to Germany, and about Count Frederiks selling off half of Russia to those same Germans. Everything makes the atmosphere of the countryside very troubled.

In the words of another delegate, 'the countryside is now passing through its most critical time, for the first time in Russian history demonstrating the antagonism of town and country: the peasant is responding to the high wages of factory labour by refusing to sell food at the old prices . . . The attitude of the countryside to the war has, right from the outset, been extremely unfavourable, for conscription had a much greater effect there than in the towns. Now in the country there is no belief that the war will be successful; in the words of insurance agents, teachers and other representatives of the 'rural intelligentsia', 'everyone wants the war to end, but no one expects that it will'. The peasantry willingly talk about politics, something which was hardly ever heard between 1906 and 1914, and say that 'Sukhomlinov should be hung', 'hang ten or fifteen generals and we might start to win'. The atmosphere in the country has become one of sharp opposition not only to the government, but to other [non-rural] classes of the population: workers, civil servants, the clergy, etc.

In the words of a third delegate, just returned from a journey to the Volga region, 'in the villages one sees extraordinary ferment, similar to that of 1906–7: political questions are discussed, resolutions are passed against landowners and merchants, branches of various organizations are being established. . . . Of course, there is no organizational centre to this, but it seems as if the peasantry are uniting through the co-operatives which are growing by the hour throughout Russia. In this way the peasantry will undoubtably be an active participant in a new and inevitable movement.'

In the words of other Kadets . . . 'across the whole of Russia the same thing is seen: everyone understands that under the old order the Germans cannot be beaten, . . . that the nation itself must interfere in the war . . . Of course, this is not heard in all provinces with the same clarity: in the north we see democratic co-operatives, fulfilling the role of the village zemstvo; in the central area of Russia the zemstva are doing more; in the south individuals are speaking out . . . This movement, which to begin with was purely economic, has become political and in the future could turn into a serious movement with a definite programme.'

Krasny Arkhiv, vol. 17 (1926), pp. 6–7, 19–20.

56   Reaction to the February Revolution

Despite widespread premonitions of trouble, the February Revolution took Russia completely by surprise. Strikes and demonstrations in Petrograd began on 23 February 1917: on 27 February the Petrograd Soviet of Workers and Soldiers Deputies was formed as was the Provisional Committee of the Duma, in defiance of the government's dissolution of the Duma. The following day the Duma Committee decided to take power as the insurrection spread to the military and the Imperial regime revealed itself as impotent. The first Provisional Government took office on 2 March and was self-elected. Also on 2 March Nicholas II abdicated. No successor was nominated since Grand Duke Mikhail would only accept the crown if proffered by the Constituent

Assembly, a new democratically elected parliament which would replace the Duma. All sections of the community welcomed the revolution. Even the military refused to take any measures aimed at restoring the old system, the autocracy. Almost everyone saw the removal of the old regime as an essential precondition of success in war and progress in political and economic matters. Just how the revolution was to develop was unclear, each citizen had his or her own view. There was no way of telling which one would prevail. However, organized political parties started with a great advantage. Nevertheless the unity of purpose, so evident in February 1917, soon vanished.

Social Democrats: Manifesto of 27 February 1917

To all citizens of Russia.

Workers of the world, unite!

Citizens! The strongholds of Russian tsarism have fallen. The prosperity of the Tsarist gang, built on the bones of the people, has collapsed. The people have risen and the capital is in their hands. Units of revolutionary troops have come over to support the uprising. The revolutionary proletariat and the revolutionary army must save the country from the downfall and final ruin which the Tsarist government was preparing.

The Russian people through its huge efforts, its blood and at the cost of many lives has thrown off the slavery of centuries.

The task of the working class and the revolutionary army is to create a Provisional revolutionary government which will stand at the head of the new-born republican order.

The Provisional revolutionary government must draw up temporary laws to defend the rights and liberties of the people, to confiscate church, landowners', government and crown lands and transfer them to the people, to introduce the eight-hour working day and to summon a Constituent Assembly on the basis of a suffrage which is universal, without regard to sex, nationality or religion, direct, equal and secret.

The Provisional revolutionary government should take upon itself the task of rapid provision of food to the population and the army, and to this end all stocks built up by the previous government and by municipal authorities should be confiscated.

The hydra of reaction can yet raise its head. The task of the people and its revolutionary government is to put down any counter-revolutionary schemes directed against the people.

An urgent and immediate task for the Provisional revolutionary government is to enter into dealings with the proletariat of the warring countries to promote a revolutionary struggle by the peoples of all countries against their oppressors and enslavers, against the imperial governments and capitalist cliques. They must aim at putting a rapid halt to the bloody human struggle which has been thrust on the enslaved peoples.

Factory workers, as well as the troops in revolt, should choose quickly their representatives to the Provisional revolutionary government, which will be created under the protection of the revolutionary people and army.

Citizens, soldiers, wives and mothers! All to battle! To open battle with tsardom and its troops!

The red flag of revolt will be raised right across Russia! Everywhere take freedom into your own hands, overthrow the tsarist lackeys, summon the soldiers to the struggle!

Government of the revolutionary people will be set up in towns and villages accross Russia.

Citizens, we have founded this new-born system of freedom on the debris of tsarism through the fraternal and concerted efforts of the rebels.

Forward, there is no return!

Merciless struggle under the red flag of revolution!

Long live the democratic republic!

Long live the revolutionary working class!

Long live the revolutionary people and the revolutionary army!

Central Committee of the RSDRP.

Velikaya oktyabrskaya sotsialisticheskaya revolyutsiya. Dokumenty i materialy. Revolyutsionnoe dvizhenie v Rossii posle sverzheniya samoderzhaviya. Moscow, 1957, pp. 3–4.

57   Resolution of the Conference of the Petrograd SRs on confidence in the Provisional Government, 2 March 1917

The conference of Petrograd SRs discussed the current political situation at its meeting of 2 March 1917 and resolved:

1 As the danger of counter-revolution has not yet disappeared, the task at the present time is to strengthen the political gains of the

revolution. The conference considers that support for the Provisional Government is absolutely necessary, whilst it carries out its declared programme: an amnesty, the granting of individual freedoms, the repeal of estate, religious and national restrictions and preparation for the Constituent Assembly. The conference reserves the right to change its attitude should the Provisional Government not adhere to the implementation of this programme. The conference also recognizes that any attempts to undermine the work of the Provisional Government in the fulfilment of its programme must be combatted.

2 The conference considers that the working masses must monitor the activity of the Provisional Government. It welcomes the entry of A. F. Kerensky in to the government as Minister of Justice to defend the interests and freedom of the people, and expresses its complete sympathy with his behaviour during the revolution. . . .

3 . . .The conference calls on all members of the SR party to play an active part in the organization of the masses through participation in the Soviet of Workers and Soldiers Deputies, in the creation of peasant unions and other organizations which aim to defend the interests of the people.

4 Whilst it supports the Provisional Government . . . the conference considers it vital to carry on energetic propaganda during the preparations for the Constituent Assembly in favour of a republican form of government and all the social and political demands which are part of the minimum programme of the SRs.

Ibid pp. 414–15.

58 Resolution of the Council of the Congress of Representatives of Trade and Industry expressing full confidence in the Provisional Committee of the State Duma, 2 March 1917

. . .the Council admires the great feat which the Duma has performed for the country. The Council firmly believes that the Duma's achievement, which has led the army and people to victory over the old regime and to the liberation of Russia, will also give the country new energy to completely defeat the invasion of the German enemy. The Council places itself at the disposal of the Provisional Committee of the Duma. It will consider the Committee's orders and instructions as binding on itself until the creation of a new and reformed administration.

At the same time the Council calls on all the commercial and industrial organizations of Russia – stock exchange committees, committees of trade and industry, merchants' guilds, factory-owners' associations, the conferences of the various different industries and the whole commercial and industrial class of Russia – to forget party and social differences, which can now be of benefit only to the enemies of the people, and to unite around the Provisional Committee of the Duma and put all their strength at its disposal.

Ibid p.410.

59   Appeal of the Central Committee of the Kadet Party in connection with the formation of the Provisional Government, 3 March 1917

The old regime has gone. The State Duma has forgotten its party differences, has united in the name of the salvation of our homeland and has taken upon itself the creation of a new regime.

All citizens should have confidence in this regime and should combine their efforts to allow the government created by the Duma to complete its great task of liberating Russia from the external enemy and establishing peace inside Russia, on the basis of law, equality and freedom.

Our valiant army and navy, which have borne the full brunt of the ruin which the old regime created in the country, and have silently carried out their great task on the field of battle, have founded an unscaleable barrier around the people's representatives and are, with them, laying the foundations of a new and free Russia.

Forget all your party, class, estate and national differences! The united Russian people should rise up and create conditions in which all citizens can live peacefully. Each class, estate and nationality should be able to express its opinions and achieve its aims. The most important slogan now is 'Organization and Unity', organization and unity for victory over the external enemy, organization and unity in internal construction. Our hearts should be inspired by the hope that this time we shall succeed in avoiding destructive disagreements.

Ibid pp. 420–1.

60 Resolution of the Council of the United Nobility on confidence in the Provisional Government, 10 March 1917

. . .In these difficult and great days for Russia, all Russians should put aside their disagreements and should unite around the Provisional Government, now the sole legal authority in Russia, dedicated to defend order and the state system and to the successful conclusion of the war.

The council . . . calls on the entire Russian nobility to recognize this authority and to cooperate in every way in the achievement of these aims. Each one of us should direct all our strength and actions to harmonious work with all devoted sons of our homeland. Internal peace is all the more important so that the Russian people can fulfil its great historical task – the establishment of a new state structure.

Ibid p. 435.

61 Peasant Recollections of the February Revolution

It took time for the news of the revolution to penetrate to all parts of the country. The return of the soldiers to their home villages was an important source of news and revolutionary ideas.

(i) Samara Province – V.G. Lysov
In March 1917 I was fourteen and had just finished the village school. My father and three uncles were in the army, fighting the Germans. In their letters they wrote that Nicholas II had been dethroned and that 'we shall soon come home and seize all the land from the rich.' The women, who had suffered much from the war, replied, 'Stop fighting and come home. Work in the field has stopped altogether here. We shall soon have to sell the last horse. Whilst you have been off fighting, we have sold everything to the rich and they have just got richer right through the war.' . . .

In 1916 the harvest was not very good and the next winter, in January 1917, there were food shortages amongst the peasantry. We too did not have enough bread to eat, and my mother and aunt sadly sold the last calf to a trader for 52 rubles and bought 12 poods of wheat from a rich peasant.

I. V. Igritsky (ed.), *1917 god v derevne; vospominaniya*

krestyan.   Moscow-Lening-
rad, 1929, pp. 287–8.

(ii) Ufa Province – G. Babich

The peasants were all living as usual: they worked for the lord,
believed in God, in the Tsar and even in the landowner, not suspect-
ing that things were astir in Petrograd. Rumours started to circulate
about the Tsar (the wave of revolution took some time to reach us): he
had fled, given up the throne, and that the soldiers and workers were
moving against him. In confirmation of these rumours a messenger
galloped into the village carrying a secret telegram.

Three days later it was announced that a telegram had been
received saying that Nicholas had abdicated and that power had
passed into the hands of a Provisional Government, which we were
now to obey. Priests were commanded to pray for the health and long
life of the Provisional Government and all the local inhabitants were
ordered to attend.

That was all that was said about the Provisional Government. The
peasants were so stunned by the news that they might as well have
been physically knocked out. They were unable to understand what
had happened.

Some soldiers then started to arrive home, full of revolutionary
ideas. They talked about freedom, about the land, and about how the
Provisional Government had promised to divide up the land amongst
all the peasants. What the peasants understood most from these con-
versations was 'land.'

Ibid pp. 301–2.

62   The February Revolution: Reaction in the Army

Here is a very perceptive account by a young officer.

Letters from an educated junior officer at the Front

4 March 1917
   . . .2 March was an eventful day . . . from the newspapers we
discovered that the Duma had been dissolved. We began to suspect
evil doings, but nothing specially terrible was suggested . . . A messenger told us that there were great disturbances in Petrograd, with
much shooting, and that the troops were evidently fighting amongst
themselves, but that, in general, they tended towards the side of the

rebels. . . . Next day we had confirmation of the rumours about a revolt in Petrograd. . . . Another officer arrived and told us that Rodzyanko was Prime Minister and some Bublikov, Minister of Communications. At the same time, the rumours about huge disturbances in Petrograd were confirmed, as well as those about some units of troops being recalled from the front. Some people cheered up at this, but others – including myself – became depressed.

. . .The lower ranks were told only that Rodzyanko had sent a telegram in which it was stated that he was Prime Minister, that a government had been formed from members of the Duma, that the government was responsible to the Duma and that the army would not want for anything. They were also told that this was the result of disturbances in Petrograd, disturbances which had already come to an end. The soldiers remained silent. I then spoke to some of them and gained the impression that whilst a substantial minority were satisfied, but did want revenge on the leaders of the old regime, the majority were completely indifferent to what had happened and wanted only one thing – peace. . . .

This morning there came news that [Grand Duke] Nikolai Nikolaevich had been appointed Commander-in-Chief. I repeated this to the troops. They again remained silent.

11 March 1917

. . .when the news arrived about the establishment of a new order, the officers began to be suspicious of the troops and the troops of the officers. We did not know how the lower ranks would react to these events, whether they would understand what had happened, and most importantly, whether they would follow the Petrograd example and take it into their heads to replace their commanders and introduce their own order; neither did we know whether they wanted to put an end to the war, or whether they would fight on to end it; finally, we did not know whether all units would take the news equally or whether regiment would fight against regiment, battalion against battalion. As the Germans were only a few miles away, what would happen if the front was broken, perhaps in several places? We agonized over how best to fulfil our duty.

At the same time, the troops did not trust their officers. They did not know which side we were on, and if we were all of one mind; they feared that we might attempt to surrender our positions to the Germans; they were sure that some sort of new instructions were being kept from them. They were also worried whether all units had gone over to the new order; they were worried whether freedom would be taken away, whether their homeland would be betrayed. They were forever clutching hold of their rifles, and several times there could have been a bloody battle.

. . .our commanders could not have behaved more stupidly. They understood nothing and thought that it was possible to return to the old order. They did nothing to contain the situation. . . .

There was a gulf between the troops and the officers which could not be bridged. However the troops might behave with individual officers, in their eyes we remained lords. When we speak of 'the people' we mean the nation, when they speak of them, they mean the democratic lower classes. In their eyes, it was not a political but a social revolution which had taken place, one which, in their opinion, we had lost, and they had won. Under the new system, they would fare better and we worse than before, and of this they were convinced. Therefore, they did not believe the sincerity of our devotion to the troops. Before, we had been the rulers – now they wanted to rule themselves. The grudges of centuries past were now being aired, we could find no common language – this was the accursed legacy of the old regime.

Krasny Arkhiv, vol. 50–1 (1932), pp. 196–200.

63   Declaration of the Provisional Government on War Aims, 27 March 1917

Revolution did not bring peace. Milyukov, the Kadet leader, was appointed Foreign Minister in the first Provisional Government and Russia's obligations to her allies weighed heavily on him. He perceived that one of the reasons for revolution had been the inefficiency with which the Imperial government had prosecuted the war. He and the government wished to remain as loyal allies but the mood of the soldiers was different.

Citizens!

The Provisional Government has discussed the military position of the Russian state and has decided that it is its duty to the country to tell the people the whole truth directly and openly.

The old regime left the defence of the country in a seriously disorganized state. Its criminal inaction and clumsy measures have brought ruin to our finances, to production and transport and to supplying the army. It has seriously damaged our economic structure.

The Provisional Government, with the vigorous and active co-operation of the people, will devote all its strength to remedying these defects which the old regime left behind. But time does not stand still. The blood of many sons of Russia has been needlessly spilt over the last 2 ½ long years of war, but the country is still exposed to a powerful enemy, occupying whole regions of our state and now, at the birth of Russian freedom, threatening us with new and decisive pressure.

The defence – at whatever cost – of our own national honour and the expulsion of the enemy from inside our borders: this is the first urgent and vital task of our troops, defending the freedom of the people.

Whilst the final solution of all the questions linked to the world war and its conclusion depends on the will of the people, in close cooperation with our allies, the Provisional Government considers it its right and duty to state that the aim of free Russia is neither domination over other peoples, nor the removal of their national dignity, nor the forcible seizure of alien territories, but the establishment of a lasting peace on the basis of national self-determination. The Russian people is not aiming to increase its external power at the expense of other peoples, its aim is not enslavement and humiliation. In the name of the highest principles of justice it has removed the fetters from the Polish people. But the Russian people will not allow that its homeland should leave this great struggle itself humiliated and with its vital forces undermined. These aims will form the basis of the Provisional Government's foreign policy. It will represent the will of the people and will protect the rights of our homeland, whilst discharging fully its obligations to our allies.

The Provisional Government of free Russia would not be correct in hiding the truth from the people – the state is in danger. We must strain every muscle to ensure its salvation. Let not the country's response to this be fruitless despair, or loss of heart, but a united effort to create a single national will. This will give us new strength for the struggle and lead us to salvation.

At this hour of severe test, let the entire country find strength in itself to develop our newly-won freedom and work industriously for the good of this free Russia. The Provisional Government has given a solemn oath to serve the people and firmly believes that with general and united support from each and everyone, it will be in a position to fulfil its duty to the country to the end.

Minister-President Prince G.E. Lvov

Velikaya Oktyabrskaya Sotsial-

*isticheskaya   Revolyutsiya.
Dokumenty i Materialy. Revolyutsionnoe dvizhenie v Rossii
posle   sverzheniya   samoderzhaviya.* Moscow, 1957,
pp. 444–5.

64   Order No 1

A major factor in the breakdown of discipline in the army was Order no 1. Originally intended only for the troops of the Petrograd garrison it was, however, quickly distributed to the troops at the front as well.

To the garrison of the Petrograd Military District, to all soldiers of the guard, army, artillery and fleet for immediate and exact execution, and to all the workers of Petrograd for their information. The Soviet of Workers and Soldiers Deputies has decreed:

1   Committees are to be elected immediately in all companies, battalions, regiments, parks, batteries, squadrons and individual units of the different forms of military directorates, and in all naval vessels, from the elected representatives of the rank and file of the above-mentioned units.

2   All troop units which have not yet elected their representatives to the Soviet of Workers Deputies are to elect one representative per company. Such representatives are to appear, with written confirmation, at the State Duma building at 10 a.m. on 2 March.

3   In all political actions, troop units are subordinate to the Soviet of Workers and Soldiers Deputies, and to the committees thereof.

4   The orders of the Military commission of the State Duma are to be obeyed, with the exception of those instances in which they contradict the orders and decrees of the Soviet of Workers and Soldiers Deputies.

5   All types of arms, such as rifles, machine guns, armoured cars and others, must be put at the disposal of company and battalion committees, and under their control, and are not, in any case, to be issued to officers, even upon demand.

6   On duty and in the performance of service responsibilities, soldiers must observe the strictest military discipline, but when off duty, in their political, civil and private lives, soldiers shall enjoy fully and completely the same rights as all citizens.

In particular, standing at attention and compulsory saluting when off duty are abolished.

7 In the same way, addressing officers by honorary titles (Your Excellency, Your honour) etc. is abolished and is replaced by the following form of address: Mr General, Mr Colonel etc.

Addressing soldiers rudely by anyone of higher rank, and in particular, addressing soldiers by *ty** is prohibited, and any breach of this provision, as well as any misunderstandings between officers and soldiers, are to be reported by the latter to the company committees.

This order is to be read to all companies, batallions, regiments, ships' crews, batteries and other combatant and non-combatant units.

Petrograd Soviet of Workers and Soldiers Deputies

M. McCauley, *The Russian Revolution and the Soviet State 1917–1921 Documents*. London, 1975, pp. 23–4. Originally in *Izvestiya*, 2 March 1917.

65 Discontent in the Army, March 1917

Report of General A.M. Dragomirov to General Ruzsky, Commander of the Northern Front, 29 March 1917

The mood in the army is becoming more tense with every passing day. That interlude of calm, which was noticeable accompanying the assembly of delegates from all units [the Fifth Army Congress of 23–7 March] has been replaced in recent days by phenomena of an extremely dangerous character. Arrests of officers and commanders have not ceased. To the former accusations of sympathy to the old regime and injustice towards soldiers have been added rotations to the line out of turn and sending people to certain death just to seize captives [that is, normal scouting operations to obtain information]. There have been cases of refusal to move into position because a unit was on the line at Eastertime last year. . . . In reserve, regiments declare their readiness to fight on till full victory, but then baulk at the command to go into the trenches . . . All thoughts are turned towards the rear. Each one thinks only of how soon his turn will come to go into reserve, or how to get a pass to Dvinsk. . . . A simple manoeuvre of

* Second person singular

replacement on the line has become a hazardous operation. . . . On these grounds, I am very anxious that the forthcoming regrouping operations will lead to serious excesses.

A. Wildman, *The End of the Russian Imperial Army*, Princeton, 1980, pp. 334–5. Originally in *Revolyutsionnoe dvizhenie v Russkoy Armii v 1917. 27 fevral–24 oktyabr. Sbornik dokumentov.* Moscow, 1968, pp. 42–3.

66   Discontent in the Army, April 1917

Report of General Alekseev, Chief of Staff, to A.I. Guchkov, Minister of War, 16 April 1917

The situation in the army grows worse every day: information coming in from all sides indicates that the army is systematically falling apart.

1 Desertions continue unabated: in the armies of the Northern and Western fronts between April 1 and 7, 7,688 soldiers are reported as deserters . . . a number manifestly and considerably under-estimated. . . .

2 Discipline declines with each passing day; those guilty of violating military duty are completely indifferent to possible criminal punishments, convinced of the extreme unlikelihood of enforcement.

3 The authority of officers and commanders has collapsed and cannot be restored by present methods. Owing to undeserved humiliations and assaults, the de facto removal of their authority over their subordinates, and the surrender of such control to soldiers' committees . . . the morale of the officer corps has sunk to a new low.

4 A pacifist mood has developed in the ranks. Among the soldier mass, not only is the idea of offensive operations rejected, but even preparations for such, on which basis major violations of discipline have occurred. . . .

5 Defeatist literature and propaganda has built itself a firm nest in the army. This propaganda comes from two sides – from the enemy and from the rear . . . and obviously stems from the same source.

Ibid pp. 335–6.

67   Lenin: The April Theses

The February Revolution caught Lenin unawares in his Zürich exile. He immediately made preparations to return to Russia and eventually succeeded, travelling by the famous 'sealed' train across Germany. Short of information about the actual course of the revolution, he nevertheless penned these famous theses or propositions and delivered them on his arrival in Petrograd. His major argument is that Russia is ripe for revolution, for proletarian revolution. Hence he advocates implacable hostility to the Provisional Government. His idea that soviets should take over power in Russia is a contribution to Marxism.

1. . . .In our attitude towards the war not the slightest concession must be made to 'revolutionary defensism', for even under the new government . . . the war on Russia's part unquestionably remains a predatory imperialist war owing to the capitalist nature of that government.

The class-conscious proletariat can consent to a revolutionary war, which would really justify revolutionary defensism, only on condition:

(a) that the power of government pass to the proletariat and the poor sections of the peasantry bordering on the proletariat; (b) that all annexations be renounced in deed as well as in words; (c) that a complete and real break be made with all capitalist interests.

In view of the undoubted honesty of the mass of the rank and file believers in revolutionary defensism, who accept the war as a necessity only and not as a means of conquest; in view of the fact that they are being deceived by the bourgeoisie, it is necessary thoroughly, persistently and patiently to explain their error to them, to explain the indissoluble connection between capital and the imperialist war, and to prove that *it is impossible* to end the war by a truly democratic, non-coercive peace without the overthrow of capital.

The widespread propaganda of this view among the army on active service must be organized. . . .

2. The specific feature of the present situation in Russia is that it represents a *transition* from the first stage of revolution – which, owing to the insufficient class consciousness and organization of the proletariat, led to the assumption of power by the bourgeoisie – *to the second stage,* which must place power in the hands of the proletariat and the poor strata of the peasantry.

This transition is characterized, on the one hand, by a maximum of freedom (Russia is *now* the freest of all the belligerent countries in the world); on the other, by the absence of violence in relation to the masses, and, finally, by the naive confidence of the masses in the government of capitalists, the worst enemies of peace and socialism.

This specific situation demands on our part an ability to adapt ourselves to the specific requirements of Party work among unprecedently large masses of proletarians who have just awakened to political life.

3. No support must be given to the Provisional Government; the utter falsity of its promises must be exposed, particularly of those relating to the renunciation of annexations. Exposure, and not the unpardonable illusion-breeding 'demand' that this government, a government of capitalists, should cease to be an imperialist government.

4. The fact must be recognized that in most of the Soviets of Workers' Deputies our Party is in a minority, and so far in a small minority, as against *a bloc of all* the petty-bourgeois opportunist elements, who have yielded to the influence of the bourgeoisie and are the conveyors of its influence to the proletariat. . . .

It must be explained to the masses that the Soviet of Workers' Deputies is the *only possible* form of revolutionary government and that therefore our task is, as long as *this* government submits to the influence of the bourgeoisie, to present a patient, systematic and persistent *explanation* of its errors and tactics, an explanation specially adapted to the practical needs of the masses. . . .

5. Not a parliamentary republic – to return to a parliamentary republic from the Soviets of Workers' Deputies would be a retrograde step – but a republic of Soviets of Workers', Agricultural Labourers' and Peasants' Deputies throughout the country. . . .

Abolition of the police, the army and the bureaucracy. . . .

6. The agrarian programme must be centred around the Soviets of Agricultural Labourers' Deputies.

Confiscation of all landed estates.

Nationalization of *all* lands in the country, the disposal of such lands to be in the charge of the local Soviets of Agricultural Labourers' and Pesants' Deputies. . . .

7. The immediate amalgamation of all banks in the country into a single national bank, control over which shall be exercised by the Soviet of Workers' Deputies.

8. Our *immediate* task shall be not the 'introduction of socialism' but to bring social production and distribution of prodcts at once only under the *control* of the Soviet of Workers' Deputies.

4 April 1917

Lenin, *Selected Works,* vol. 6.
Moscow–Leningrad, 1935,
pp. 21–4.

68   The Kerensky Offensive

Responding to appeals from the Allies for a Russian offensive to complement
an Allied offensive on the Western Front, Kerensky and the Provisional
Government believed that the Russian Army was still capable of launching
successful attacks. Kerensky was a brilliant orator and moved many soldiers
by his emotive words. However when he had left the effect wore off. The
offensive was a disaster and demonstrated finally that the Russian Army was
no longer a fighting force.

Russia, having thrown off the chains of slavery, has firmly resolved
to defend, at all costs, its rights, honour and freedom. Believing in the
brotherhood of mankind, the Russian democracy appealed most earnestly to all the belligerent countries to stop the war and conclude a
peace honourable to all. In answer to our fraternal appeal, the enemy
has called on us to play the traitor. Austria and Germany have offered
us a separate peace and tried to hoodwink us by fraternization, while
they threw all their forces against our Allies, with the idea that after
destroying them, they would turn on us. Now that he is convinced that
Russia is not going to be fooled, the enemy threatens us and is concentration his forces on our front.

WARRIORS, OUR COUNTRY IS IN DANGER! Liberty and
revolution are threatened. The time has come for the army to do its
duty. Your Commander-in-Chief, beloved through victory, is convinced that each day of delay merely helps the enemy, and that only by
an immediate and determined blow can we disrupt his plans. Therefore, in full realization of my great responsibility to the country, and in
the name of its free people and its Provisional Government, I call upon
the armies, strengthened by the vigour and spirit of the revolution, to
take the offensive.

Kerensky,
Minister of War and Navy.
16 June 1917

F.A. Golder, *Documents of*

Russian History, 1914–1917.
New York, 1927, pp. 426–7.

69   The July Days: The Bolshevik Proclamation of 5 July 1917

The disasters at the front led to demonstrations at home. The Bolshevik slogan of 'All Power to the Soviets', immediate peace and the transfer of land to the peasantry gradually gained a mass following in the two capitals of Petrograd and Moscow. The Bolshevik proclamation was in response to a Petrograd Soviet appeal not to go out on to the streets armed. Hence the Bolsheviks backed down. The Provisional Government seized the initiative and published material, purporting to show that Lenin was receiving large sums of money from Germany. The mood of the population changed and Lenin went into hiding in Finland.

COMRADES! On Monday you came out on to the streets. On Tuesday you decided to continue the demonstration. We called you to a peaceful demonstration yesterday. The object of this demonstration was to show to all the toiling and exploited masses the strength of our slogans, their weight, their significance and their necessity for the liberation of the peoples from war, hunger and ruin.

The object of the demonstration was achieved. The slogans of the vanguard of the working class and the army were imposingly and worthily proclaimed. The scattered firing of the counter-revolutionaries could not disturb the general character of the demonstration.

Comrades! for the present political crisis, our aim has been accomplished. We have therefore decided to end the demonstration. Let each and every one peacefully and in an organized manner bring the strike and the demonstration to a close.

Let us await the further development of the crisis. Let us continue to prepare our forces. Life is with us, the course of events shows the correctness of our slogans.

Central Committee, RS-DLP
Petrograd Committee, RS-DLP
Interborough Committee, RS-DLP
Military Organization of the Central Committee, RS-DLP
Commission of the Workers' Section of the Soviet of Workers' and Soldiers' Deputies.

M. McCauley, *The Russian*

*Revolution and the Soviet
State 1917-1921 Documents*.
London, 1975 p. 33.

70   The Kornilov Affair

After the July Days the Provisional Government felt stronger. It appears to
have feared demonstrations on the demi-anniversary of the revolution in
Petrograd on 27 August 1917. Talks between Kerensky, the Prime Minister,
and General Kornilov, the Supreme Commander-in-Chief, led to the latter
believing that he had a mandate to enter Petrograd and deal with any trouble
which might arise. This would have meant arresting or attempting to arrest
the leaders of the Petrograd Soviet. Kerensky got cold feet and denied all
knowledge of such an understanding. He placed all the blame on Kornilov's
shoulders and ordered him to surrender his command. This is Kornilov's
response. The affair was the final nail in the coffin of the Provisional Government. Kerensky appealed to the Petrograd Soviet for support and provided
arms to defend the capital. There was no fighting since Kornilov's troops
never reached Petrograd but the Soviet kept the arms. It then became possible
to plan an armed seizure of power.

Appeal to the People to be Circularized in All Cities and Railways

I, General Kornilov, Supreme Commander-in-Chief, declare
before the whole nation that my duty as a soldier, as a self-sacrificing
citizen of free Russia, and my boundless love for my country oblige me
at this critical hour of Russia's existence to disobey the orders of the
Provisional Government and to retain the Supreme Command over
the Army and Navy. I am supported in this decision by all of the
commanders-in-chief of the fronts, and declare to the Russian people
that I prefer to die rather than give up my post of Supreme Commander-in-Chief. A true son of Russia remains at his place to the end
and is always ready to make for his country the greatest of all sacri-
fices, which is his life.

In these terrible moments through which our country is passing,
when the approaches to both capitals are almost open to the victorious
advance of the triumphant foe, the Provisional Government forgets
the great question of the independence and the very existence of the
land and frightens the people with phantoms of counter-revolution,
which it is calling forth by its inability to govern, by its weakness and
indecision.

Is it not for me, a son of the people, who has devoted himself heart
and soul to the service of the people, to stand guard over the great

liberties and great future of Russia? But at the present moment this future is in weak and hesitant hands. The arrogant foe, by using bribery and treachery, has made himself master here as if he were at home, and carries destruction not only to liberty but to the very existence of the Russian nation.

Russian people, shake off your madness and blindness and look into the bottomless pit into which our country is rushing.

Desiring to avoid all collision, all shedding of Russian blood in civil war, and forgetting all insults and injuries, I, in the presence of the whole nation, say to the Provisional Government: come to Head-quarters where your safety and freedom are guaranteed by my word of honour, and together we will work out and form such a government of national defence as will assure liberty and will lead the Russian people to its great future, worthy of a free and mighty people.

29 August 1917

F.A. Golder, *Documents of Russian History, 1914–1917.* New York 1927, pp. 522–3.

71   Proclamation of a Republic, 1 September 1917

Despite the fact that it was generally agreed that the proclamation of a republic would be left to the Constituent Assembly when it convened, the Provisional Government sought to increase its authority by declaring Russia a republic.

. . .Believing it necessary to terminate the outward vagueness of the form of government, and mindful of the whole-hearted and enthusiastic acceptance of the republican idea that was shown at the Moscow State Conference, the Provisional Government declares that the political form under which the Russian State is governed is a republican form, and it proclaims the Russian Republic. . . .

A.F. Kerensky, Minister-President Zarùdny, Minister of Justice

M. McCauley, *The Russian Revolution and the Soviet State*

1917–1921   *Documents*.
London, 1975, p. 44.

72   The Bolshevik Seizure of Power

Immediately after the Kornilov Affair the Petrograd Soviet set up a Military
Revolutionary Committee to consider all military questions especially re-
quests by the Provisional Government to move troops from Petrograd.
Trotsky became chairman of the committee and the armed uprising was then
feasible. The Bolshevik seizure of power coincided with the convocation of the
II Congress of Soviets. The October Revolution was a Soviet Revolution.

To the Citizens of Russia!
    The Provisional Government has been overthrown. State power
has passed into the hands of the organ of the Petrograd Soviet of
Workers' and Soldiers' Deputies, the Military Revolutionary Committee, which stands at the head of the Petrograd proletariat and
garrison.
    The aims which the people have struggled for: the immediate pro-
posal of a democratic peace, the abolition of landlords' estates, workers' control over production, the creation of a Soviet government – all
this has been guaranteed.
    Long live the workers', soldiers' and peasants' revolution!
                The Military Revolutionary Committee of the Petrograd
                        Soviet of Workers' and Soldiers' Deputies.

25 October 1917

V.I. Lenin, *Polnoe Sobranie
Sochineniy*, vol. 35, Moscow,
1959–p. 1.

III   Foreign Affairs

73   Relations with Germany

In mid-October 1904, Wilhelm II proposed a Russo-France-German agreement directed against Great Britain. Germany dropped the idea after Russia had insisted on giving France prior knowledge of a Russo-German agreement.

Letter from Lambsdorf, Minister of Foreign Affairs, to Count K. R. Osten-Sacken, Russian Ambassador to Berlin, 28 October 1904

Strictly confidential and personal.

. . .These favourable proposals from Berlin demand our most careful consideration. It is clear that the Germans want to use present circumstances to discover the contents of our agreements with France and to find out precisely what we can depend on from our ally. They have no compunction about provoking a quarrel between us and the French, to make us distrust the Franch and force them into a corner. It is obvious that in Berlin they would be glad to see our differences with England continue and intensify; and best of all – to isolate Russia completely by making touching promises, which would lead us to trust exclusively Germany. If this occurred, the Germans would not miss the opportunity to make Russia bear the full burden and cost of such iron bonds. On the other hand, the friendship of our powerful neighbour is, of course, vital for the sake of tranquillity along our long frontier, and in view of our need to be supplied with coal and other contraband. This must all be seriously considered and we must try not to do anything which would damage our relations with Germany, whilst at the same time keeping France's friendship. Only by maintaining this balance can we succeed in getting such benefits as are possible from both sides.

Krasny Arkhiv, vol. 5 (1924), pp. 14–15.

74 Relations with Germany: Björkö Agreement

A year later Wilhelm II tried again. This time the French government was apprised of German proposals but refused to contemplate any form of alliance.

Letter from Lambsdorf, Minister of Foreign Affairs, to A.I. Nelidov, Russian Ambassador to Paris, 26 September 1905

Strictly personal.

. . .I must send you this personal communication, which I beg you to keep to yourself and not to mention in your letters. It must be kept absolutely secret. I have to tell you that it is now almost a year since Kaiser Wilhelm repeated to our poor dear Tsar the necessity of them both signing a defensive alliance and of obliging France, as our ally, to join it. I had succeeded in standing in the way of this crude policy and made the Tsar understand that the most important aim of the Kaiser, if not his sole purpose in this is to make us quarrel with France and to get Germany out of her isolated position – at our expense. I am convinced from long experience that for us to have genuinely good relations with Germany, we need our alliance with France. Otherwise we should lose our independence. . . . Up to now, whilst maintaining the most cordial relations with Berlin, we have very tactfully opposed all attempts to compromise us. But then, during that ill-starred meeting at Björkö, Kaiser Wilhelm succeeded, by insidious flattery, in assuring our dear Tsar that he was our sincere friend and ally and that the sole means of salvation for Russia and Europe was a new Triple Alliance which, he believed, France would willingly join. He later made the Tsar sign *a sort of defensive alliance* with Germany against any European power which attacked either of the two countries. The Kaiser also managed to keep the details of what had been signed secret from everyone . . . and it was planned to come into force only after we had concluded peace with Japan.

Our august sovereign apprised me of all this on 30 August (12 September) on his departure for Finland. I did not conceal from His Imperial Majesty that he had been made to do something which was unbelievable and that the undertakings which he had given were in complete contradiction to those which his august father had made in the agreements with France between 1891 and 1893. It was therefore necessary that, before the ratifications of the Treaty of Portsmouth were exchanged, the Kaiser should agree to redraft his agreement so that it bore no mention of France, or else to secure from the French government a review of our alliance so that the French would join this defensive Triple Alliance which, of course, would be directed against England.

I did not conceal from the Tsar that I doubted the possibility of the success of this policy, to which His Majesty, under the influence of all the fine assurances of the Kaiser, told me 'I think all the same that if the matter is dealt with skilfully, than it can succeed'.

. . .At my request the Tsar wrote to the Kaiser, warning him that the agreement signed at Björkö could not come into force until the attitude of the French government was clear, or else the conditions set out by the two emperors in June 1905 had been adjusted in accordance with our obligations to France. . . .

We must try to come out of this with the very least damage. Our retreat will, of course, enrage the Kaiser and he will try, using his own unscrupulous means, to create repercussions in Paris and London which will be harmful to Russia. Most importantly, however, we must do everything we can to maintain our friendly relations with France. I am sure you will give warning of any displeasure with us on the part of Paris. A rift in the alliance between Russia and France would be a true disaster, from which you can save our beloved Sovereign and our homeland which has already suffered so much.

Ibid pp. 35-7.

75   Anglo-Russian Relations: Minutes of Meeting on Persia

The Anglo-Russian Convention of 1907 was not a formal alliance and was not directed against Germany. It was restricted to dealings concerning Persia, Afghanistan and Tibet. However, relations between the two countries, especially in Persia, continued to be strained.

Minutes of the meeting of 1 February 1907 concerning an agreement with England on Persian affairs in connection with the Baghdad Railway

Izvolsky said that . . . it was now necessary to come to a conclusion on the main proposal of the British government – the delimitation of spheres of influence in Persia. Until recently this idea had not met with sympathy in Russian public opinion, and in governing circles there was a firm conviction that Persia should come completely under Russian influence and that we should aim at gaining an exit onto the Persian Gulf, with the building of a railway right through Persia and the establishment of a fortified position on the Gulf. Events of recent years had demonstrated the impossibility of this plan and had raised the question of the need to remove the grounds for any possible conflict with England. The most appropriate means for this was the delimitation of spheres of influence. . . .

The meeting accepted this principle as the only possible basis for an agreement with the British government and Izvolsky then, in view of the wide ramifications of the subject, indicated its close links with the proposed Baghdad railway. An agreement with England could bring unexpected results and he warned of the possibility of international difficulties if there were objections from third parties, especially, of course, from Germany which, as the events in Morocco had shown, took offence at any agreement which could in any way affect her status as a Great Power concluded without her knowledge. Such dangers had even greater foundation as Germany, according to the information he had, was already turning its attention towards Persia and was preparing to establish its interest there. . . . Of course, to protect Russia fully from that quarter there was a need for a better method of consultation with our western neighbour and for a definition of the areas of our mutual interests. The Baghdad railway could serve as a natural basis for such an agreement, since Russia, in conjunction with France and England, had attempted with all the means at her disposal, to delay its development. It was therefore desirable that the meeting should decide whether it considered it useful for Russia to continue to approach the subject from this angle.

Kokovtsov firstly noted that the widespread belief in Germany about the existence of large industrial and economic resources in Persia was substantially exaggerated. On present information, the banks which specialized in the financing of German trade and industry in Asia were so overburdened with business that they were in no condition to embark on new enterprises in Persia, all the more so as the unstable situation there was far from favourable to the growth of economic activity. . . . Even so, the presence of German interests in Persia could not be denied, and therefore such an agreement as the Minister of Foreign Affairs mentioned was in principle highly desirable.

Moving to deal with the question of the Baghdad railway, Kokovtsov stated that . . . as an important transit route between Western Europe and Asia, it would replace existing sea communications, but as it would not cross our borders we would receive none of the benefits of this transit route. The Baghdad railway would, of course, increase the productivity of those fertile areas of Asia Minor and Mesopotamia which it crossed and would create a new and serious competitor to our grain exports to European markets. Of special danger to our economic dominance in northern Persia were the proposed branch lines leading towards the Persian Gulf, which would allow access for German and British goods to the main area where we were economically dominant.

However, we must remember that it is not within our power to interfere with the construction of the railway, or even to seriously delay it. The only method of doing this – by pressure on France – would be unreliable and we could hardly hope to prevent the participation of French capital in the project for long.

In the same way, we must reject the idea that we can neutralize the danger of the Baghdad railway by the building of another route in competition with it, in particular, by linking the Russian and Indian railway systems through Afghanistan. England would doubtless regard such a transit route as more dangerous for her than the Baghdad railway and would be unlikely to agree to such a project. It remained therefore to come to terms with the inevitable construction of the railway and to try, at the price of non-opposition, to gain some compensation from Germany. In any case, the Minister of Finance considered it undesirable for Russia to take part in the building of the railway. The state of our finances meant that our direct participation was not possible, whilst indirect participation, through some private credit institution and with the assistance of French bankers, promised us no benefits and would give us no real influence in the project.

Krasny Arkhiv, vol. 69 (1935), pp. 19–21.

76   Anglo-Russian Relations: Minutes of Meeting on Afghanistan

Minutes of the Special Conference on Afghanistan, 14 April 1907

Izvolsky noted that . . . it was extremely important for Russia that our relations with England took on that amicable character which best corresponded with our own interests. The Anglo-Russian agreement would be a new and powerful guarantee of peace, something especially necessary for us now. It follows that we should make every effort to bring the negotiations with England to a successful conclusion, and carefully avoid anything which could adversely affect them.

These negotiations, now at their most critical point, are directly linked to our talks with Japan, which should shortly achieve their desired result, and will end in a series of conventions, partly in fulfilment of conditions in the 1905 Treaty of Portsmouth, and partly as new agreements. It is intended that, as a result of these conventions, Russia and Japan will guarantee the integrity of each other's territory and safeguard their own interests at points where they meet, as well as the treaty obligations, which link both states to the Chinese Empire.

The agreement with Japan will, however, be incomplete if, alongside it, we do not obtain safeguards from England, allied to Japan by treaty. An agreement with her would give us a much-needed stability in our foreign relations, something which is lacking at the present moment. Our general situation after the Japanese war and the subsequent internal disturbances means that we must avoid any schemes which will not strengthen our country and we must protect only our most vital interests. In line with this, we must deal with the question of Afghanistan and look at the points suggested by England. These do not represent a draft agreement, but are merely a set of desiderata which, if they are followed, could bring about a concordance of Russian and English interests in Afghanistan. Russian counter-proposals will be drawn up in accordance with decisions taken at this meeting.

Ibid pp. 25–6.

77 Anglo-Russian Relations: Minutes of Meeting on Afghanistan

Minutes of the meeting of the Special Conference on the conclusion of an agreement with England concerning Afghanistan, 11 August 1907.

In exchange for the obligations assumed by England in Articles I and V, we relinquish our right to political relations with Afghanistan. This is, however, a purely theoretical concession, since in reality we have never had direct political links with Kabul and could probably only establish them by means of a succesful war. As regards the right of direct frontier relations, which we have long wanted, Article II of the draft agreement will guarantee them for us, as well as giving them legal sanction. . . .

The final draft of Article III, dealing with Russo-Afghan trade, omits certain details which were included in one of the first drafts of the convention. In place of these is a more general statement which gives our trade all the advantages given to English trade; in this way we guarantee for ourselves complete equality with England in trading questions . . .

Finally, Article IV, which states that the agreement will come into force only at the moment we are informed of the consent of the [Afghan] Emir to its provisions, is the result of long and persistent negotiations with the English and is a vital element in the convention, since without such a clause, the whole significance of the convention would be lost if the Emir refused to agree to it.

After this review of individual clauses, Izvolsky stated that, in his opinion, it was impossible to expect further concessions from England. It fell to the meeting to take a final decision – should we accept the draft agreement or not? It must be borne in mind that the decision had to be taken, not just in the light of the interests of individual branches of government, but from a wider national point of view.

Looking at our agreement with England on Afghanistan in this way, we must recognize that we were at a turning point in our whole foreign policy. We were also close to agreement, not just over Afghanistan, but also over Persia and Tibet, and both these questions have been a permanent threat to our relations with England. The war with Japan and our internal problems have put Russia in a difficult position. The opinion is often heard that we are close to a new war with Japan and her ally, England, and there have been moments when there were grounds for believing that this was a serious danger. Our policy should, therefore, be aimed at protecting us from such threats. We have succeeded in coming to an agreement with Japan, which gives us a significant guarantee of peace, as it is part of a whole network of international agreements linking Japan, England and France. To break one of the agreements in this network would be extremely dificult, since it would affect the very complex and interlocking interests in the Far East. The protection of our own interests and the strengthening of peace in those areas is of no less importance for Russia than for the other Powers. The general political situation is such that we can expect great upheavals in Europe, for example in Austria and the Balkan peninsula. If Russia continued to be tied by the uncertain position in the Far East and could not make her voice heard at a moment of decision in European questions, she would immediately descend to the level of a second-rate Power. We should put our Asian interests in their proper place, otherwise we ourselves will become an Asiatic state, and this would be a great tragedy for Russia.

On the strength of these considerations the Minister of Foreign Affairs attached the greatest significance to the satisfactory conclusion of the negotiations with England.

The Chairman of the Council of Ministers said that, in his opinion, the succesful conclusion of an agreement with England was a matter of great national importance. Our internal situation did not allow us to pursue an aggressive foreign policy. For us the absence of anxiety in our foreign affairs was extremely important, since it would give us the chance to devote all our energies to internal matters with complete confidence. In such conditions the making of an agreement of Asian questions should be seen as very advantageous for us. The agreement which had already been made with Japan and the imminent agreement with England were victories for our diplomacy. Without going into the details of the agreement, Stolypin recognized the advantages of the latest draft, which contained concessions from England, and spoke in favour of its acceptance.

Ibid pp. 32–7.

78 Constantinople and the Straits

Since Russia perceived this area to be of great strategic significance she was naturally very concerned with German moves. Distrust of German motives and strength led to Russia drawing closer to her allies, especially England.

Report of Sazonov, Minister of Foreign Affairs, to Nicholas II, 26 December 1913

On 26 December 1913 Sazonov reported to Nicholas II that . . . the deliberate dragging-out of the negotiations showed the desire to win time, in order to prevent the possibility of concerted action by the Triple Entente, so that all we would be able to do was reconcile ourselves to an accomplished fact. . . .

In reality, if Russia, France and England decided to repeat their joint representations in Constantinople as to the inadmissability of a foreign general commanding the corps there, they must be prepared to back up their demands with force. We therefore need to know whether France and England are, in principle, prepared to use force and if so, exactly how.

Whilst we must leave it to our military and naval experts to say which military options are most favourable, I beg to report that from the political point of view it would be most appropriate to plan, in the event of an unsatisfactory reply from the Porte, for the simultaneous joint occupation of certain places in Asia Minor by Russia, France and England, together with an announcement that the Powers would continue in occupation until their demands were satisfied.

Should this principle be accepted, England and France could occupy such ports as Smyrna and Beirut; we would have the choice of occupying Trebizond or Bayazid or embarking on some other operation, should this seem more appropriate to our military and naval staffs.

In coming to a decision, we must not forget that whilst pressure is being applied to the Porte, we cannot exclude the possibility of active support for her from Germany. In this event the solution of the problem could be transferred from Constantinople and Turkey to our western frontier, with all the resulting complications. . . .

Should we decide to press our demands to the limit, the risk of serious complications in Europe must be borne in mind, although it is likely that a determination not to shift from our position will be sufficient to ensure a satisfactory outcome. On the other hand, if Russia acquiesces in such a central question as the command of a corps in Constantinople by a German general, this would be tantamount to a severe political defeat and could have fatal consequences. Firstly, it would not protect us from the growing ambitions of Germany and her allies, who are all the time adopting a more and more intransigent tone in questions touching on their interests. However, in France and England the dangerous conviction is growing that Russia is prepared to make any concessions for the sake of peace. If this belief takes hold amongst our friends and allies the Triple Entente could be finally destroyed and each member would try to find ways of protecting its interests in conjunction with Powers of the opposing camp. It is precisely such an outcome which is being hoped for by Germany, who under various strange pretexts is complaining about the compensation being offered her in the form of the removal of the English admiral who commands the Turkish fleet from Constantinople to some other base. . . .

If this turns out to be the case, Russia will eventually find herself politically isolated, for we could hardly rely on France, who has no desire to sacrifice her general political interests for the sake of advantageous financial conditions.

. . .If our military and naval experts for their part feel that it is worth taking the risk of serious complications, on condition, of course, that France shows a corresponding determination to support us with all her might and England gives mutual cooperation, we could embark on a trusting exchange of opinions on the matter with both Powers. If this exchange of views results in our allies adopting an evasive stance, then we of course should have to consider the serious risks inherent in Russia acting alone. . . . If the response of France and England is satisfactory then whilst observing the necessary restraint and care to prevent complications, we could press our interests to the limit.

Krasny Arkhiv, vol. 7 (1924), pp. 41-3.

79 Constantinople and the Straits

A striking feature about this document is the exaggerated belief in Russia's military power held by the Minister of War and the Chief of the General Staff. Such a belief was catastrophically misplaced. Kokovtsov, on the other hand, had a good grasp of the realities of the situation.

Minutes of Ministerial meeting, January 1914

. . .The meeting then moved to consider other measures which could be adopted, in particular Sazonov's suggestion of the occupation of certain ports in Turkish territory.

The Minister of Foreign Affairs confirmed that such measures were envisaged, assuming the cooperation of the other Powers of the Triple Entente, but pointed out that it was unclear how ready England was to act. As regards France, the Russian government could rely on her total and active support. The Minister had received an assurance from Delcassé in the name of the French Minister of Foreign Affairs that France would go as far as Russia desired.

Although he recognized that . . . the result of pressure on Turkey could be war with Germany, Sazonov, however, did not see that this was inevitable.

The Minister of Foreign Affairs drew the meeting's attention to the possibility of achieving success through energetic, but at the same time cautious, joint action by the three Powers and, in Sazonov's opinion, this need not necessarily bring war with Germany. In reality an attack on Germany by Russia, supported only by France, would not be especially dangerous. The two Powers combined would be hardly able to deal Germany a fatal blow, even assuming success on the field of battle – something which was problematical. Such a struggle, but with the participation of England, could be fatal for Germany, who clearly recognized the danger of an English attack leading to an internal social catastrophe within six weeks. Germany was afraid of England, and this explained the hatred which the Germans had for the

growing might of Great Britain. It was therefore vital for the Russian
government, prior to making any decisive moves, to secure the support of the British cabinet, whose active participation was, in
Sazonov's view, not guaranteed. British intervention was certain
should Russia and France suffer military reverses. Such intervention
could either be directed towards putting an end to a European confrontation which was harmful to British interests, or could take the
form of active support for those powers whose defeat would be against
the aims of British policy. The necessity for the Russian government
to act only with a guarantee of active support from England was, of
course, a weak point in Russia's position.

. . . The Chairman of the Council of Ministers, supposing that such
measures (as the occupation of Turkish territory) would inevitably
bring war with Germany, posed the question: was such a war desirable and could Russia proceed on this course?

Sazonov . . . agreed with Kokovtsov that war with Germany was in
principle undesirable, but did not feel able to judge whether Russia
would be able to fight such a war.

The Minister of War and the Chief of the General Staff stated
categorically that Russia was able to take on Germany single-handed,
not to mention a conflict with Austria; however such a war was hardly
likely, since the whole Triple Entente would become involved.

Three basic positions were expressed, which can be formulated
thus:

1 Kokovtsov (Chairman of the Council of Ministers and a strong
   opponent of war with Germany) believed that the measures proposed by Sazonov against Turkey could lead to war with Germany,
   and he therefore opposed them. Kokovtsov stated that, in an
   attempt to avoid actions which could increase the risk of military
   confrontation, he was prepared to implement a financial boycott,
   though this was not guaranteed to produce the desired result. . . .
   As regards direct means of compulsion, including the seizure of
   Trebizond, Kokovtsov felt it desirable to refrain from them.
2 Diametrically opposed were the war and naval ministers together
   with the Chief of the General Staff, who, whilst like Kokovtsov
   admitted the possibility of German intervention, unlike him felt
   war to be a feasible option and even a desirable one.
3 Finally, Sazonov recognized a certain risk but believed the risk of
   German intervention to be small (especially if Russia were to have
   French and English support) and therefore supported categorically
   decisive measures against Turkey.

This last view was eventually accepted by the meeting.

Ibid pp. 47–8.

80   The Moroccan Crisis

Concern about German power reinforced the need to cleave close to England.

Letter from Benkendorff, Russian Ambassador to London, to Nervatov, acting Minister of Foreign Affairs, 2 July 1911.

. . .For my part, I see the enormous expansionist force of Germany, with its influence and flag, at the bottom of everything. If the Press is correct we face a new test today in Morocco. This expansionist force in no way implies that the German cabinet is trying deliberately to pursue an aggressive policy; but it occurs as a consequence of counter-measures on the part of other Powers and this always presents the danger of conflict.

In Asia, in present circumstances, I see no other course than to maintain our solidarity with England.

The force of German expansion is such that to hope for concessions from that side is, I believe, only to deceive ourselves.

> *Mezhdunarodnye otnosheniya v epokhu imperializma, seriya vtoraya, 1900–13*, Moscow, 1929, pp. 160–1.

81   The Balkan Wars

In autumn 1912, Serbia, Bulgaria and Greece attacked Turkey. Both Russia and Austria-Hungary increased the readiness of their forces to take offensive action. The war lasted a month and ended in defeat for Turkey. The peace settlement was disadvantageous to Russia: however the victors fell out over the spoils and this led to the Balkan states fighting one another in June 1913.

Letter from Izvolsky, Russian Ambassador to Paris, to Sazonov, Minister of Foreign Affairs, 10 October 1912.

. . .In my view there are the following three possible outcomes to this situation: a decisive victory by the Balkan States; a similar victory by Turkey; the prolongation of hostilities and, as a result, disturbances among the Christians in Constantinople or elsewhere in the Ottoman Empire.

I feel that the first of these possibilities is the least likely, and would at the same time be the most fraught with danger for peace in general: it would immediately raise the question, in all its historical magnitude, of the struggle of Slavdom not only with Islam, but also with the Teutons. In this case we could hardly put our trust in palliative measures and would have to prepare for a great and decisive European war.

Less dangerous from the general European point of view, but more awkward for us would be a convincing Turkish victory. This would excite our domestic public opinion and place upon us the moral duty to go to the aid of the Balkan States. . . .

It seems to me that we must expect that events may compel us to resort to the . . . comparatively dangerous, but at the same time effective, method of putting pressure on Turkey. As I see Poincaré almost every day I touched upon this question, making it clear that I was only giving my own personal observations, and was, as it were, thinking aloud. At first the idea evidently frightened him. He told me that any such isolated action by Russia would destroy the united method of action of the Powers, and could spur Austria to take parallel action. In his opinion, this would cause serious displeasure against Russia in England and would lead to the dissolution of the Triple Entente. I replied that this option was foreseen only in the case of decisive Turkish success. Austria was not interested in seeing Turkey strengthened, but only in the weakening of the Slav states, and, therefore, in the event of these latter being defeated, she would hardly try to find a way to interfere and would probably react with equanimity to hostilities between us and Turkey in Asia. For Germany such hostilities, which would divert our attention from our western frontier, would be advantageous and desirable. As regards England, it is not in her interests to allow a conflict between Turkey and ourselves and she would intervene as a mediator and peacemaker.

. . .I feel that it is to our advantage to impress upon Poincaré that our intervention in certain circumstances is inevitable; if we refrain from intervening we will therefore deserve the gratitude of France; if we do intervene, Poincaré will be forewarned and can give us valuable diplomatic assistance in keeping the conflict localized. I believe that if events make us decide on mobilization or even only on moving our Cossack troops, we shall have to warn Poincaré about this in good time so that he can assist us in clearing the ground in London.

The third possibility – the prolongation of hostilities without any great success on either side – would be especially suitable for collective mediation by the Powers and would probably avoid the need for us to intervene alone. On the other hand, such a situation would be likely to produce, either in Constantinople or in other areas of the Ottoman Empire, internal disturbances and the slaughter of Christians.

> *Materialy po istorii franko-russkikh otnosheniy za 1910–1914 gg. Sbornik sekretnykh dokumentov.* Moscow, 1922, pp. 289–91.

82 The Balkan Wars

Letter from Izvolsky, Russian Ambassador to Paris, to Sazonov, Minister of Foreign Affairs, 25 October 1912

. . .Turning to Poincaré's suggestion as to the means of preventing the seizure of territory in the Balkans by Austria, I, first of all . . . must inform you of the exact text of Poincaré's note to me on this subject. . . . The suggestion was made after discussion in the French cabinet and represents a new view by France of the question of territorial expansion by Austria at the expense of the Balkan States. Whilst France has up to now held that local, purely Balkan, events would only result in her taking diplomatic and not any active moves, she now recognizes that territorial gains by Austria would disturb the general European balance and therefore France's own interests would be affected. I did not omit to mention to Poincaré that, in suggesting joint discussions with us and England as to ways of preventing such gains, he was raising the question of the practical consequences of this suggested agreement. From his reply I concluded that he was fully aware that France could be drawn into military action on this score. Whilst he was only putting forward this question for discussion, Paléologue, in conversation with me, fully recognized that such a proposed agreement could lead to some form of action. . . . It seems that all this deserves the most serious attention on our part, and that we should not pass up this opportunity to strengthen the French government's view of the possibility of Austrian expansion in the Balkans. We should prepare the ground for joint action in the future by Russia, France and England if, in the course of events, Austria draws back from her present statements which reject the option of territorial compensation.

Ibid pp. 295–7.

83   German-Turkish Relations

The defeat of Turkey opened up the possibility of Germany increasing her influence in Constantinople and the Straits. The appointment of a German general as commander of the Constantinople military district intensified Russian concern. Pressure from Russia, France and Great Britain, however, led to the appointment being rescinded.

Letter from Benkendorff, Russian Ambassador to London, to Sazonov, Minister of Foreign Affairs, 28 January 1914

. . .The initiator of the crisis is not Germany, even less perhaps, Turkey. The real reason lies in the German-Turkish agreement, which establishes solidarity between the two powers. In the case of conflict it would be a matter of honour and dignity for Germany to take up arms in defence of Turkey. Consequently, any threat to Turkey, whatever it may be – and military preparations all the more so – is directed straight against Germany and can have no less effect in Berlin than in Constantinople. On the other hand, such an act would offend Berlin more than it would Constantinople. In the Bosphorus they are used to such things. But it seems to me absolutely inconceivable that Germany, only recently having gained imperial status, and now a prominent political and military power, still proud of her brilliant victories of not so many years ago, would be reconciled to a diplomatic defeat which was insulting to her dignity. I cannot believe that this would happen. I therefore conclude that to take measures against Turkey means to head directly for war, . . . a course which, I fear, will not find special approval in Paris and which Grey will definitely reject.

Further, I believe that the atmosphere now is so filled with electricity that it only needs the Powers of the Triple Alliance to be confronted face-to-face with the Powers of the Entente – or vice versa – and war will break out. Even a declaration by each of the three Entente Powers made in Berlin, official declarations, more or less identical, could not make the cabinet – or rather Germany – give way. She is far from being like that. . . .

On the other hand, whatever the German game is, it makes me think that they understand that they have made an error and would give much to get out of it, with the vital condition that it was not made into a question of honour. They well know in Berlin that France, always ready it seems for a fight with Germany, would side with us. They well know what Grey's opinion is and what significance is attached to this question in England. I know that is quite sufficient to make them think, because from their point of view it would require the greatest self-confidence to imagine that in the event of a general war England would not be drawn into it little by little. At the least they have no such assurance that this will not occur. This warning, I feel, needs only lightly underlining – but it would mean risking war without it being absolutely necessary. Our negotiations with Berlin, supported if necessary by France and England individually, in a form which would not offend Germany's dignity, appear to me to be the only possible method for the peaceful attainment of our goals; in this case war could break out only as a result of Germany's political and diplomatic obstinacy. . . .

A financial boycott, insofar as it is possible, appears to me to be the only method of putting direct pressure on Turkey. But I do not place any great reliance on it. As regards other measures which you may like to suggest – whilst considering German *amour-propre* and the very restricted position in which, in my opinion, Germany would be placed – I strongly doubt whether an agreement could be reached by such measures. No one will risk embarking on a political course which does not meet with sympathy in Paris and London – especially by means which in themselves are not agreeable there. Action by us in Asia Minor could by itself be the motive for a German ultimatum. . . .

. . .The essence of any idea is that to strongly offend Turkey, as would happen when she is isolated, would mean on this occasion to offend Germany, and I can see no benefit for our diplomacy in this.

> *Mezhdunarodnye otnosheniya v epokhu imperializma. Seriya tretya, 1914–17 gg.* Moscow, 1931, pp. 137–41.

84   Russia in Asia

The 'official' view of Russian foreign policy and its development is provided by Prince G.N. Trubetskoy, a senior member of the Ministry of Foreign Affairs for most of his career but who in 1906 turned to journalism. In 1912, however, he was recalled to the Ministry of Foreign Affairs as special adviser on Near East Affairs, and during the war acted as envoy to Serbia.

. . .As regards Russian foreign policy, all considerations as to its future direction and handling must stem from an evaluation of [the Treaty of Portsmouth] and its consequences for us in both the long and the short-term.

. . .The treaty may be summarized thus: the elimination of Russian 'imperialism' in the Far East and its replacement by Japanese 'imperialism'.

. . .Russian imperialism, forced out from China and Korea, continued to be dangerous to both Japan and England. The former feared its rebirth in its former haunts, the latter had not lost its centuries-old fear of the spectre of a Russian invasion of India. On the basis of this common enemy the Anglo-Japanese defensive alliance developed, directed, of course, against Russia. . . .

It would not be a mistake to say that against the phantom of Russian imperialism in Asia there developed two very real imperialisms – English and Japanese – which tried to delimit the spheres of their 'special' interests in Asia. It is no use hiding the facts from ourselves: the force represented by the Anglo-Japanese alliance is so imposing that it was able to destroy any hope of a rebirth, on previous conditions, of Russian imperialism in Asia. This would still have to be come to terms with, if the results of the alliance had brought such a reduction in our active policy in Asia, and the Anglo-Japanese alliance had really guaranteed the staus quo in Asia in accordance with the pledges of the former architect of English policy.

. . .Can we oppose the Anglo-Japanese alliance with another real power which could face up to it in Asia? For all its worth, our alliance with France cannot serve as a counterweight in this case. Both our rivals have vigourous interests in Asia, defendable, in case of war, by the entire military and naval weight of Japan and England. France's possessions in Asia, despite their importance for the mother country, are far from being of the first importance, and France could only defend them from China. In our Press we hear the idea of a rapprochement with Germany to serve as a desirable counter balance. . . . But Germany could not, in time of peace, support us by maintaining a sizeable army in Kiao-Chou, since this would definitely not correspond with her interests in this insignificant colony. And how, should it be necessary, could we, together with our own troops, transport German forces by rail to the theatre of war, across enormous distances and therefore separated from their natural base. It is not difficult to see that such an alliance is clearly impracticable and unrealizable. . . .

The practical upshot of this is that we should not reject the hand which England if offering us with a possible agreement. Our Asian policy should be directed towards restricting the extension of Japanese imperialism with all the diplomatic methods at our disposal. We can achieve practical results in this respect by voluntarily rejecting our previous pretensions and by appearing as the champion of interests common to the whole world. Such actions could form the basis for the creation of a system of political balance in Asia. . . . We desire only the preservation of neutral buffers between us and British possessions. Our interests in this respect hardly differ from English ones; it is safer to bet on them coinciding over this problem. More difficult is the problem of delimiting our spheres of influence in Persia and the Persian Gulf. In Northern Persia our influence is established and we have real interests there. In Southern Persia and the Gulf our rivalry with England could not produce such a favourable result, for it is on a very different basis. The question of India plays a very great role here in English policy. . . .

In the field of Asian policy an agreement with England appears far from impossible from our point of view. It could be retorted, however, that England would find such an agreement useless, since she has nothing to fear from us in Asia and the key to the solution of Asian problems is out of our hands.

> *Pamyati Kn. G.N. Trubetskogo Sbornik dokumentov.* Paris, 1930, pp. 55–63, Originally in *Polyarnaya Zvezda*, 27 January 1906, a weekly edited by P. B. Struve.

85   Russia in Europe

. . .Russia has no need to make fresh territorial acquisitions. . . . To search for new lands would only mean a further complication in the presently almost impossible task of governing our state. Besides, Russia has no need to pursue hegemony over the Slav states or to interfere in their internal affairs in any way. Our unfortunate experience since the time of the Treaty of Berlin should teach us that assiduous guardianship over our brother Slavs does not increase their sympathy for us, but rather repels them. All the same, as far as one can judge from the general course of European national and state development, the process of national differentiation is accompanied by the no less strong development of tribal integration. . . . Panslavism cannot, of course, be compared as an idea to Pan-Germanism. The analogy can be continued only in relation to Russia and Poland. As regards the independent Slav states, then neither our own interests, nor their interests, nor historical and geographical conditions would be satisfied should they merge into a single unit, and such an idea should not appear in even our most ambitious programme. The community of interests of Russia and the Slav states requires the free development of their national individuality.

This is how Russian 'imperialism' should be seen in future, and we think that on this basis it will not come into conflict with the interests of the civilized world; for in this way the Slav idea will become one of the foundations of the system of political balance. . . .

The key to our policy in Asia is linked to the solution of the problem of our relations with England. We have seen that our interests in Asia present no obstacle in principle to the amicable definition of spheres of influence with England. It remains to be seen whether England desires such an agreement, and what strength we represent for her in Europe.

. . . In time of war Germany succeeded in concluding a trade agreement with us for the same period as the Anglo-Japanese alliance, an agreement by which our agriculture was burdened down for the benefit of German farmers. Germany saw that we were up to our necks in the mess in the Far East and took in into her head to deal with our ally – France. The Morocco crisis was a convenient pretext for this. . . .

It firstly appears vital to us that Russia should refuse to contemplate any military adventures. On the contrary, she should aim at consolidating the general peace and at establishing a peaceful political balance.

The main short-term aims of our foreign policy should be to protect the status quo in Asia from attacks by Japanese or any other imperialism, and in Europe to counter any attacks by a single imperial power.

We consider that a method of achieving this in present conditions is by the improvement of our relations with England with the help of our ally France.

Such a move ought not to exacerbate military differences with anyone, and ought not, of course, to arouse German fears, for it is very desirable that we should have good-neighbourly relations with Germany. Political agreements and alliances should retain their character as mutual guarantees.

Ibid pp. 64–72, Originally in
Polyarnaya Zvezda, 3 February
1906.

86   The Durnovo Memorandum, February 1914

Not all official opinion was in favour of Russia's alignment with England.
P.N. Durnovo was a member of the State Council, a former Minister of
Internal Affairs and an associate of the court coterie, who argued, harking
back to the traditional relationship between Russia and Prussia, that alliance
with Germany was a more sensible course for Russia to pursue.

. . .The vital interests of Russia and Germany do not conflict.
There are fundamental grounds for a peaceful existence of these two
states. Germany's future lies on the sea, that is, in a realm where
Russia, essentially the most continental of the great powers, has no
interests whatever. We have no overseas colonies, and shall probably
never have them, and communication between the various parts of
our empire is easier over land than by water. No surplus population
demanding territorial expansion is visible, but, even from the viewpoint of new conquests, what can we gain from a victory over Germany? Posen, or East Prussia? But why do we need these regions,
densely populated as they are by Poles, when we find it difficult
enough to manage our own Russian Poles? . . .

Exactly the same thing applies to Galicia. It is obviously disadvantageous to us to annex, in the interests of national sentimentalism, a
territory that has lost every vital connection with our fatherland.. . . .

The obvious aim of our diplomacy in the rapprochement with
England has been to open the Straits. But a war with Germany seems
hardly necessary for the attainment of this object, for it was England,
and not Germany at all, that closed our outlet from the Black Sea. . . .

Also, there is reason to believe that the Germans would agree
sooner than the English to let us have the Straits, in which they have
only a slight interest, and at the price of which they would gladly
purchase our alliance. . . .

It may be argued, however, that, under modern conditions in the
various nations, territorial acquisitions are of secondary importance,
while economic interests take first rank. But in this field, again,
Russia's advantages and needs do not conflict with Germany's as
much as is believed. It is, of course, undeniable that the existing
Russo-German trade agreements are disadvantageous to our agriculture and advantageous to Germany's, but it would be hardly fair to

ascribe this circumstance to the treachery and unfriendliness of Germany.

It should not be forgotten that these agreements are in many of their sections advantageous to us. The Russian delegates who concluded these agreements were confirmed protagonists of a development of Russian industry at any cost, and they undoubtedly made a deliberate sacrifice, at least to some extent, of the interests of Russian agriculture to the interests of Russian industry. . . .

It would seem that the conclusion of a commercial treaty with Germany, entirely acceptable to Russia, by no means requires that Germany first be crushed. It will be quite sufficient to maintain neighbourly relations with her, to make a careful estimate of our real interests in the various branches of the national economy, and to engage in long, insistent bargaining with German delegates, who may be expected to protect the interests of their own fatherland and not ours.

But I would go still further and say that the ruin of Germany, from the viewpoint of our trade with her, would be disadvantageous to us. Her defeat would unquestionably end in a peace dictated from the viewpoint of England's economic interests. The latter will exploit to the farthest limit any success that falls to her lot, and we will only lose, in a ruined Germany without sea routes, a market which, after all, is valuable to us for our otherwise unmarketable products.

In respect to Germany's economic future, the interests of Russia and England are diametrically opposed. For England, it is profitable to kill Germany's maritime trade and industry, turning her into a poor and, if possible, agricultural country. For us, it is of advantage for Germany to develop her sea-going commerce and industry which serves it, so as to supply the remotest world market, and at the same time open her domestic market to our agricultural products, to supply her large working population. . . .

We must not forget that Germany herself is, to a certain extent, interested in our economic well-being . . . In her capacity of permanent – although, of course, not unselfish – middleman for our foreign trade (Germany) has an interest in preserving the productive resources of our country, as a source of profitable intermediary operations for her.

. . .A war (against Germany) will demand such enormous expenditures that they will many times exceed the more than doubtful advantages to us in the abolition of the German (economic) domination. More than that, the result of such a war will be an economic situation compared with which the yoke of German capital will seem easy.

For there can be no doubt that the war will necessitate expenditures which are beyond Russia's limited financial means. We shall have to obtain credit from allied and neutral countries, but this will not be granted gratuitously. As to what will happen if the war should end disastrously for us, I do not wish to discuss now. The financial and economic consequences of defeat can be neither calculated nor foreseen, and will undoubtedly spell the total ruin of our entire national economy.

But even victory promises us extremely unfavourable financial prospects; a totally ruined Germany will not be in a position to compensate us for the cost involved. Dictated in the interest of England, the peace treaty will not afford Germany opportunity for sufficient economic recuperation to cover our war expenditures, even at a distant time. . . .

It should not be forgotten that Russia and Germany are the representatives of the conservative principle in the civilized would, as opposed to the democratic principle, incarnated in England and, to an infinitely lesser degree, in France. . . .

From this point of view a struggle between Germany and Russia, regardless of its issue, is profoundly undesirable to both sides, as undoubtedly involving the weakening of the conservative principle in the world of which the above-named two great powers are the only reliable bulwarks. More than that, one must realize that under the exceptional conditions which exist, a general European war is mortally dangerous both for Russia and Germany, no matter who wins. It is our firm conviction, . . . that there must inevitably break out in the defeated country a social revolution which, by the very nature of things, will spread to the country of the victor. . . .

A rapprochement with England does not promise us any benefits, and the English orientation of our diplomacy is essentially wrong. We do not travel the same road as England; she should be left to go her own way, and we must not quarrel on her account with Germany.

The Triple Entente is an artificial combination, without a basis of real interest. It has nothing to look forward to. The future belongs to a close and incomparably more vital rapprochement of Russia, Germany, France (reconciled with Germany), and Japan (allied to Russia by a strictly defensive union). A political combination like this, lacking all aggressiveness towards other states, would safeguard for many years the peace of the civilized nations, threatened, not by the militant intentions of Germany, as English diplomacy is trying to show, but solely by the perfectly natural striving of England to retain at all costs her vanishing domination of the seas.

F.A. Golder (ed.), *Documents of Russian History, 1914–1917*. New York, 1927, pp. 12–23.

IV   The Economy

87   Basic Statistics

	1900	1910	1913
Population (millions)	132.9	160.7	175.1 (1914)
Pig iron production (m. poods)	179.1	185.8	283.0
Coal production (m. poods)	986.3	1,526.3	2,200.1
Railways ('000 km end yr.)	53.2	66.6	70.2
Consumption of cotton (m. poods)	16.0	22.1	25.7
Imports (m. rubles)	626.3	1,084.4	1,084.4
Exports (m. rubles)	716.2	1,449.0	1,520.0
Budget revenue (ordinary, m. rubles)	1,704.1	2,780.9	3,417.3
Budget expenditure (ordinary, m. rubles)	1,599.1	2,473.1	3,094.2

O. Crisp, *Studies in the Russian Economy before 1914.* London, 1976, p. 112.

88   Savings Banks

Banks attracted savings for various reasons: interest rates were good (*c.* 4-5 per cent); it was easy to make deposits as there were bank branches at every railway station so there was no need to make a journey into a town; this was a good way of saving to buy land; the currency was stable at this time and there was no risk attached to putting money in a savings bank; there was confidence in the state banks because it was recognized that savings were secure with no risk of the government taking arbitrary action to confiscate them. (Olga Crisp, unpublished)

(i) The Growth of accounts

Year	No. of accounts ('000)	Deposits (m. R)
1905	4988	831
1906	5665	1035
1907	6210	1149
1908	6560	1208
1909	6940	1283
1910	7436	1397
1911	7972	1503
1912	8455	1595
1913	8992	1685
1914	9241	1835
1915	9985	2449
1916	12161	3890

P.A. Khromov, *Ocherki eko-
nomiki Rossii perioda mono-
polisticheskogo   kapitalizma.*
Moscow, 1960, p. 97.

(ii) Savings Banks Deposits by Occupation of Account Holder

Occupation	1903		1912		1915	
	m. R	%	m. R	%	m. R	%
Landowning, agriculture and rural trades	201.6	24.7	453.2	27.8	641.4	28.4
Urban trades	96.4	11.8	174.5	10.7	223.5	9.9
Factory work	32.3	3.6	67.5	4.1	100.2	4.4
Service ind.	65.1	8.0	110.9	6.8	126.3	5.6
Trade	92.7	11.4	168.6	10.3	307.8	13.6
Clerics	64.8	7.9	88.6	5.4	90.0	4.0
Military	32.5	4.0	51.5	3.2	111.4	4.9
Civil service	59.4	7.3	91.6	5.6	129.1	5.7
Professions	111.5	13.7	273.8	16.8	382.1	16.9
Other	59.4	7.3	151.4	9.3	149.1	6.6

*Ocherk razvitiya i deyatelnosti
gosudarstvennogo   sberegatelnykh
kass.* St Petersburg, 1912,
Table 4.

89   Number of Wage Earners

1897	9,156,620
1900	10,375,080 (non-agricultural)
1913	17,815,000

The figures . . . present difficulties with regard to full-time, seasonal, or casual and sporadic wage-earning activities. The data for 1897 are based on Russia's first population census. However, Russian peasants – conditioned by past experience to associating censuses with new taxation, stricter assessment, or punishment for evasion – refused to complete, or gave inaccurate answers to question 4 on the census form, which concerned sources of income other than the family farm. The most frequent answer was that the family farm was the one and only source of livelihood. Only about one in fifteen of the seventy-million-strong peasant population of European Russia declared subsidiary earnings, a proportion which would have to be doubled for the active population and increased still further for adult males, as women took outside employment less frequently.

> Olga Crisp, 'Labour and Industrialization in Russia', in P. Mathias and M.M. Postan (eds.), *The Cambridge Economic History of Europe,* vol. VII, part 2. Cambridge, 1978, p. 332.

90   Distribution of Workers in Different Forms of Employment

Groups		Number of persons (thousands)			Index (1860 = 100)	
		1860	1913	1917	1913	1917
I.	Industrial workers					
	(a) in factories and mines	860	3,100	3,643	360.5	423.6
	(b) employed in their own homes, in rural or urban industry not under (a)	800	3,000	3,500	375.0	437.5
	Total industrial	1,660	6,100	7,143	367.4	430.3
II.	Employed in building	350	1,500	1,500	428.6	428.6

Groups	Number of persons (thousands)			Index (1860 = 100)	
III. Transport					
(a) water	500	500	1,857	100.0	363.4
(b) railways	11	815		7,409.1	
Total transport (approx.)	511	1,315	1,857	257.3	363.4
IV. Agricultural wage-earners	700	4,500	5,000	642.8	714.3
V. Other persons working for wages (urban unskilled and day labourers, and apprentices in commerce, restaurants, and domestic service)	800	4,065	4,465	508.1	558.1
Total non-industrial wage-earners (total II-V)	2,361	11,380	12,822	482.0	543.0
Overall total	4,021	17,480	19,965	434.7	496.5

Ibid p. 332.

91 Share of Different Industries in Employment and Production, 1897 and 1908 (per cent)

Group of industries	No. of workers		Gross value of production	
	1897	1908	1897	1908
Textiles	30.6	36.5	33.3	29.8
(Cotton)	–	(22.7)	–	(21.0)
Foodstuffs	12.2	17.1	22.8	33.9
Mining and metallurgy	25.9	24.5	13.9	16.4
Metal goods and machinery	10.2	–	10.9	–
Timber-processing	4.1	4.1	3.6	3.7
Livestock products	3.1	2.8	4.7	3.5
Ceramics (inc. building materials)	6.8	–	2.9	–
Chemicals	1.7	2.9	2.1	3.8
Paper	2.2	3.9	1.6	2.8
Others	3.2	8.2	4.2	6.1

No separate figures for cotton in 1897 data

Ibid p. 354.

92   Number of Workers per Factory

These figures were compiled on the basis of reports from the Factory Inspectorate and included only enterprises which had more than 16 workers. There is therefore a significant underestimation of the number of small enterprises. *Vsaya Rossiya,* an industrial directory covering the period 1898–1900 notes 142,000 firms with 1,695,000 workers: an average of 12 per enterprise, whilst the Inspectorate's figures give an average of 93. The truth is that there were large numbers of both very small and very large factories. (Olga Crisp, unpublished)

No. of workers in one factory	No. of factories					
	1901		1910		1914	
	No.	%	No.	%	No.	%
- 50	12740	70.5	9909	65.7	8929	63.6
51- 100	2428	13.4	2201	14.6	2088	14.9
101- 500	2288	12.6	2213	14.7	2253	16.0
501-1000	403	2.2	433	2.9	432	3.1
1001-	243	1.3	324	2.1	344	2.4
	18,102		15,080		14,046	

Size of factory by no. of workers	No. of workers					
	1901		1910		1914	
	No.	%	No.	%	No.	%
- 50	243,615	14.3	219,665	11.6	199,922	10.2
51- 100	171,170	10.1	158,704	8.3	148.954	7.6
101- 500	492,095	28.9	507,886	26.7	504,440	25.7
501-1000	269,133	15.8	302.840	15.9	296,347	15.1
1001-	525,637	30.9	713,648	37.5	811,197	41.4
	1,701,650		1,902,743		1,960,860	

P.A.   Khromov,   *Ocherki ekonomiki   Rossii   perioda kapitalizma.* Moscow, 1960, p. 7.

93   Russian Industry and Monopoly: Prodameta and Produgol

The Prodameta and the Produgol were incorporated joint stock companies, founded in 1902 and 1904, respectively, with the avowed aim of setting up collective organizations for the sale of metallurgical products and coal of the member enterprises. . . . The idea of the Prodameta came from Paris.

The negotiations were protracted because of the conflict of interests between various groups of enterprises, and the initial scope of an organization, embracing all types of metallurgical products, had to be abandoned for more modest agreements on specific products. Subsequently various changes took place and as a result a loosely knit association of some 30 metallurgical enterprises placed in the main in South Russia, but with a few also from the Polish and the central areas, eventually emerged. Within this association there was a number of more closely knit smaller groups, with specific and detailed agreements. These 30 enterprises, though they represented a mere 17 per cent of the total number of Russian metallurgical enterprises, accounted for 70 per cent of the share capital of the metallurgical industry, for 33 per cent of its labour force, for 88 per cent of its production of assorted iron, 82 per cent of the total production of sheet and ordinary iron and for 74 per cent of the output of tyres and axles. The contract of association did not embrace iron ore or pig iron, but indirectly affected them.

By 1910 the French had become the dominant element in the Prodameta. . . .

The second syndicate, the Produgol, was run from the beginning of its formation in 1904 by a Paris committee. It was confined to the Donetz basin alone, and its constituent enterprises accounted for 60 per cent of the country's output.

The formation of the two syndicates was prompted by the desire to remedy the disastrous position in which the enterprises, controlled by a large proportion of French capital, found themselves when struck by the crisis of 1900–3, followed by a depression lasting until 1909. It was thought desirable to create an agency which would be able to seek out new markets and reduce overhead costs, by rendering obsolete the separate sales agencies of the individual enterprises and by reducing transport costs over long distances, by means of the allocation of orders to enterprises nearest to the place of destination. These objectives were for the most part achieved.

As it happened, during the long years of crisis and depression, the policy of the syndicates could have little unfavourable effect on the economy. On the contrary we find that, though there had been a certain reduction in the output of pig iron by 1908, the output of manufactured metal products had increased. Moreover this increase was due almost entirely to the better equipment and mechanisation of the industries concerned.

The policy of restricting production and raising prices had become a real danger during the boom of 1909–14, when it led to a virtual 'coal and pig iron famine' in the years 1911–12. . . . But the restrictive policies of the syndicates were not the only reasons for the shortages in coal and pig iron. Technical difficulties, in particular in the coal industry, made it impossible for the latter to cope with the unaccustomed demand. The high prices were among other things due to increased production costs as a result of the rise in wages, the cost of assistance to workers, and industrial taxation imposed by post-revolutionary legislation.

Whatever the position may have been, the Russian government was not unarmed vis-à-vis the syndicates, though the latter had grown considerably in power. In 1908 the government was instrumental in preventing the formation of a cartel of the metallurgical industry, which was sponsored by the Belgian and French banks. Court proceedings were opened against the Produgol in 1914 and warnings were issued that, if production failed to catch up with demand, the government would proceed with the setting up of enterprises of its own to meet state needs, and moreover duty free imports of metallurgical products and coal were to be temporarily admitted.

Olga Crisp, *Studies in the Russian Economy before 1914*, London, 1976, pp. 175–7, 190–1.

94   Budget Expenditure as a Proportion of National Income, 1900–1913

These figures cited by Khromov were originally computed by Prokopovich in 1913. Though government involvement was obviously less pronounced than in 1900, judging by the share of budgetary expenditure relative to national income, it was still very substantial in 1913. (Olga Crisp, unpublished)

1. National Income (50 provinces)
   1900   5,891 million rubles
   1913   11,805 million rubles
2. Budget Expenditure (Ordinary plus extraordinary)
   1900   1,883 million rubles
   1913   3,383 million rubles
3. Proportion
   1900   31.9%
   1913   28.6%

P.A. Khromov, *Ekono-micheskoe razvitie Rossii v XIX-XX vekakh, 1800-1917.* Moscow, 1950, pp. 524-9; M. E. Falkus, 'Russia's National Income, 1913: A Revaluation', *Economica,* vol. 35 (1968), p. 53.

95   Comparative Agricultural Yields, 1911-1915 (Poods per desyatina)

	Wheat	Rye	Oats	Maize	Potatoes
Russia	45	54	52	74	489
USA	69	68	77	111	440
France	86	68	83	81[2]	570
Great Britain	146	–	119	–	1012
Germany[1]	146	120	127	–	904

1: 1911-14
2: 1911-14

P.A. Khromov, *Ocherki eko-nomiki Rossii perioda mono-polisticheskogo kapitalizma.* Moscow, 1960, p. 195.

96   The Stolypin Land Law of 9 November 1906

By allowing peasants to leave the commune and to consolidate their holdings into a single farm, Stolypin hoped to create a class of small peasant landowners with both the incentive and the opportunity to increase levels of production. The government hoped that by satisfying peasant demands it would remove the causes of the discontent manifested in 1905.

By Our Manifesto of 3 November 1905 redemption payments by peasants for allotment land were abolished as from 1 January 1907. From then on those lands will be free from any restrictions imposed on them because of this payment and peasants will be granted the right to leave the commune freely and individual households will be able to obtain part of the communal land stock as their own property.

However, the actual implementation of this legal right will, in most cases, meet with serious difficulties connected with the impossibility of deciding on the size of holdings to be allocated to those households wishing to leave the commune. . . .

In view of this, we recognize that those obstacles which exist in law to a peasant being able to exercise this right to allotment land must be removed . . . and We . . . lay down the following regulations:

1 Each householder, holding allotment land from the commune, can at any time request that his due share of this land be transferred to him as his private property.

2 In communes where there has been no general redistribution for the 24 years preceding such a request, a householder wishing to leave the commune will receive . . . all those areas of communal land which are in his permanent use (excluding rented land).

3 In communes where there has been a general redistribution within the 24 years preceding such a request, each householder wishing to leave the commune will receive all the land which was granted to him by the commune for the period until the next redistribution. . . .

6 Requests for land to be transferred to private property shall be submitted to the commune through the village elder, who, after approval by a simple majority in the commune, must, within a month from the date the request was made, allocate the area of land which is to become the private property of the individual householder. . . . If the commune has not made such a decision within the stated time, then, following a request by the householder concerned, this action will be taken by the local Land Captain who will hear all disputes on the matter and give his decision. . . .

12 Each householder who has had land transferred to him as a result of the procedure in this law has the right to demand at any time that the commune should provide him with a single piece of land in exchange for his various separate pieces.

13 In cases where such a request does not coincide with a general redistribution, or where such a request would be awkward or impossible to fulfil, the commune can satisfy it by making a monetary payment to the householder concerned. Any dispute about the size of the payment shall be settled by the local Peasant Court. . .

Whole communes, both those where land is held in communal tenure as well as those where it is held by individual tenure, may change to a system of consolidated holdings for each peasant, by a two-thirds majority of peasants eligible to vote at the village meeting.

Nicholas.

Polnoe Sobranie Zakonov Ros-
siyskoy Imperii, 3rd ed., vol.
XXVI/I, no. 28528.

97   Lenin on Stolypin's Agrarian Policy

If Stolypin's agrarian policy was maintained for a very long period,
and if it succeeded finally in transforming the whole structure of rural
landholding on a bourgeois pattern, it could make us abandon any
attempt at an agrarian policy in a bourgeois society. . . . But
Stolypin's policy can in no way make us alter our present tactics. . . .
The 'success' of Stolypin's policy in the countryside in the next few
years can only lead to an intensification of the struggle within the
ranks of the peasantry, rather than to any lessening of it, for the final
aim of establishing a purely bourgeois peasant economy will take
much time. Stolypin's 'success' in the short term might at best bring
about the isolation of a section of consciously anti-revolutionary
Octobrist peasants, but it is precisely this transformation of a prosperous minority into a politically conscious and united force that
would provide a substantial impetus for the development of the politically conscious and united masses against such a minority.

V.I. Lenin, *Polnoe Sobranie*
Sochinenii, 5th ed., vol. 17.
Moscow, 1961, p. 275.

98   Stolypin's Land Reform – Octobrist Reaction: Speech by A.D. Golytsin in the Third Duma, 7 November 1908

. . . .This edict of 9 November results from the eventual recognition
of the need to discuss the question of our decrepit and obsolete forms of
land ownership. to rescue our millions of peasants from the stagnant
swamp of the commune, from general ignorance, lack of culture and
inertia . . . which provides a fertile ground for all kinds of propaganda. I tell you straight out: the opponents of the 9 November edict
have understood this better than we have. They have understood that
this edict pulls away the rug on which they stand, that the break-up of

the commune will deprive them of that cannon-fodder without which any active struggle is impossible . . . I can partly understand the desire of some parties to preserve the commune in its present form at whatever cost. It is true that with the commune it is possible to continue that domination over the masses which we have seen up to now, that obedience which the masses have shown to advice from all sorts of national organizations and unions. But we are not aiming at ruling over anybody, at giving orders to anyone, and therefore the economically free and energetic individual holds no fears for us, and in this sense we welcome the edict of 9 November. . . .

The defenders of the commune for the same reasons support . . . the belief that there is a great reserve of land available . . . which has been discussed in connection with the problems of land shortage and additional provision through compulsory expropriation. . . . I want to say that if we finally succeed in dispelling this belief in land being available, this will be recognized as one of the Third Duma's great services to history. . . . Whilst the peasantry retain this belief, no educational or cultural measures will make them introduce improved methods of cultivation on their own lands. Whilst there is other land close by, there will always be an urge, impermissible in a cultured state, to appropriate it, and this will make the peasant eye these lands greedily. There will not be sufficient stimulus for him to improve his own lands to produce benefits for himself, and this land will remain in its primitive state until the land shortage question again comes to the fore. . . . It is time to stop appeasing our people with unrealizable dreams, which nobody takes seriously – not even those people who propound them. It is time to demonstrate to them the real way to achieve wealth, happiness and material security, as long proven in other countries, and we appeal to them to choose this path. It leads to freedom from the oppression of the commune, to education, culture and sustained and honest work protected by law. All our agrarian legislation should be directed this way.

Gosudarstvennaya Duma. *Stenograficheskie otchety,* sozyv III, session II, vol. 1, cols. 805–10.

99   Stolypin's Land Reform – Kadet Reaction: Speech by A.E. Berzovsky in the Third Duma, 27 October 1908

. . .we are not ardent defenders of the commune, we are not convinced that the commune is the perfect way of holding land. Communal ownership is just one stage in the evolution of landholding. When economic conditions change sufficiently that it is necessary to move to another form of landholding, then the commune loses its *raison d'être* and another type of landholding appears. Therefore we have introduced an amendment to the bill . . . we declare that anyone who wishes to leave the commune can do so at any time . . . society must satsify this desire for severance either by land or by a cash payment. . . . Finally, the quantity of land which each person who does leave is entitled to shall be set out by the commune, either on the basis of the last redistribution, or if it is taking place at a time of redistribution, on the basis of that. This is completely fair for the commune itself. . . . Further, we have limited the buying-up of land. This is the core of the material rights which we will give to the commune and to individual households leaving it.

I have listened with interest to what the deputy minister said about our proposals. Unfortunately, I heard no analysis of the actual content of our amendment. I heard only a general complaint that the Kadet proposals did not, in essence, provide the freedom for each peasant to leave the commune, and that they established a three-year period during which the commune had to deal with requests to leave; in other words, the attacks dealt only with the procedural part of the proposals. We shall in due course defend them, but they are not essential and can be altered, as long as they define clearly the rights of the peasant who wants to leave and the rights of the commune, and unambiguously set out the procedure by which a peasant can claim his right to leave the commune. We have clearly stated that if the commune does not fulfil its legal duty to allow a peasant to leave and does not give him either land or money, then the matter should be dealt with by the courts, and the court should make him a payment, or if this is not possible, should compulsorily apportion him a piece of land.

It seems to us that our proposals are free of elements of force and will not bring discord into the heart of the commune. They recognize the authority of the commune, but at the same time give it the duty of fulfilling the request of a peasant who wants to leave. And even if he settles on land which has been compulsorily acquired from the commune, this is not putting him on top of a volcano, such as the law of 9

November 1906 does to a peasant who wants to go counter to the
wishes and convictions of the commune. What sort of farm would it be
if the land had been seized from the commune, without its acknowl-
edgement or desire? In our proposals, we want only to co-operate in a
natural evolution, and not to introduce any artificial methods to
hasten the process of the dissolution of the commune.

Ibid cols. 385–400.

100   Stolypin's Land Reform: Implementation

Number of peasants leaving the commune, 1907–15
    There were an estimated 10–12 million peasant households.

Year	No. of households applying to leave.	No. of households finally leaving.
1907	211,922	48,271
1908	840,059	508,344
1909	649,921	579,409
1910	341,884	342,245
1911	242,328	145,567
1912	152,397	122,314
1913	160,304	134,554
1914	120,321	97,877
1915	36,497	29,851
Total	2,755,633	2,008,432

S.M. Dubrovsky, *Stol-
ypinskaya zemelnaya re-
forma.* Moscow, 1963, p.
200.

By 1 May 1915 14% of all communal allotment land had passed into private
consolidated ownership. Ibid p. 576.

101   Landed estates

Imperial Russia had no single register of farming units. Russian statistics
classified land according to three main juridical categories: (i) land belonging
to the state, Imperial family, the church and other foundations, (ii) allotment
(*nadel*) land – owned by communes, (iii) privately owned land (*chastno-*

vladelcheskaya). Category (iii) only concerns us here. In 1905 about 86 million desyatinas of land in 50 provinces of European Russia were classified as *privately* owned and consisted of over 752,000 units, giving an average of about 114 desyatinas per unit. Some 619,000 or over 82 per cent of the total were less than 50 desyatinas in size and covered an area of 6.5 million desyatinas or 7.5 per cent of the total land area of privately owned land. In 1905 peasants owned 44 per cent of the privately owned properties of under 100 desyatinas, the average being 27 desyatinas.

Structure of privately owned landed property in 1905

Groups by size (desyatinas)	No. of units	% of total number of properties	Total land area (thous. des.)	% of total area
Small – 200	695,248	92.5	14,323	16.7
Medium 201–1000	43,782	5.7	19,336	23.0
Large 1001 –	13,851	1.8	52,175	60.3

While large estates accounted for a substantial proportion of the total of privately owned land it is significant that the overwhelming majority of all estates fell within the category of small estates, emphasizing again a duality in the agrarian structure not unlike that obtaining in industry. It is also of interest that the peasant share of privately owned land in 47 provinces of European Russia grew from 6.2 per cent in 1877 to 12.6 per cent in 1887 to 24.8 per cent in 1905 and to 30.4 per cent in 1913. In addition the peasant was entitled to a share in the *nadel* land held by the commune.

A significant proportion of the large estates by 1913 were under peasant leases so that the economic impact of the large estates in terms of output was relatively insignificant though their contribution to marketings was considerable. It is estimated that estates accounted for about 12 per cent of grain output and for about 22 per cent of grain marketings by 1913.

Olga Crisp, unpublished manuscript.

102   The Development of Siberia

Here are some of the conclusions of a report by the Prime Minister, P.A. Stolypin, and the Minister of Agriculture, A.V. Krivoshein, on a working visit to Siberia and the Volga in 1910. Their aim was to assess the economic potential of the regions.

Conclusions

. . .whilst the work of the government migration organization is in many ways imperfect and does not always meet up to the demands placed upon it, the actual business of migration and the continual acquisition of new areas for Russian culture, an example of the creative force of the people, is being carried out with unshakeable firmness and with a natural inevitability. Unpopulated Siberia is rapidly coming to life and growing stronger. . . .

. . .the most important conclusions we have reached, indicating fundamental measures which should be taken immediately, are . . .

1 The land which is held by the original inhabitants of Siberia, as well as that of the migrants, should be held by them not just as tenants, but as landowners. Only the right of ownership of land provides the peasant economy with stability, and serves as a basis for subsequent proper division of land between different landholders. . . .

2 Government policy in Siberia and in European Russia should gradually be harmonized. . . . With this in mind, when land is given to migrants and to the original Siberian inhabitants, a village zemstvo should be established. . . .

3 In the best areas of Siberia there should, at an appropriate time, be a move towards selling land to migrants. . . . The correct valuation and sale of the best land, with the simultaneous strengthening of government help in bleak areas, is the best way of achieving the planned and permanent settlement of Siberia. . . .

4 The freedom to scout should be restored . . . and it is desirable to continue the reduced railway fares for migrants and scouts. . . .

5 Monetary grants for setting-up house should not be allocated according to the circumstances of individual migrants, but according to the difficulty of settling in a particular region. . . .

6 Agricultural help to the population must be established and developed. . . . The proper organization of this agricultural aid requires the rapid establishment of agricultural colleges in Siberia.

7 As well as establishing small peasant holdings, larger private estates must also be set up in Siberia. . . . The proximity of larger and more cultured areas than those of the ordinary migrant will also assist in the general improvement of agriculture in Siberia. It will bring variety and improved techniques and will give the peasant population a supplementary source of income. . . .

8 A market must be provided for Siberian grain and other products of the Siberian economy. . . .

9 In general, migration must be extended; the strengths of the migration organization must be in accordance with the material significance of settling Siberia, and in connection with this, more money must be made available for the migration organization.

A.V. Krivoshein and P.A. Stolypin, *Poezdka v Sibir i Povolzhe*. St Petersburg, 1911, pp. 75–8

103   Migration to Siberia, 1905–1913

	Total migrants and scouts.	Irregulars %	Returners
1905	44,029	92.6	11.524
1906	216,648	50.8	46,262
1907	567,979	19.7	117,518
1908	758,812	47.7	121,204
1909	707,463	47.9	139,907
1910	353,000	(c. 20%)	(70,000)*
1911	226,100	–	(64,000)
1912	259,600	–	(34,000)
1913	327,900	–	(23,000)
	3,461,531		

Note *Figures in parentheses do not include scouts, whose return movement accounts for a large percentage of the earlier returner figures. For example, of the 117,518 who returned in 1907, 90,323 were scouts; out of 121, 204 for 1908, 76, 102 were scouts. The peak of the return movement of direct migrants was therefore reached in 1910.

D.W. Treadgold, *The Great Siberian Migration*. Princeton, NJ, 1957, p. 34.

104   The Village and the First World War

These two accounts come to quite different conclusions about the impact of the war on the village.

(i)

The total personal needs of the peasantry, and, in the first place, the consumption of food, decreased as the result of eleven million consumers being taken for the army. . . . The quantity of grain and potatoes saved was approximately as much as could be obtained from 3 to 6 million desyatinas of arable land. . . . decrease in the consumption of meat equaled 7 to 18 per cent of the total amount of meat produced in Russia; the savings in milk, butter, etc., equaled the average amount produced yearly by 500,000 to 1,600,000 cows. . . .

Two circumstances characterized the peasant money budget during the War. On the one hand the expenditure had greatly decreased. It is difficult to calculate the financial consequences of such facts as the decrease in the number of men who went to earn their living in the towns (and the corresponding decrease in the expense of providing them with outfit, fares and ready cash), the decline in the number of marriages and births etc . . . (but solely) the decrease in expenditure brought about by prohibition equaled 950 to 1,000 million rubles a year. . . .

While reducing the peasants' expenditure, the War enormously increased their revenue . . . to form a general idea of the increase in the peasants' revenue it is sufficient roughly to cast up the sums received by them in cash in connection with mobilization and requisitions. . . .

1 Compensation for horses, carts and harness requisitioned by the army. . . .
2 Payments for cattle which under normal conditions would not have been put on the market but during the war were either requisitioned or taken from the peasants in some other semi-compulsory way. . . .
3 Government allowances to the dependents of the mobilized men. . . .

Considerable increase of income and reduction of expenditure naturally led to the peasants having a surplus of cash. Students of village life observe that one of the peasant difficulties at the period was superabundance of money. The fact that the peasants had really accumulated more cash than they could profitably use is proved by an immense increase in deposits in the cooperative banks and a decrease in the number of loans made by the latter. There are grounds for asserting that during the war the need for money as distinguished from the need for goods was replaced by a desire to get rid of cash.

A.N. Antsiferov *et al.*, *Russian Agriculture during the War*. New Haven, Conn., 1930, pp. 132–8

(ii)

The idea [that the peasantry was becoming wealthier during the war] is based on a number of erroneous assumptions. Firstly, the view of the peasantry as a uniform group in economic terms; secondly, the mechanical transfer of amounts spent on vodka into income; thirdly, that the amounts paid by the government in compensation for horses and carts etc. corresponded to their real value and that they all reached the peasantry and, fourthly, the calculation of new income without any reference to the old or to peasant expenditure.

. . .V.A. Fedorov wrote that . . . the 'peasantry . . . are at once producers of agricultural produce and vendors of labour'. But the agricultural producers are not the same people as the vendors of labour, since the latter, whilst selling their labour, have to buy produce from the former. The rise in bread prices . . . hit the peasantry who bought it most, since the rise in wages was not as great as that in the prices of manufactured goods. . . .

As regards the effect of the prohibition of the sale of vodka, only that part of the expenditure which was made by those who remained in the village during the war can be counted as income. This was, in the main, old people, women and children. Whilst the sale of vodka was officially forbidden, demand did not dry up: expenditure now went, not to the Treasury, but to illicit distillers, speculators, etc. . . .

The requisitioning of horses brought only loss to the peasants . . . since they could only purchase another horse at double the price they had received in compensation for the requisitioned animal. . . . Not all the money paid by the Treasury for requisitioned items found its way to the peasantry: . . . in a number of areas the local administration kept sums back in settlement of tax arrears. . . . Whilst the payments made by the government to the families of those called-up . . . rose by one third, prices for manufactured goods rose by 500 per cent.

A.M. Anfimov, *Rossiyskaya derevnya v gody pervoy mirovoy voyny*. Moscow, 1962, pp. 242-7.

105   Peasant Disturbances, 1914–1917

	Number of disturbances	Number where troops used
1914 (from 17 July 1914)	265	35
1915	177	19
1916	294	91
1917 (to 26 February 1917)	51	4
Total	787	149

A disturbance is defined as a separate uprising of peasants from one or more villages regardless of the length of time it lasted or the form it took.

> *Krestyanskoe dvizhenie v Rossii v 1914–1917 gg.* Moscow–Leningrad, 1965, pp. 513–14.

106   The Gross National Debt

Year	Million rubles
1.1.1911	9,014
1.1.1912	8,958
1.1.1913	8,858
1.1.1914	8,825

Approximately 45 per cent of the debt was held abroad.

> A.L. Vaynshteyn, *Narodnoe bogatstvo i narodnokhozyaystvennoe nakoplenie prerevolyutsionnoy Rossii.* Moscow, 1960, p. 435. Olga Crisp brought this source to our attention.

107   Foreign Investment: Witte's Views

Only capital, knowledge and enterprise can hasten the formation of a completely independent national industry. . . .

Accumulation of capital is possible only to the extent that the economy produces surplus over demand. In Russia, where the overwhelming majority of the population is still engaged in agriculture, this excess of income over expenditure is too small to serve as a source of the accumulation of new capital. . . .

The inflow of foreign capital is, in the strong conviction of the Minister of Finance, the only way to bring our country's economy quickly up to the level where it can provide us with cheap and plentiful goods. Each new wave of capital from abroad beats down the immoderately high level of profits of our monopoly enterprises and makes them seek compensation in new technical improvements, which brings with them cheaper goods. The propping-up of the meagre reservoir of domestic capital by foreign funds gives all the capital in the country the chance to move more freely across a wider area and to add to both large and small sources of profit. Thanks to this, the natural wealth of Russia and the labour of its people is utilized much more fully, the entire economy functions at a greater intensity and it becomes difficult to say whether it is foreign capital or native productive forces, newly enlivened and expanded with the help of this capital, which has the greater effect on the growth of industry.

Lately, voices have been raised against this flow of capital from abroad, insisting that it damages our fundamental national interests by aiming at swallowing up all the profits of growing Russian industry and that, in essence it will lead to our productive wealth being sold off. It is no secret to the Minister of Finance that the inflow of foreign capital is unpalatable to precisely those enterprises who dislike any competition from newly established companies. Domestic industries jealously guard their monopoly profits as much as foreign companies which have already established a firm place in Russian industry.

'Vsepoddaneyshey doklad Ministra Finansov S. Yu. Witte Nikolayu II o neobkhodimosti ustanovit i zatem neprelozheno priderzhivatsya opredelennuyu programmy torgovo-promyshlennoy politiki Imperii, 1899 (January-February)', in I. F. Gindin, 'Ob osnovakh ekonomicheskoy politiki tsarkogo pravitelstva v

kontse XIX-nachale XX
v', in *Dokumenty po istorii
monopolisticheskogo kapitalizma
v Rossii, Materialy po istorii
SSSR*, vol 6. Moscow, 1959,
pp. 181–5.

108   Foreign Capital: Note from V.A. Maklakov to Poincaré, French Minister of Finance, 18 April 1906 (New Style)

Maklakov was a leading Kadet.

Witte . . . has characterized the parliamentary system as the 'great illusion of our century' and cannot consequently be considered as a sincere supporter of a representative regime. . . . There is a court clique which undermines him behind the scenes and counters each of his liberal wins. . . . It has forced the Tsar . . . to promulgate the edict of 20 February which destroyed the authority of the Duma by the creation of a second chamber, half of whose members are high officials nominated by the government. . . .

Such are the sentiments of the government and its advisers, at the very moment when the elections to the Duma, despite great pressure from the regime, have produced a body with a clear majority of convinced constitutionalists. . . .

In contracting a loan just before the opening of the Duma on the eve of this inevitable crisis [between government and Duma] the government has shown that it wants to keep the operation out of the Duma's control because the elected representatives would not approve of the reasons for the loan. Otherwise, with the assent of the Duma, the government could act in more favourable conditions and, at the same time, in greater conformity with the rules of the constitutional regime. In Russia there is no doubt that the government wants to obtain its material needs at its own inclination and to suppress from the start the national representative assembly – but only after this ghost of a Duma has played its part and has served to draw in money from Europe by creating a false belief in the imminent arrival of a stable regime.

For all Russia it would be an atrocious deception to think that material help provided to an authoritarian and bureaucratic regime came from democratic France. The young Russian democracy would not be able to forget where the dying regime got its last resources from.

Translated from the original
French given in Olga Crisp,
'The Russian Liberals and
the 1906 Anglo-French loan
to Russia', *Slavonic and East
European Review*, vol. 39
(1960–1), pp. 509–10.

109   Foreign Investment in Russian Companies, 1914

	Capital of Russian joint stock companies	Foreign capital
	million rubles	million rubles
Share capital	4721	2186
Debenture capital	398	281
	5119	2467 (48%)

B. Bonwetsch, 'Das auslän-
dische Kapital in Russland',
*Jahrbücher für Geschichte
Osteuropas*, vol. 22 (1974), p.
416

110   The Share of Foreign Capital in Productive and Non-productive Investment, 1861–1914

Year	Total of productive investment (Million Rubles)	Foreign Capital m. R	%	Russian Capital m. R	%
1900	6121	4003	65.4	2118	34.6
1908	7503	4356	58.1	3147	41.9
1914	10089	5776	57.3	4313	42.7
	Total of non-productive investment (m. R.)				
1900	5787	729	12.7	5058	87.3
1908	9011	2070	23.0	6941	77.0
1914	11069	1858	16.8	9211	83.2
Increase 1. Productive					
1900–1908	1382	353	25.5	1029	74.5
1908–1914	2586	1420	54.9	1166	45.1

Year	Total of productive investment (Million Rubles)	Foreign Capital m. R	%	Russian Capital m. R.	%
2. Non-productive					
1900–1908	3224	1341	41.6	1883	58.4
1908–1914	2058	(212)	–	2270	100

V.I. Bovykin, 'Probleme der industriellen Entwicklung Russlands', in D. Geyer, ed., *Wirtschaft und Gesellschaft im vorrevolutionären Russland*. Cologne, 1975, p. 197.

The division into productive and non-productive investment is probably untenable in the sense that investment deemed non-productive by Bovykin, i.e. government debt and mortgage bonds, could be used for productive purposes, e.g. improvement of estates, whilst investment in municipal debt, if used, for example, for the building of sumptuous town halls, could be non-productive. There is also a problem with the so-called productive application of banking shares. Nevertheless with all these reservations there is no doubt that a larger share of foreign investment was in productive enterprises. (Olga Crisp, Unpublished paper delivered at the Historical Congress in Bucharest in 1981.)

111   Distribution of French Investment in Russian Industries, 1914

		million francs Russia	Russian Poland
Mining:	Coal	165.1	171.9
	Iron	15.0	
	Gold	5.1	
	Platinum	48.8	
	Other	61.0	
Iron and steel		604.6	126.1
Metallurgy and metal industries		90.1	0.2
Electrical ind.		4.2	
Copper ind.		43.0	
Oil		214.1	
Chemical ind.		114.3	0.2
Textiles		129.6	56.4

	million francs Russia	Russian Poland	
Cement, public works	10.3		
Rubber	95.1		
Food ind.	21.4		
Water, gas, electricity	64.9	27.7	
Banks	284.6		
Insurance cos.	50.9		
Trade and transport	15.7		
Total	2,126.2	383.3	2,509.5

R. Girault, *Emprunts russes et investissements français en Russie 1887–1914*. Paris, 1973, p. 516

112   The First World War and Public Finance: Note by the Minister of Finance, P.L. Bark, to the Finance Committee, September–October 1914

In the two months which have elapsed since the declaration of war with Germany, our expenditure has already reached very significant levels, in many respects exceeding that on the Russo-Japanese war. Up to 26 September, the Treasury had disbursed 1,014 million rubles in extraordinary expenditure. . . . This sum does not include the large amounts spent on mobilization . . . which will probably amount to some 400 million rubles.

This evidence of the growth of government expenditure and condition of the Treasury shows that in the near future the resources of the Treasury may be insufficient to cover our expenditure on the war.

In view of this the Minister of Finance considers it his duty to present his ideas on how futher resources for the war can be provided through credit operations, and proposes that a new short-term loan issue of 400 million rubles be made by the Treasury. . . .

The Minister of Finance also considers it his duty to inform the Committee of the state of our foreign holdings and of his proposals to concentrate them in London, in view of the need for resources to pay the huge sums due on military orders and the necessity to help our own commerce and industry so that it can settle its debts in sterling.

On 10 July 1914 the Ministry of Finance held 666.3 million rubles abroad, distributed as follows:

Country	Million rubles
France	463.0
England	80.9
Germany	110.9
Austria	3.2
Others	8.3
Total	666.3

Immediately after Austria presented her ultimatum to Serbia the Ministry of Finance removed all its holdings from Austria and Germany . . . (so that) at the beginning of the war the Ministry of Finance's sums held abroad amounted to 540 million rubles, made up of 431.3 million rubles in France, 78.4 million rubles in England and 30.3 million rubles elsewhere.

In normal times these sums would be sufficient to cover all the expenditure of the Ministry of Finance abroad – to pay both our loans and our normal foreign debts – for a year and a half.

However, the almost universal imposition of a (financial) moratorium following the outbreak of war prevented the Ministry of Finance from arranging its foreign holdings as it would like. A particularly difficult situation has arisen in France . . . where our Ministry of Finance has only with difficulty been able to make payments on our loans, and the French banks have refused to pay our other debts, in particular those requiring the transfer of funds to other countries, because of the moratorium.

'O predstavlenii Ministru Finansov prava sovershit kreditnye operatsii na vnutrennem angliyskom denezhenykh rynkakh', in A.L. Sidorov, *Finansovoe polozhenie Rossii v gody pervoy mirovoy voyny (1914–1917).* Moscow, 1960, pp. 532–4

V   Social Development

113   Zemstvo activity

Zemstva (local provincial and district councils) were introduced to Russia in 1864. By the beginning of the twentieth century they had become the major provider of social services in the provinces. It was in the zemstva that the moderate political parties had their genesis.

. . .the overall number of district electors in all 34 provinces was severely reduced – from 13,329 to 10,229. Substantially more than half were gentry. Peasant electors were reduced to 3,167 from a previous total of 5,357. Excluded from voting were priests, merchants and the owners of trading enterprises. . . . [Effects of the revised Zemstvo Statute of 1890].

. . .the zemstva duties were laid down as follows: to provide provisions for police patrols, to pay JPs and judges, to set aside money for detention cells and for the transport and upkeep of convicts. In the main these responsibilities were inherited by the zemstvo and bore no relation to local affairs. As they were necessary for the state, they were to be compulsory for the zemstvo. Matters which were difficult to deal with from St Petersburg were also transferred to the zemstvo: fire insurance, famine relief, the upkeep of roads and bridges and of state hospitals and workhouses. The government required little else from the zemstvo. The remainder of the duties of the zemstvo enumerated in the law were not compulsory . . . in the draft law there was not even any mention of the zemstva right to concern themselves with education, health or veterinary matters. And if the State Council had not, in its examination of the 1864 Regulations, remembered this, there would have been no zemstvo schools or zemstvo doctors. . . . Educational and health matters developed and became firmly established as a zemstvo activity. Gradually the zemstvo took on other responsibilities: in many areas they combatted epidemics, and it was recognized as desirable to give aid to agriculture and peasant industries. Zemstvo activity developed and grew, and with it expenditure increased. Over the last 35 years it has grown from 30.5m rubles in 1876 to 36m in 1880, 43m in 1885, 48m in 1890, 66m in 1895, 88m in 1900, 124m in 1906 and 168m in 1910.

. . .as an example, expenditure in 1912 was made up thus:

	Rubles
Education	66,473,300
Health	57,704,800
Administration and staff	15,467,500
Roads, bridges and fords	15,201,200
Debt repayment	14,296,700
Assistance to agriculture, animal husbandry and peasant industry	13,979,900
To reserves	9,752,400
Upkeep of posting stations for police, government servants and zemstvo employees.	7,131,300
Miscellaneous	6,972,900
Veterinary medicine	6,238,200
Workhouse upkeep and assistance to the poor	3,603,700
Government expenditure	3,346,300
Total	220,168,200

. . .estimates for income were made up as follows. Firstly, any surplus from the previous year was taken into account, together with recoverable debts. Interest on zemstvo capital and income from zemstvo estates and enterprises [agricultural equipment and book shops], tolls levied on roads and bridges, charges levied on strangers using zemstvo hospitals and fines for late payment of debts were added to this. . . . When all the income which could be relied upon was reckoned up, it became clear what the shortfall would be against projected expenditure. This was the sum to be raised by taxation. In 1912, for example, definite income for the zemstvo in 34 provinces amounted to 74m rubles. The remaining 146m had to be collected from zemstvo taxpayers. . . . Of this, about 103m was raised on land and forests, some 25m from industrial and commercial enterprises, 15m from urban property and 2½m from rural property.

G.E. Lvov and T.I. Polner,
Nashe Zemstvo i 50 let ero raboty.
Petrograd, 1917, pp. 17–30.

114   Formation of the United Nobility

At the same time as political parties were being formed in Russia, the nobility felt the need to unite its provincial noble assemblies into a national organization. Each district (uezd) and province (guberniya) had its own noble assembly, consisting of the nobility of the area. The assembly elected one of its number chairman, as spokesman of the nobility in the region and as marshal of the nobility. The United Nobility held annual congresses after 1906 and was able to exert considerable influence on policy through its close contacts with court circles and its privileged access to the Tsar.

Declaration of the Council of the United Nobility, 21 May 1906

On 21 May the first congress of representatives from noble assemblies convened, at the request of the assemblies in 29 of the 37 provinces of Russia which have gentry representation. The task of the congress was, firstly, to explain and coordinate the views of the noble assemblies on the most important questions of national life and, secondly, to agree on the future activity of the united Russian nobility in the political and economic life of the country so as to strengthen, defend and develop the foundations of the state. The congress . . . included 133 gentry as representatives from 29 provincial assemblies, and 61 gentry from various provinces, invited to the congress as observers. . . .

The results of the work of the congress were seen both in its acceptance of general matters put to it which had been drafted previously, and in a series of proposals on questions of national importance which were to be investigated before the next congress, to take place no later than January 1907. The former of these included, firstly the coordination of the views of the assemblies' representatives on the political significance of the historical period through which Russia was passing and the role which the gentry should play in the political life of the country . . .; secondly, the setting out of definite views on the agrarian question, views which in the opinion of the congress should form the basis of the agrarian legislation . . .; and thirdly, the organization of . . . gentry congresses and their executive organ. . . .

The congress's proposals were, in principle;

1 The creation of an all-estate Russian union of agrarian property-owners, to support and defend the principles of property, as a foundation of the state, and of agricultural work, as an economic principle.

2 The organization of migration for 'land-shortage' peasants and surplus workers. . . .

3 The creation of an all-estate mortgage bank. . . .
4 The preparation of an electoral system which will guarantee that
   the needs of the country, and particularly its agrarian demands, are
   represented; this is necessary so that the opinions of the gentry
   are heard when the bills on the reform of local government are
   discussed.
5 Finally, the organization and development of the press so as to
   ensure the dissemination of sensible views on political and other
   questions, in particular to achieve a greater unity in the work of
   noble assemblies.

> *Sbornik dokumentov po istorii*
> *SSSR (period imperializma).*
> Moscow, 1977, pp. 23–5

115 Working-Class Life

The average Russian worker's living standards were very low but even lower
living standards in many country areas led to an influx of peasants into cities
and towns. The overcrowding and lack of sanitation in, for example, St
Petersburg, were appalling. Bogorod and Seredsk were in Moscow province.

(i) Workers' daily Diet

	St Petersburg textile workers	Baku oil workers	Bogorod textile workers	Seredsk textile workers
Calories:				
Vegetable	2740.9	2932.2	2755.9	2850.5
Animal	514.5	409.1	151.5	185.8
Total	3255.4	3341.3	2907.4	3036.3
Grammes:				
Protein: Vegetable	73.83	72.84	62.96	68.0
Animal	37.7	39.53	10.47	14.58
Total	111.53	112.37	73.43	82.58
Fats: Vegetable	16.62	16.12	47.4	29.00
Animal	36.26	14.65	7.53	9.56
Total	52.88	30.77	54.93	38.56
Carbohydrate.	562.39	593.10	504.79	564.40

Expenditure of workers' families

	St Petersburg %	Kiev %
Housing	20.7	22.4
Clothing and footwear	12.2	12.9
Food	48.7	49.9
Alcohol and tobacco	5.0	3.8
Medicine and hygiene	5.3	4.2
Cultural and educational	3.3	3.5
Help to relatives	2.2	0.3
Miscellaneous	2.6	3.0
inc. social and political	1.2	0.5

Source of main meal for St Petersburg workers

	Place of work	% Tavern	Home	No info.
Single workers	9.5	34.6	46.4	9.5
Married workers	0.3	5.2	88.3	6.2

Occupation of different types of accommodation

	St Petersburg		Kiev	
	Single	Married	Single	Married
Separate flat	0.9	46.5	11.3	67.0
Single room	35.7	45.8	28.0	30.6
½ room	17.6	0.7	15.8	0.9
Part of a room	37.0	4.0	39.0	1.5
A bed	3.7	–	5.9	–
½ bed	2.3	–	–	–
No info.	2.8	3.0	–	–

N.K. Druzhinin, *Usloviya byta rabochikh v dorevolyutsionnoy Rossii*. Moscow, 1958, pp. 14, 35, 40, 46.

(ii) British worker's diet: from a survey by Dr T. Oliver, 1894

In order to put the Russian diet in perspective, a comparison is drawn with a British worker's diet in 1894. It is interesting to note that the figures for energy value and protein are roughly the same. The Russians, however, ate far less fat and far more carbohydrate.

Male worker's daily diet

Energy value	Protein	Fat	Carbohydrate
Kcal	g.	g.	g.
3,321	114	146	387

D.J. Oddy 'Working-Class Diets in Late Nineteenth-Century Britain', *Economic History Review*, vol. 23 (1970), p. 320.

116 Peasant Life

These descriptions of peasant housing come from studies conducted in two poor villages in Voronezh province, in the central black earth (chernozem) region. However they should not be taken as typical for all parts of Russia. Even in Voronezh province there were better-off villages. Shingarev was known for his strong, pro-peasant views. He was Minister of Agriculture in the first Provisional Government and Minister of Finance in the first coalition government.

. . .The living accommodation and homesteads in both villages are typical of the whole northern part of the province, and are distinguished only by the mediocrity of the buildings. The plan of a cottage and yard of average size in these villages in generally as follows:

The cottage is almost square with a porch on the right or left side, and often without a storeroom (if there is one, it is located on the other side of the porch). It faces the street and has two windows on that side. From the porch there is access into both the yard and the street. In front of the cottage, on the street, is a small earthen or stone-faced cellar. The yard is usually enclosed by a wattled fence: this forms the walls for the awning which runs around the yard and the enclosure for the animals, opposite the cottage. Sometimes there is a small storehouse on one of the sides of the yard. The area of the yard is no more than 20–40 sq. sazhen. (1 sazen = 2.13 metres) Inside the cottage, directly opposite the entrance from the porch, is a Russian stove, occupying a substantial proportion of the building. Around the walls to the right run benches, and in a corner to the left of the entrance is the dining table. In the corner opposite the opening of the stove is a small stand or shelf for crockery. From the stove to the opposite wall there stretch, just under the ceiling, benches for sleeping on, but these are far from being a feature of every cottage. Such is in the simple arrangement inside a cottage, devoid of furniture except for one or two wooden benches, and without any hint of luxury or decoration, apart from the icons in the corner above the tables. Even cheap pictures are a great rarity and curtains, photographs and flowers – often seen in villages in industrial regions – are completely absent. A little crockery, some clothing, and in the winter, a spinning-wheel or loom complete the beggarly picture of the peasant house. . . .

In both villages the general condition of the cottages is quite satisfactory, thanks to their predominantly brick construction. Most of the brick cottages, built some 15–20 years ago, looked as new and were in good condition. On the other hand, the wooden buildings were in many cases rotted and dilapidated. In (both villages) some 20 per cent of all the cottages were in a tumbledown state. In particular, 17 cottages had rotten walls, 16 rotten flooring and 16 rotten roofs, so that a fifth of all buildings were decrepit, hardly fit to live in and threatening to collapse. . . .

The cottages are built close together, have little air inside, are full of fumes and at the same time are too cold, badly lit and completely lacking in ventilation. . . .

The furnishing of the cottages corresponds to their general condition. . . . Bare walls, benches, a table, sleeping benches, stands with kitchen utensils, a little clothing and a few household articles – that is all there is inside a cottage.

Almost the only furniture is the dining table – which is also used for preparing food. Various other domestic tasks are also performed on it: harnesses are repaired, linen and clothing embroidered . . . The table is near the benches along the walls, for many cottages have nothing else to sit on. If the family is small, then everyone can sit at the table for meals. In large families, only the adult males and old women sit at table; the other women eat standing up and spoon their food from the communal bowl between the heads of those sitting down. The small children sit on benches at some distance from the table. In summer only the very young, very old and sick sleep inside the cottage – everybody else goes outside to sleep in the yard, the porch, the threshing barn, etc. In winter, of course, everyone sleeps inside. . . . The most favoured place for sleeping when inside is on the stove. This is the warmest place of all, and so children, old people and the sick go there . . . In 83 per cent of all cottages, the stove was a place for sleeping on. The remaining members of the family, who could not find space on the stove (and frequently the entire family did sleep on the stove) slept on benches along the wall opposite the door.

> A.I. Shingarev, *Vymiryayu-shchaya derevnya*, 2nd ed. St Petersburg, 1909, pp. 31–2, 48–9.

117 Stolypin's Land Reform: Vendors of Allotment Land in Voronezh Province, 1914

The extract reproduced in document **116** is typical of the 'literature of social lament'. Shingarev chose a particularly poor village for his survey so as to underline the sufferings of poor peasants. He is typical of many members of the intelligentsia who felt guilty about their privileged position in life. Documents **117** and **118** present the other side of the picture. However whereas they refer to 1914 – after the good years of 1908–13 – Shingarev was writing slightly earlier. Factors which would point towards poverty as a reason for selling (F, G and I) only account for 10.4 per cent of the total number of vendors. (Olga Crisp, unpublished)

Groups by qty. of land before sale.	Land sold As % of pre-sale holding	As % of total land sold	No. of vendors %	As % of those engaged in agriculture
I. –7 des.	76.2	61.6	81.0	70.5
II. 7–15 des.	55.3	30.7	15.9	86.1
III. 15–20 des.	33.5	4.1	1.8	83.8
IV. 20– des.	25.1	3.6	1.3	89.2
	61.5	100	100	73.4

Reasons for selling land

Group	Reason – % of vendors A	B	C	D	E	F	G	H	I	J	K	L
I.	5.9	25.7	6.2	11.5	28.1	6.2	2.4	6.5	1.1	1.5	1.2	2.7
II.	9.2	27.8	5.9	7.6	21.2	9.0	1.6	7.8	3.4	3.4	0.3	2.8
III.	8.0	14.0	10.0	9.0	29.0	4.0	3.0	14.0	15.0	6.0	–	5.0
IV.	14.1	14.3	19.7	4.2	25.3	1.4	1.4	8.4	1.4	2.8	–	7.0
	6.6	25.7	6.4	10.7	27.6	6.5	2.3	6.8	1.6	1.9	1.0	2.8

A: Purchase of land in European Russia
B: Migration

C: Transfer to members of family
D: Income from service or craft
E: Lack of manpower in family
F: Decline in economy
G: Drunkenness and spendthrift nature
H: Change in place of residence
I: Payment of taxes
J: Improvement of economy
K: Allotment not wanted
L: Other reasons

M.S. Simonova, 'Mobilizat-
siya krestyanskoy nadelnoy
zemli v period stolypinskoy
agrarnoy reformy', in *Materialy po istorii selskogo khozyay-
stva i krestyanstva SSSR.*
Sbornik 5, Moscow, 1962, p.
457.

118   Stolypin's Land Reform: Purchases of Allotment Land in Voronezh Province, 1914

Many peasants in Voronezh Province had accepted 'beggar holdings' at the time of Emancipation. Many of these had done so in anticipation of low prices of land in the region. Some succeeded in purchasing land, especially since there were opportunities for earning money, but many others were left with inadequate holdings. It is instructive that 37 per cent of the land purchased was acquired by landless peasants and that the most affluent, those with over 20 desyatinas, only acquired 4 per cent of the purchased land. If 15 desyatinas is taken as an adequate holding, then 90.7 per cent of the land purchased was acquired by those in Groups I, II and III. Indeed the proportion of the land held by better-off peasants declined. The beneficiaries were poor and middle peasants. Hence the experience of Voronezh Province does not support Lenin's thesis that capitalist relations in agriculture were leading to a situation where the better-off peasants (kulaks) were acquiring land at the expense of middle and poor peasants and that the middle peasant was being squeezed between the rich and poor peasants with most of them tending to fall into the less-well-off category. Indeed the greatest vitality was demonstrated by poor peasants (Groups I and II) who acquired 68.1 per cent of the land on the market. It is quite possible that a similar trend was evident in many other provinces. (Olga Crisp, unpublished)

Amount of land before purchase (grouped)	Desyatinas		
	Amount before purchase	Land bought	Land after purchase
I. Landless	–	5426	5426
II. –7 des.	6913	4595	11508
III. 7–15 des.	10754	3322	14076
IV. 15–20 des.	4379	781	5160
V. 20– des.	6350	577	6927
	28,396	14,701	43,097

Group	No. of transactions		% of land bought
	No.	%	
I.	2016	36.0	36.9
II.	2079	37.1	31.2
III.	1096	19.4	22.6
IV.	265	4.7	5.3
V.	154	2.8	4.0
	5610		

Ibid p. 458

119 Merchant Life

The family life of the Buryshkins was a far cry from that of the average worker's family. Buryshkin, however, reveals how far merchant life had advanced from its introverted and fiercely patriotic nature described as the 'kingdom of darkness' by Dobrolyubov in the 1860s.

. . .I want to give an impression of how the middle ranks of the Moscow merchant class lived – the last survivors of the 'kingdom of darkness'. The style of our life was extremely simple, devoid of any external manifestations of wealth. We had no manservant at home, nor did we eat from gold and silver dishes. Our dinner service was quite plain . . . but our home was a place where there was an atmosphere of plenty. . . .

Both my sisters were students: Shura, training to be a teacher, and Nadya studying science, and later medicine. . . .

At dinner there would always be some of the family's friends, most often girls who knew my sisters and relatives – usually female. We always waited for my father to arrive from the warehouse, but here the resemblance to the 'kingdom of darkness' stopped. The meal was substantial, although we rarely had wine, and I never recall spirits being drunk. Over dinner the talk was mostly of the theatre. We were all, as was often the case in Moscow, passionate theatre-goers. We talked about music, about literature. There was comparatively little about politics: all the same we had a variety of different opinions. One of my sisters was a fervent populist and preferred not to get into arguments. . . .

My father was not a collector in the strict sense of the word, but he did buy pictures and our house contained a number of good examples of the work of Russian artists. After his death, the paintings were divided amongst his three children. It was I who inherited the collecting urge, although I was unsuccessful in completing the task he had begun. . . .

Our house was not particularly suitable for living in, or rather it did not correspond to the needs of modern technology. It needed rebuilding or else to be put to some other use. So my father decided to bequeath it to the city of Moscow to be turned into a museum or a library, on condition that my mother could have the use of the house during her lifetime. My mother spent very little time there after my father died and moved into an adjacent flat to mine. The war was not long in coming and our old house was turned into a hospital, with my sister as the senior doctor.

. . .My collecting concentrated on Russian items, especially anything I could find which concerned Moscow. In time the collection became enormous . . . and I intended to give it to the city to organize a museum in memory of my father. It is now the basis for the Museum of Old Moscow.

P.A. Buryshkin, *Moskva kupecheskaya*. New York, 1954, pp. 221–4

120   Bourgeois Life

. . .Amalia Karlovna Guishar, the widow of a Belgian engineer and herself a Russianized Frenchwoman, arrived in Moscow from the Urals with her two children – her son Rodion and her daughter Larissa. She placed her son in a military academy and her daughter in a girl's high school. . . .

· Madame Guishar's husband had left her his savings, stocks which had been rising and were now beginning to fall. To stop the drain on her resources and to have something to do, she bought a small business; this was Levitskaya's dressmaking establishment near the Triumphal Arch; she took it over from Levitskaya's heirs together with the firm's goodwill, its clientele and all its seamstresses and apprentices. . . .

[The family] moved into the small three-roomed flat adjoining the workshop.

This was the most sordid part of Moscow – slums, shady dives . . . and whole streets given up to vice.

The children were not dismayed by the dirt in their rooms, the bedbugs and the wretchedness of the furniture. Since their father's death their mother had lived in constant fear of destitution. Rodya and Lara were used to being told that they were on the verge of ruin. They realized that they were different from the children of the street, but, like children brought up in an orphanage, they had a deep-seated fear of the rich. . . .

The workshop was in a single-storeyed house near the corner of Tverskaya Street, in a quarter invaded by the Brest railway with its engine depots, warehouses and lodgings for the clerks. . . .

Nothing had changed since Levitskaya's day. The sewing machines whirred frantically under the tread of tired seamstresses or their hovering hands. Here and there a woman sat at a table, sewing quietly with a broad sweep of the arm as she pulled the needle and long thread. The floor was littered with scraps. You had to raise your voice to make yourself heard above the clatter of the machinery and the fluted warbling of the . . . canary in its cage in the window. . . .

In the reception room the ladies clustered in a striking group round a table heaped with fashion journals; they stood, sat or reclined in the poses they had seen in the fashion plates, and discussed the models and the patterns. Sitting in the manager's chair at another table was Faina Silantyevna Fetisova, a bony woman with warts in the recesses of her flabby cheeks, who was a senior cutter and Madame Guishar's assistant.

A cigarette in a bone holder clamped between her yellowed teeth, her eyes with yellow eyeballs screwed up against the yellow jet of smoke from her nose and mouth, she jotted in a notebook the measurements, orders and addresses of the clients.

Madame Guishar had no experience of running a workshop. She felt that she was not quite the boss, but the staff were honest and Fetisova reliable. All the same, there were troubled times and she was afraid to think of the future; she had moments of paralysing despair. . . .

Lara and Rodya realized that nothing in life would come to them easily. Unlike the idle and the well-to-do, they had not the leisure for premature theorizing and curiosity about things which did not as yet concern them in practice.

> B. Pasternak, *Doctor Zhivago*, trans. by M. Hayward and M. Harari, London, 1961, pp. 30–4.

121   Official Petersburg

There, where nothing but a foggy damp hung suspended, at first appeared the dull outline, then descended from heaven to earth the dingy, blackish grey St Isaac's Cathedral: at first appeared the outline and then the full shape of the equestrian monument of Emperor Nicholas I. At its base the shaggy hat of a Nicholas grenadier thrust out of the fog.

The carriage was flying towards Nevsky Prospect.

Apollon Apollonovich Ableukhov was gently rocking on the satin seat cushions. He was cut off from the scum of the streets by four perpendicular walls. Thus he was isolated from people and from the red covers of the damp trashy rags on sale right there at this intersection . . .

The houses merged cubelike into a regular, five-storey row. This row differed from the line of life: for many a wearer of diamond-studded decorations, as for so many other dignitaries, the middle of life's road had proved to be the termination of life's journey.

Inspiration took possession of the senator's soul whenever the lacquered cube cut along the line of the Nevsky: there the numeration of the houses was visible. And the circulation went on. There, from there, on clear days, from far, far away, came the blinding blaze of the gold needle, the clouds, the crimson ray of the sunset. There, from there, on foggy days – nothing, no one.

And what there was there was lines: the Neva and the islands. Probably in those distant days, when out of the mossy marshes rose high roofs and masts and spires, piercing the dank greenish fog in jags –

> -on his shadowy sails the Flying Dutchman winged his way toward Petersburg from there, from the leaden expanses of the Baltic and German seas, in order here to erect, by delusion, his misty land and to give the name of islands to the wave of onrushing clouds.

> Apollon Apollonovich did not like the islands: the population there was industrial and coarse. There the many-thousand human swarm shuffled in the morning to the many-chimneyed factories. The inhabitants of the islands are reckoned among the population of the Empire: the general census has been introduced among them as well.

> Apollon Apollonovich did not wish to think further. The islands must be crushed! Riveted with the iron of the enormous bridge, skewered by the arrows of the prospects.

A. Bely, *Petersburg*, trans. by R.A. Maguire and J.E. Malmstad. Brighton, 1978, pp. 10–11.

122   The Co-operative Movement

Co-operatives, especially consumers' and credit co-operatives expanded rapidly before 1914 and even during the war. They became especially widespread in the south and east of Russia, and in 1912 the Moscow Narodny Bank was set up as a central credit institution for co-operative banks.

Credit Cooperation Before the War

The membership of credit cooperatives in Russia aggregated 8.2m on 1 January, 1914. By 1 January 1917, it had further increased to 9.8m, not including organizations located in the evacuated territories of Poland and of the Baltic provinces. According to conservative estimates, the households affiliated with cooperative credit organizations represented on the latter date a total population considerably over sixty millions, of whom over fifty millions were covered by credit associations. Its bulk was formed by the peasant element. . . .

Professor Tugan-Baranovsky, the noted Russian economist, states that 'our peasant cooperation is free of the influence of the landed gentry . . . while the credit associations originally attracted the better-situated groups, they have been gradually enlisting, as they grew stronger, the poorer peasants as well. The proportion of horseless peasants in the cooperatives of Ufa province doubled in the course of five years, while the proportion of peasants owning more than four horses decreased by more than one third. "The cooperative movement in Ufa province originated among the well-to-do elements of the rural population" says M. Krassilnikov, "but it gradually came to embrace poorer households as well, and as a result its nucleus was in later years formed of the intermediate groups, those which actually constitute what is known as the mass of the people." '

> E.M. Kayden and A.N. Antsiferov, *The Cooperative Movement in Russia during the War*. New Haven, 1929, pp. 260–4

Consumers' Co-operation in Siberia.

. . .the Union of Siberian Cooperative Unions *Zakupsbyt* was set up on 15 August 1916 and a campaign of publicity was at once mapped out for the organization of local consumers' societies into district unions, and their consolidation for larger wholesale activities in the *Zakupsbyt*. . . .

The advent of the *Zakupsbyt* was the opening of a new epoch in the history of Siberian cooperation. Before its formation the work of the various unions was lacking in unity, planning, and in conscious direction; their financial resources were weak and unintegrated; their knowledge of the various markets was limited, resulting not infrequently in competition among themselves. The *Zakupsbyt* was more than a central federation of unions for wholesale supply and sale called into being by the conditions of war and disorganized markets; it was principally an ambitious economic experiment on an all-Siberian scale to establish a coordinated form of producer-consumer mutualism, to abolish waste and overlapping in the distribution of goods, and to bring about a system of planned, disciplined and coordinated operations binding into one the ancient conflicting interests of country and town. So vast and impressive was its achievement in a comparatively brief period that it was soon in a position to exert an ever increasing influence on political authorities, no matter what government was in the seat of power.

Before the war, and the coming of the *Zakupsbyt*, there was only one district consumers' union in the entire territory of Siberia and the Ural, uniting a small groups of 16 primary societies. So rapid was the growth of local consumers' societies during 1916, following the first evidences of economic scarcity, and so widespread the trend toward unification, that at the time of its foundation the *Zakupsbyt* was at once joined by thirteen district and regional unions carrying with them a total of 1,958 affiliated primary societies. By the end of 1918 the shareholding membership had grown to thirty unions with 10,262 societies. . . .

The appearance of the *Zakupsbyt* and of its member unions in any market had an immediate effect on prices, often liberating the masses from the grasp of profiteers. And the cooperative unions penetrated even into the remotest corners of Siberia. An example of their far-reaching activities is the case of the fur-hunting region of Turukhansk beyond the Arctic Circle. Itinerant merchants from the south had long monopolized the field, buying the furs at greatly depressed prices and supplying the natives with their wants at inflated prices. The trappers were perpetually in debt, driven by necessity to hunt even the young fur-bearing animals in order to increase the stock they might offer in trade to the merchant. . . . Then in 1917 the Yenissei Union of Cooperatives jointly with the *Zakupsbyt* federation assembled parties of furs, selling the goods direct to America and China, and repaying their full realized value to the natives, less handling charges. The Yenissei Union supplied them with powder at 400 rubles a pud, when the private dealers were charging 1,400 to 1,600 rubles, and with small shot at 140 rubles a pud against the dealers' charge of 300 to 320 rubles. The union also supplied tea, textiles, soap, salt, flour, tobacco, and other goods at prices two to four times lower, and it established a permanent agency with a cooperative inn at Turukhansk for the visiting natives.

Ibid pp. 169–70, 184–5.

123   Living Conditions in the Army: Report of the Chief Military Hygiene Officer, 1910

. . .At the present time, the most serious defect in our army from the point of view of hygiene is that very many barracks are a long way from meeting the most modest hygienic requirements as living accommodation. Firstly, of course, the cramped conditions and lack of air must be mentioned. This is made all the worse by the absence of separate dining halls and recreation rooms. . . . In almost all barracks, the natural ventilation does not satisfactorily air the living quarters. Poor air-flow is noticeable by the existence of a certain smell, specific to barracks, which usually intensifies at night.

Damp and cold barracks are far from rare. In many places the latrines are of primitive construction, extremely cold and far from the barracks; those inside barracks or close by are often so badly built that the stench permeates through to the living areas. . . .

The barrack accommodation of the troops of the Amur military district is particularly poor. Only half (54 per cent) of the lower ranks live in stone barracks. These are the best type from the point of view of hygiene, but are very few in number and are therefore insufficient for the pressing needs of the troops. Besides this, there is a completely understandable desire to move the troops out of bad accommodation into new barracks, with the result that the latter become very crowded. About 25 per cent of troops are accommodated in wooden barracks of temporary construction, with single-thickness wooden floors or even with just a wooden plank between the beds. About 8 per cent of troops live in old and dilapidated wooden barracks, completely unsuited to the severe and changeable climate of the region. Some 6 per cent of troops live in temporary wooden barracks constructed for the last war (with Japan) and therefore fundamentally unsuitable for permanent use. The remaining 5 per cent exist in dug-outs or other such primitive constructions, which satisfy no hygienic criteria. . . .

The list of grave hygienic deficiencies is added to by the lack, in many places, of baths and laundries, so that the soldiers have to use private bath-houses, thus increasing the chances of bathers catching various infectious diseases, and washing is either given to some laundress operating unofficially, or else is done quickly at the baths. Besides, the baths which are used by many troops are distant from their barracks, which is very inconvenient in the cold winter weather.

Krasny Arkhiv, vol. 98 (1940),
pp. 160–1

124   Selected Professions: Employment Statistics

The expansion of numbers in the various professions in the years before 1914 is most impressive.

1 Agronomists
– 1909–13, growth in nos. from 2,541 to 9,112.
   But the number with an educational qualification dropped from 54

per cent to 43.4 per cent: evidence of the shortage of specialists.
- about one third worked for the Ministry of Agriculture, the remaining two thirds for the zemstva and other such organizations.
- in 1913, the zemstva employed 4,300 agronomists.

2 Veterinary medicine
- 1912, 3,400 vets and 3,800 assistants (*feldsher*).
- 1914, a different source records 5,200 qualified vets.
- 1914, Ministry of Agriculture recorded 5,000 vacancies for vets in government service, excluding the army and the zemstva.

3 Doctors
- 1897 census recorded *c*. 17,000 doctors.
- 1912, 22,772 doctors and 28,500 assistants; 8,100 hospitals with 220,000 beds.
- 1914, The Russian Medical Register recorded 42,700 names, including 28,240 doctors, 3,120 female doctors, 5,330 pharmacists, 112 'master pharmacists' and 5,800 dentists.
- 1913, fewer than two doctors per 10,000 of population.

4 Teachers
- number of teachers with higher education teaching in secondary schools: 1906 – 11,647; 1914 – 20,956.
  1914: another 3,185 and 3,085 in private and commercial schools respectively – total figure of 27,226.
- Teacher training colleges for secondary school teachers: 1900 – 10, 1916 – 48.
  Number of primary school teachers: 1906 – 69,200 in rural areas, 2,800 in towns. 1914 – 128,000 and 3,500.
- separate primary teacher training colleges: 1906 – 70, 1916 – 189.
  1900–13, trained a total of 20,300 primary school teachers.
- 1911, census of primary schools: 100,700 schools with 153,300 teachers. 52 per cent of teachers had a secondary education, 48 per cent with a lower level. 32 per cent had a teaching qualification.
- to implement universal primary education it was calculated that 370,464 teachers were needed: 307 colleges would be needed to train this quantity.

V.R.   Leykina-Svirskaya,
Russkaya   Intelligentsiya   v

1900–1917 godakh. Moscow, 1981, pp. 47–64.

125   Public Health in Russian Cities

Health care was inadequate in Russia as a whole but in the overcrowded capital the authorities were quite unable to cope.

Stolypin's speech to the Third Duma on a government bill to install a sewerage scheme in St Petersburg, 19 January 1911

. . .Nobody will be able to deny that the government should take special measures to deal with a city where the number of deaths exceeds the number of births, where one third of the deaths are caused by infectious diseases, where typhoid claims more victims than in any West European city, where smallpox is still rife, where recurrent typhus, a disease long eradicated in the West, is still occasionally seen, and which is a favourable breeding-ground for both cholera and plague bacteria.

. . .It is the capital's poor who most need this sewerage scheme. I have seen them in the city's hospitals, resignedly submitting to death, poisoned because they have had no access to clean water. I am well aware of the 100,000 deaths from cholera over the last year; I feel hurt and ashamed when my country is singled out as the source of all types of infections and diseases.

. . .There is a whole series of towns from which infections spread across the whole of Russia. Cast your minds to the Volga valley: Astrakhan, the gate through which plague and cholera reach us, Astrakhan with its notorious sewage pipes discharging straight onto the banks of the Volga, making it into a cess-pit filled with pollutants. Then Tsarytsin and its infamous ravines where the River Kavkaz rises, its high banks piled with accumulations of refuse, centres of infection, and people live lower down, breathing the germ-laden air carried down to them. The way the river gets cleaned, of course, is when it catches fire. Next comes Saratov and its no less notable Glebuchev and Beloshinsky valleys, places I have walked through and could tell you some stories about. And Samara, elegant Samara, and its Vedeneva pit, now more of a mound than a pit and the source of the liquid filth which finds its way into the River Samara. Kazan too has its city centre sights: the River Bulak and Lake Kaban which collect all Kazan's sewage.

Gosudarstvennaya Duma. *Stenograficheskie otchety*. Sozyv III, session IV, vol. II, cols. 98–106.

126 A Country Doctor Looks Back

Mikhail Bulgakov, the well known writer, was also a qualified doctor. Here he describes his experiences during the year 1915–16 as a country doctor. It was his first taste of medicine after qualifying.

We are cut off: the nearest kerosene lanterns are seven miles away at the railway station, and even their flickering light has probably been blown out by the snowstorm. The midnight express to Moscow rushes moaning past and does not even stop; it has no need of this forlorn little halt, buried in snow – except perhaps when the line is blocked by drifts.

The nearest street lamps are thirty-two miles away in the district town. Life there is sweet: it has a cinema, shops. While the snow is whirling and howling out here in the open country, there on the screen no doubt . . . palm trees sway as a tropical island comes into view . . .

Meanwhile we are alone. . . .

In that year of unique experience . . . I had done two amputations at the hip, and I had lost count of all the fingers. There were eighteen curettages listed, a hernia and a tracheotomy, all of them successful. And the number of gigantic abscesses I had lanced, not to mention broken limbs set in plaster or starch. I had corrected dislocations. Intubations. Childbirth. Whatever they come with, I've dealt with it. Admittedly I won't undertake a caesarian section; I send them into town for that. But forceps, versions – any number. . . .

And the wounds I have stitched – the cases of suppurating pleurisy when I have had to prise the ribs apart; the cases of pneumonia, typhus, cancer, syphilis, hernia (successfully treated), haemorrhoids, sarcoma.

In a moment of inspiration I opened the out-patients register and spent an hour analysing and totalling. In a year, up to the very hour of that evening, I had seen 15,613 patients; 200 in-patients had been admitted, of whom only six died.

I closed the book and tottered to bed. At twenty-five years old and celebrating my first professional anniversary, I lay in bed and thought as I fell asleep that I was now vastly experienced. What had I to fear? Nothing. I had extracted peas lodged in little boys' ears, I had wielded the knife countless times. . . . My hand had acquired courage and did not shake. I spotted all the tricky complications and had acquired a unique ability to understand the things that peasant women say. I was able to interpret them like Sherlock Holmes deciphering mysterious documents. Sleep is creeping up on me.

'I cannot', I mumbled, growing sleepier, 'honestly imagine being brought a case that would floor me . . . perhaps in Moscow they might accuse me of an amateur (*feldsher*) attitude to medicine . . . well, let them . . . it's all right for them in their clinics and teaching hospitals, X-ray cabinets and so on . . . whereas here there's just me . . . peasants couldn't live without me . . . How I used to shudder whenever there was a knock at the door, how I winced with fear . . . Now, though . . .'

M. Bulgakov, *A Country Doctor's Notebook*, trans. by Michael Glenny. London, 1976, pp. 41, 106–7

127   Literacy of the Rural Population of twelve Provinces of European Russia, 1908–1912

Province	Period of census	Literate, semi-literate and students (per cent)		
		Men	Women	All
Moscow	1909–12	58.6	25.9	41.7
Tver	1911–13	51.0	18.5	34.1
Olonets	1909	45.0	13.5	30.4
Tula	1910–12	46.3	11.0	28.5
Kharkov	1913	39.1	10.6	25.1
Poltava	1910	38.2	8.7	23.7
Vologda	1908–11	39.3	5.3	22.0
Novgorod	1907–8	35.9	7.7	21.6
Kaluga	1910–11	–	–	20.3
Samara	1911–13	31.1	8.1	19.5
Simbirsk	1910–11	27.6	3.8	15.6
Penza	1910–12	25.9	3.8	14.8
Average		39.8	10.6	24.8

A.G. Rashin, *Naselenie Rossii za 100 let*, Moscow, 1956, p. 294.

128   Urban Literacy, 1897–1912

Town	Years of census	literate (per cent) Men	Women	All
St Petersburg	1897	71.8	51.5	52.6
	1910	76.1	56.7	66.9
Moscow	1897	66.9	42.3	52.3
	1912	74.6	51.3	64.0
Kharkov	1897	61.7	41.9	52.5
	1912	74.2	58.6	66.6
Voronezh	1897	60.4	43.4	52.1
	1911	–	–	61.2
	1916	–	–	65.8
Baku	1897	39.4	22.1	32.4
	1913	43.0	32.5	38.8

Ibid p. 298

129   Literacy of the St Petersburg Population* in 1910 by Age and Sex

Age group	literate (per cent) Men	Women	All	Age group	literate (per cent) Men	Women	All
Average	85.2	64.3	75.6	36–40	83.6	56.7	71.5
				41–45	82.1	56.0	70.1
6–10	53.4	50.2	51.5	46–50	79.6	52.7	65.9
11–15	95.3	91.5	93.6	51–55	79.5	52.8	65.4
16–20	93.4	80.5	87.5	56–60	78.2	49.6	61.2
21–25	89.6	71.7	81.6	61–65	81.7	50.9	61.7
26–30	88.7	62.5	77.0	66–70	79.3	46.2	55.4
31–35	86.8	61.8	76.0	70-	76.1	46.7	53.6

* Figures include the population of the suburbs.

Ibid p. 300

130   Bill on Universal Primary Education Introduced in the Second Duma by the Minister of Education, 20 February and 1 November 1907

The government failed to enact its bill to introduce universal primary education and educational matters continued to be a major topic of debate.

1 All children of both sexes shall be offered the opportunity, on reaching school age, of taking a full course of instruction in

a properly organized school.

2 Responsibility for providing a sufficient quantity of schools . . . is the concern of the institutions of local self-government; the number of schools is to be calculated according to the number of children aged between 8 and 11.

3 The normal duration of primary school education is to be four years.

4 The normal number of children per teacher in a primary school is 50.

5 One school should normally serve an area with a radius of 3 versts.

6 Each institution of local self-government is obliged to prepare, within two years of the present bill coming into force, a plan for the establishment of a set of schools and a time limit for the introduction of universal primary education in their area. . . .
   NB: The local church school administration should participate in the planning of a network of schools.

7 For a school to be included in the network it must satisfy the following conditions: it must have a religious instruction teacher and a teacher who has the legal right to teach; it must have premises which are suitable from both the educational and sanitary points of view; it must have sufficient text books and educational supplies; it must provide children with free education.

8 The local organs of self-government must submit the plans for the establishment of a network of schools to the Ministry of Education, which will consult with the Ministry of Internal Affairs before making a decision on them. If it approves the plans the Ministry will provide funds for the minimum pay of teachers, reckoned at R360 per teacher and R60 per religious instruction teacher. The overall quantity of subsidy provided to a given region should not exceed R300 for every 50 children of school age.
   Note: Church schools which become part of the general school network will receive subsidies on the same level as those schools under the control of the Ministry of Education, but from the funds assigned to the Holy Synod. Church schools which remain outside the network must exist on local funds.

. . . .

10 The receipt of a subsidy does not restrict the rights of a school's founders in relation to the management of a primary school. Local self-government is responsible for the organization and

ordinary management of primary schools under the guidance and supervision of the Ministry of Education.

11 Private persons and other organizations whose schools join the general network may receive a subsidy from the Ministry of Education . . . on the same basis as the institutions of local self-government.

12 The Ministry of Education can distribute subsidies in accordance with local demands and needs before the receipt of plans for universal primary education.

> *Khrestomatiya po istorii peda-gogiki*, vol. 4, part 2. Moscow, 1933, pp. 358–9

131   School discipline

Many conservatives were deeply worried about the effect of education on the nation's youth. Radical ideas were all-pervasive and a solution suggested was to eliminate all radicals in universities by denying them access to higher education in the first place.

Speech by B. S. Chebotarev to the VII Congress of the United Nobility, February 1911

. . .I recall the time when all the further education establishments in Russia were involved in the general strike. How did our secondary schools react to this? Did they remain calm? Did they remain on one side as disinterested spectators? On the contrary, many grammar schools announced their solidarity with the strikers and stated that they wanted to strike as well. Remember the petitions which were presented to headmasters by their pupils. Finally, remember what state our secondary schools were in and what is happening in them now. It was impossible to avoid reading about murders which grammar school pupils had committed, both on and off school premises. Finally, see how many grammar school pupils have already been tried for their part in robberies and demonstrations. It therefore seems to me that to combat the revolution only in further education institutes would be just a palliative in the fight against a movement which is growing each year and which, each year, requires that we combat it all the more energetically. To destroy this viper we must catch it in its nest, and this is located in the secondary school. . . .

The first step should be . . . not only to punish the 'infected' elements, not only to 'throw them overboard', but to prevent others sliding further down the slippery slope. I believe that we should add a section to the secondary school curriculum which will examine political theories, making them comprehensible to the young so that they can be directed towards critical analysis of the tendentious rubbish which they get in the cheap pamphlets which fill the bookshops. . . . Surely the Ministry of Education . . . cannot afford to ignore this question, cannot avoid it by remaining silent, thereby providing our dying youth with nothing at all. Another step would be for each pupil to have his own record card, showing his spiritual and moral qualities, and if a young man wanted to go to university, and this record card did not give an altogether sparkling picture of him, but on the contrary showed that he was likely to be a potential danger to the state, he should be told that, regrettably, the gates to university were closed for him.

Ibid pp. 378-9

132   The School Curriculum

One of the problems facing conservatives was that the textbooks available were so unsatisfactory. Hence books giving the correct point of view had to be commissioned.

. . .We must pay great attention to the fact that our schoolchildren, peasant children, are being suffocated perhaps by grammar, arithmetic and other such complicated subjects, and are not learning about history, about their homeland and are not being inculcated with a love for Russia – their homeland – and her history. . . . Every school council and every teacher must note that the first task of anyone who considers themselves to be educated is to give the growing peasant population a knowledge of Russia and her history and a love for their heritage. Thank God that religious instruction is a compulsory subject in schools and that a love for God and the true religion are obligatory. We must instil a love for Russia in our schoolchildren at the same time as they learn their ABC. But here we come to the sad question of books. . . . How are school libraries chosen? Very simply, their content is approved by the Ministry of Education, but what they have approved in past years gives little confidence for the future. Anyone who has seen the books recommended by the Ministry for teaching can testify as to their lack of suitability. Let us take for example Vakhterov's book, which has enjoyed great success amongst teachers.

We need say no more about it than that every ten pages – and this a fairly thick book – there is a story about prisons, or a convict's tale, or a prisoner's song. . . . What merit does this book have? . . . Should we not bring our children up to see that there is something more in the world than prison walls? . . . Let us turn to pieces on Russian history. There are no religious chapters in the book. The catalogue of such school books contains neither a single saint's life, nor any sacred writing. . . .

. . .Our Council should petition the Ministry of Education to pay great attention to the text books for primary schools and should suggest that prizes be instituted – without skimping on money – so that good teachers can devote themselves to compiling suitable texts.

Ibid pp. 381–2

133   The Goal of Education

Resolutions of the All-Russian Conference on Educational Questions, 1913

The Tasks of the Primary School
In its contribution to the physical, moral, aesthetic and intellectual development of the child, the primary school should foster the adult in him and prepare him for the rational and honest development of his personal and social life. The primary school, as the first stage in the general educational system, should not pursue purely utilitarian aims. There can be no place in its course for the teaching of vocational subjects. The demand of the working population for knowledge in the primary school can only be satisfied through general subjects: pupils should, before all else, become acquainted with those features of nature and human life which they will meet most often. The demand for professional education can only be satisfied by the provision of an adequate number of special schools and extra classes. . . .

The Primary School Curriculum
The present primary school course provides only scanty educational material. The primary school curriculum needs reviewing and amending. Science, geography and history should be recognized as school subjects, and should have distinct places in the curriculum, as each of them has particular educational value; their teaching presents different problems and requires special methods. . . .

Teaching ought to be based on concrete material, taken from life and the environment, on direct experience and observation and on the children's active use of these materials. To do this schools must have excursions and nature study . . . drama, individual reading and conversation, and creative writing (essays, diaries, magazines, etc.) The school itself and the teaching in it must be organized on the principle of free discipline and the individuality of the child.

Individuality and Creativity
The task of developing all sides of a child's personality and of preparing him for life can only be achieved by a school based on the ideas of the activity and creativity of children. These principles . . . can be put into practice only by a change in the legal position of teachers, by (1) a recognition of the teacher's right to take part in the development of the school curriculum; (2) the recognition of their right to choose freely their teaching materials . . .; (3) freedom for teachers to select their own books; (4) the recognition of their right to choose their own teaching methods – this necessitates the removal of superfluous reglementation by the administration and the local authorities, and of excessive interference by the inspectorate. . . .

Freedom of Education and Discipline
We see school discipline as possible only to the extent where it does not harm the development of the free and individual personality of the pupil. Favourable external circumstances and a working atmosphere which interests the pupils are more sensible ways of maintaining discipline. We firmly condemn the use of corporal punishment and other methods of discipline which humiliate the pupil . . . and call upon comrade-teachers to recognize that these punishments are degrading to the profession of teacher and that they deserve to be completely eradicated from school practice.

The General Demands on a Teacher
Taking into account (1) that a teacher in a local school must guide the all-round development of the growing generation; (2) that the low cultural level of the environment in which the pupils of the primary school live does little to help the work of the teacher; (3) that as a result of this the teacher must extend his activity outside the school and must assist in raising the cultural level of the area, we believe that, in order to fulfil his duties adequately, the teacher must: (1) have been educated to a level higher than that of a general secondary course; (2) have had a specialized course of teacher-training and (3) must work

unceasingly to supplement and extend his knowledge.

Ibid pp. 384-7

134 Number of Primary Schools under the Ministry of Education, 1905-1914

Year	No. of schools	% growth	No. of pupils (000's)	% growth
1905	43,551		3350.4	
1906	45,629	4.8	3596.4	7.3
1907	47,838	4.8	3783.7	5.2
1908	50,876	6.4	3933.6	4.0
1909	54,726	7.6	4204.9	6.9
1910	59,000	7.8	4541.7	8.0
1911	64,279	8.9	4860.3	7.0
1912	69,318	7.8	5155.5	6.1
1913	76,416	10.2	5559.7	7.8
1914	80,801	5.7	5942.1	6.9

1905-14: 77.3 per cent growth in number of pupils; 85.3 per cent growth in number of schools.

A.G. Rashin, *Naselenie Rossii za 100 let.* Moscow, 1956, p. 315.

135 Science in Russia

Ever since Peter the Great the Russian state had furthered science. The Academy of Sciences, founded in 1725, initially concerned itself with the surveying of natural resources. A prominent early scientist was M.V. Lomonosov (1711-65), an internationally known chemist. Despite the founding of half a dozen universities and learned societies, the impact of government censorship during the first half of the nineteenth century still affected all fields of intellectual endeavour. This brought Russian intellectuals working in diverse fields together and an inclination towards broad generalization which involved important philosophical implications was characteristic of much of the original thinking of important Russian scientists in the pre-revolutionary era. Scientists often clashed with the authorities. For instance, D.I. Mendeleev (1834-1907), who introduced the concept of evolution to chemistry was never elected a member of the Academy of Sciences and had to give up his chair at the University of St Petersburg after transmitting a students' petition to the Ministry of Education. Space was an area of great interest and scientists such as N.E. Zhukovsky (1847–1921) and K.E. Tsiolkovsky (1857–1935) made fundamental contributions to aerodynamics, thus preparing the way for Soviet success in space. A feature of Russian science and medicine was the role played by the army. Hence quite a few scientists, doctors and surgeons were army officers and they conducted their research under army auspices.

. . .Most scholars, including V.I. Vernadsky, a prominent philosopher and historian of science, emphasized three basic social, cultural and political conditions that hampered a more impressive development of Russian science: government policy, the absence of a 'scientific' class or estate in Russia, and Russia's dependence on the West. . . .

Because it controlled the university curriculum, the government was the sole authority in defining the social value of individual sciences. . . . 'It can be said', Vernadsky argued, 'that the research activities of university professors were carried out not according to but in spite of the will of the government.' The physicist P.N. Lebedev agreed with Vernadsky and lamented the general absence of research centres that were unencumbered by teaching and uninterrupted by the chronic disorders common in university communities since 1860. Among other things, the educational overcommitment of university laboratories prevented a mutually beneficial interaction between industry and research institutions.

The basic complaint voiced by prominent professors was that the 1884 charter made them 'government bureaucrats', with no freedom of action. . . . In January 1905 the St Petersburg professors and academicians issued the famous 'Note of 342' so called because it was signed by 342 persons. . . . 'A stream of government decisions and regulations has reduced professors and other instructors at the institutions of higher education to the level of bureaucrats, blindly executing the orders of higher government authorities. . . . Science can develop only when it is free, when it is protected from external interference, and when it is unhindered in its efforts to illuminate every aspect of human existence.' . . .

Drastic limitations on the enrollment of Jewish students came just as Russia was developing a Jewish intellectual community imbued with values that encouraged scientific exploration and possessed of huge reserves of capable young people who were eager to obtain higher education. . . .

Even when discrimination in Russia slacked off, Jewish students faced many obstacles. In 1912 there were at least 8,000 Russian students in Western European universities, and Jews made up the bulk of this contingent. . . .

Russia's third handicap in science was her disproportionate economic dependence on the West. . . .

At a meeting of the St Petersburg Academy of Sciences in 1915, Vernadsky summed up the economic causes of the national predicament: 'We have suddenly awakened to the inexcusable magnitude of our country's economic dependence on Germany. The experts have known about this dependence for a long time; now the entire nation knows about it. In peacetime this dependence was considered harmless and inconsequential; the current world crisis has unveiled the full range of its injurious and crippling effects.

This dependence is undoubtably behind many problems in our country. . . . One of these problems . . . is the glaring inadequacy of our knowledge of the productive forces that nature has given us. . . . Our dependence on foreign products . . . has kept us from searching for scientific answers to our economic needs. We do not even know whether some of the important natural resources are available to us, or in what quantities. . . . This is the present situation with regard to such metals as bismuth, antimony, molybdenum, cerium, zinc, aluminium, nickel, barium, tungsten, tin and vanadium.'

> A. Vucinich, *Science in Russian Culture, 1861–1917.* Stanford, 1970, pp. 481–7.

136 The Cinema

The cinema gained in popularity in Russia very rapidly. In a country of high illiteracy it was more easily accessible for the masses.

. . . Just look into any cinema. The composition of the audience will amaze you. All sorts of people are there – students and policemen, writers and prostitutes, the bearded and bespectacled intelligentsia, merchants, high-society ladies, models, civil servants – in a word, everyone. . . .

The cinema moves on like a mighty conqueror. I repeat, this is nothing to rejoice about or to despair of. It is spontaneous. The approaching reign of the cinematograph is inevitable. . . .

The book has passed through many stages in its development. It once deluged the masses with . . . all sorts of rubbish and rot. Then came men of conscience and honour . . . literacy committees and such like, and the book brought the fruits of human talent and genius to a mass readership.

The cinema at the moment is akin to popular literature. It appeals to the same base tastes and instincts.

And, looking back over the past year, filled with the lights of cinemas, and when the book continued steadily into decline, as in previous years, we hope that men of conscience will come forward for the cinema. The cinema needs people of humility who will pour the pure wine of creation into new jars.

S. Ginzburg, *Kinematografiya dorevolyutsionnoy Rossii*. Moscow, 1963, pp. 87, 105, 157. Originally in A. Serafimovich, 'Mashinnoe nadvigaetsya', *Russkie Vedomosti*, 1 January 1911.

Educational films available through Pathé in Moscow, January 1914

Agriculture (inc. farming, meadow cultivation, sowing, market-gardening, gardening, forestry, machinery and implements, livestock and processing)	81
Physics and related disciplines	64
Technology	3
Chemistry	5
Zoology and botany	10
Medicine	8
Economic aspects of agriculture (co-operatives, local industries)	13
	184

Razumny Kinomatograf, 2nd ed., St Petersburg, 1914.

Number of films produced in Russia

1913	129
1914	232
1915	370
1916	499

V. Vyshnevsky, *Khudozhestvenny Filmy dorevolyutsionnoy Rossii*. Moscow, 1945.

137 The Content of Books and Magazines Published in Russia, 1901–1916

The expansion of book publishing during this period was very marked with the greatest increase coming in science and related topics.

According to figures issued by the Chief Press Directorate, printed book production in the Russian language amounted, in 1901, to 10,200 titles and in 1913 to 26,000 titles, whilst the corresponding figures including all the languages of the Russian Empire were 15,900 and 34,000. Excluding reference, official and special publications, this left in 1908, for example, almost 7,000 Russian-language titles, and this included both literature and such things as religious writings, school text-books, popular literature and children's books.

The Growth of Book Production, 1901–13

Year	No. of titles on science, applied science and social science	No. of titles on literature, drama and poetry
1901	1,477	1,165
1908	4,570	1,577
1913	6,590	2,012

Between 1901 and 1913, the first category grew by 440 per cent and the second by 170 per cent.

. . .In looking at the figures for periodicals, it must be realized that the absolute figures conceal the dynamics of new periodicals appearing and others closing down. In 1896, there were 697 Russian-language periodicals, and in 1900 – 1,002, but over this five-year period 794 new publications appeared. In 1905 in Russia there were 1,350 newspapers and magazines and in 1910 – 2,400, but between 1901 and 1916 over 14,000 appeared at different times. . . .

In 1915, 1,381 magazines were published in Russia (1,088 in Russian) and 916 newspapers (728 in Russian). Current affairs, politics and literature were dealt with in only 235 magazines (128 in Russian) and 739 newspapers (569 in Russian). There were also a number of publications devoted to satire and humour, the theatre and bibliography and almost a hundred dealing with the world war.

V.R. Leykina-Svirskaya,
Russkaya Intelligentsiya v

1900–1917 godakh. Moscow, 1981, pp. 122–3

138   The Bureaucracy

The Russian bureaucracy was renowned for its cumbersome nature. H.W. Williams, a long-time British resident of Russia, describes the huge volume of paperwork the system generated.

. . .From the big dreary-looking yellow or brown buildings in St Petersburg where the Ministries are housed, currents of authority, of directive energy go forth to all the ends of the great Empire in the form of telegrams or occasional oral messages by special couriers, but above all in the form of endless 'papers'. Pens scratch, typewriters click, clerks lay blue covers full of papers before the 'head of the table'; the 'head of the table' sends them on to the 'head of the department', to the Assistant Minister, if need be, and in the more important cases, the Assistant Minister to the Minister. Then back go the papers again with signatures appended, down through various grades for despatch to a judge, to another department, to a Governor, to a chinovnik on special service, or to some petitioner from the world without. Incoming and outgoing papers are the systole and diastole of the Chancelleries. All sorts of documents go under the general name of *bumaga* or 'paper', from a warrant for arrest to a report on a projected railway, or a notification of taxes due. There are *doklady* or reports, and *otnoshenia* or communications between officials of equal rank, and *donesenia* or statements made to superiors, *predpisania* instructions or orders, and *proshenia*, applications and petitions. These and a hundred others besides are all 'Papers', and there is a special style for each of them, and a general dry and formal style for all of them known as the 'Chancellery Style', which permeates Russian public life, and creeps into private letters and concert programmes, and newspaper articles, and into the very love-making of telegraph clerks waiting for trains on wayside stations. The 'papers', their colour, the stamps upon them, their style, create an immense uniformity of mental content, and tend to level down the striking differences that exist between say, the Tartar policeman in a town on the Caspian Sea, and the son of a Russian priest who serves as a clerk in the financial department in Tver. It is extraordinary discipline. The lack of variety in the system increases its hold on all its members. There are hardly any of the curious divergencies and inconsistencies of which the English administrative system is so full, hardly any quaint anachronisms left to linger on because of some wise use they have for the affections. There are certain inevitable modifications in the Caucasus, in Central Asia, in Bessarabia and in Siberia, Poland and the Baltic Provinces. But generally speaking the system as outlined in mathematical order on smooth white paper is embodied with surprising accuracy in the network of institutions that cover the great plain from limit to limit. Authority is delegated from the big yellow Ministries in St Petersburg to the dreary white buildings in the head towns of the provinces into which the whole Empire is mapped out, and from the provincial towns to the head towns of the districts into which each province is divided, and then down to the smallest towns. . . . The uniformity of it all is both imposing and depressing and as wearying as the inevitable red-capped stationmaster and brown-coated gendarme on every one of the scores of railway stations between Wirballen and Harbin.

> H.W. Williams, *Russia of the Russians*. London, 1914, pp. 57–9

139 Corruption

Corruption was endemic in the bureaucracy but it had also penetrated the Orthodox Church.

To a man unaccustomed to this scheme of things it is all the more difficult, because for one and the same thing it is necessary to give in several different places – to different persons. It is necessary to give to the district priest; bribes must be given . . . to the consistory members, to the clerk, to the porter; they must be given in the consistory chancery – to the secretary, to the chief clerk, to his assistant, to the protocolist, to the archivist, to the clerks, to the porters – for forwarding the case, for a report, for verification, for the seal – and God knows how much and to whom. Experienced men know this; for each service there is an accepted price, determined by the nature of the service and by the position of the person interested in the case. But for special cases – difficult ones – they charge more than the usual rates; they take several times more, by threats and by violence – money and things; they take as much as they can.

> J.S. Curtis, *Church and State in Russia*, New York, 1940,

p. 59. Originally in A.M.
Ivantsov-Platonov, *O Rus-
skom Tserkovnom Upravlenii*.
St Petersburg, 1898, pp. 25,
32.

VI   Culture and Religion

140   Tolstoyanism

By the end of his life, Tolstoy's main interests were in the moral and philosophical fields. He was born in 1828 and died in 1910

Letter from Tolstoy to Gandhi, 7 September 1910

The longer I live . . . I want to tell others what I feel so particularly keenly about, and what in my opinion is of enormous importance, namely what is called non-resistance, but what is essentially nothing other than the teaching of love undistorted by false interpretations. The fact that love, i.e. the striving of human souls towards unity and the activity resulting from such striving, is the highest and only law of human life is felt and known by every person . . . [Christ] pointed to the danger of its [this law's] distortion which comes naturally to people who live by worldly interests, namely the danger of allowing themselves to defend those interests by force, i.e. as he said, returning blow for blow, taking back by force objects which have been appropriated etc., etc. He knows, as every reasonable person is bound to know, that the use of violence is incompatible with love as the basic law of life, that once violence is tolerated in any cases whatsoever, the inadequacy of the law of love is recognized and therefore the law itself is repudiated. The whole of Christian civilization, so brilliant on the surface, grew up on this obvious, strange sometimes conscious but for the most part unconscious misunderstanding and contradiction.

Essentially speaking, once resistence was tolerated, side by side with love, there no longer was or could be love as a law of life, and there as no law of love except violence, i.e. in the power of the stronger. For 19 centuries Christian mankind has lived in this way. True, people at all times have been guided by violence alone in organizing their lives. The difference between the lives of Christian peoples and all others is merely the fact that in the Christian world, the law of love was expressed so clearly and definitely, as it hasn't been expressed in any other religious teaching, and that people in the Christian world solemnly accepted this law but at the same time allowed themselves to use violence and built their lives on violence. And so the whole life of Christian peoples is an outright contradiction between what they profess and what they build their lives on; a contradiction between love, recognized as the law of life, and violence recognized even as a necessity in various forms such as the power of rulers, courts and armies – recognized and extolled. This contradiction kept growing with the advancement of the peoples of the Christian world and has recently reached the ultimate degree. The question now obviously amounts to one of two things – either we recognize that we don't recognize any religious and moral teaching and are guided in the organization of our lives only by the power of the strong, or that all our taxes collected by force, our judicial and police institutions and above all our armies must be abolished.

. . .Socialism, communism, anarchism, the Salvation Army, the growth of crime, unemployment among the population, the growth of the insane luxury of the rich and the destitution of the poor, the terrible growth in the number of suicides – all these things are signs of this internal contradiction which ought to and must be solved – and, of course, solved in the sense of recognizing the law of love and renouncing all violence. . . .

In recognizing Christianity, even in the distorted form in which it is professed among Christian peoples, and in recognizing at the same time the necessity for armies and arms to kill in wars on the most enormous scale, there is such an obvious and crying contradiction that sooner or later, probably very soon, it will be exposed and will put an end either to the acceptance of the Christian religion which is necessary to maintain power, or to the existence of an army and any violence supported by it, which is no less necessary to maintain power. This contradiction is felt by all governments . . . and from a natural feeling of self-preservation is prosecuted more vigorously than any other anti-government activity, as we see in Russia and as is seen from the articles in your journals. Governments know where their main danger lies, and in this question are keeping a careful eye not only on their own interests, but on the question: to be or not to be.

With the utmost repect,
Leo Tolstoy

R.F. Christian (ed. and
trans.) *Tolstoy's Letters*, vol 2.
London, 1978, pp. 706–8

141 Impact of Tolstoy's Death on Russia

Tolstoy died on 7 November 1910

. . .on another bitterly cold morning, I came out to find special editions of the newspapers with black borders on the front, bewildered lost-looking people in the streets, and crowds of students in front of the university. They stood in complete silence. Every one had a black crepe arm band. Someone I didn't know pinned an arm band to the sleeve of my greatcoat.

I walked on to school. Posses of mounted Cossacks were slowly patrolling the streets. Knots of policemen stood in the gateways. I caught up with my classmates and saw that they all had arm bands like mine. In the cloakroom we took them off our coats and pinned them on our jackets. The school was unusually silent.

K. Paustovsky, *Childhood and
Schooldays*, trans. by M.
Harari and M. Duncan.
London, 1966, pp. 108–9

142 Futurism

The Futurists dedicated themselves to the destruction of the old harmonies and the traditional ways of looking at the world.

We and the West (Poster no. 1)

(i)
Europe's cultural seekings – there have been no achievements – have reached a crisis, seen externally in her attitude to the East. IT IS NOT WITHIN THE POWER OF THE WEST TO UNDERSTAND THE EAST, for the West has lost all sense of the boundaries of art (philosophical and aesthetic questions have been confused with the methods in which they can be embodied in art). EUROPEAN ART

IS OUTDATED AND THERE IS NOT, AND CANNOT BE ANY NEW ART IN EUROPE as new art is based on cosmic elements. All Western art is TERRITORIAL. RUSSIA is the only country which, up to now, has not had territorial art. All the West's efforts are directed to the FORMAL BASIS of the achievements of the old art (the old aesthetic). All attempts by the West to construct a new aesthetic are, both a priori and a posteriori, a FATAL CATAS-TROPHE: a new aesthetic can only follow a new art, and not vice-versa. We believe that the difference between the development of Western and Eastern art is that Western art is the embodiment of a geometric perception of the world, moving from object to subject, whilst the art of the East is the embodiment of an algebraic perception of the world, from subject to object. We assert as a common basis for art, poetry and music:

1 An arbitrary spectrum
2 An arbitrary perspective
3 Self-sufficiency, of tempi, both in artistic methods and in immutable rhythms;

and in PARTICULAR,

FOR PAINTING:

1 The negation of conical construction and trigonometric perspective.
2 Dissonances.

FOR POETRY

1 The continuity of the unity of the verbal mass.
2 The differentiation of masses of different degrees of rarefaction; lithoid, fluid and phosphenoid;
3 The overcoming of the accidentalist approach.

FOR MUSIC

1 The overthrow of linearity (architectonics) through an internal perspective (primitive synthesis);
2 The substantianality of the elements.

Georgy Yakulov
Benedikt Livshits
Arthur-Vincent Lure.

1 January 1914

Manifesty i programmy russkikh futuristov. Munich, 1967, pp. 138–9.

(ii) A Slap in the Face of Public Taste
Our First New Surprise for readers.

Only we are the face of our Time. The trumpet of time sounds through us in literary art.

The past is constricting. Hieroglyphics are more understandable than the Academy and Pushkin.

Pushkin, Dostoyevsky, Tolstoy and the rest should be thrown overboard from the ship of modernity.

Whoever does not forget his first love will not recognize his last. Who would be so credulous as to point his last love towards the profound lechery of Balmont? Will he find a reflection of today's courageous soul there?

Who would be so cowardly as to be afraid of ripping the paper armour from the warrior Bryusov's black tail coat? Or is the dawn of unknown beauties to be found there?

Wash your hands as they have touched the filthy slime of books written by those countless Leonid Andreyevs.

All that these Maksim Gorkys, Kuprins, Bloks, Sologubs, Remizovs, Averchenkos, Chernys, Kuzmins, Bunins etc need is a villa by a river. This is the reward which fate gives to tailors.

We gaze at their insignificance from the heights of skyscrapers! . . . We command that there should be respect for a poet's rights:

1 To increase vocabulary as a whole with arbitrary and derivative words. (A word is an innovation.)
2 To feel absolute hatred for the language which has gone before them.
3 To rip the laurel of shoddy glory which you made from the bathhouse birch twigs from their proud brows.
4 To stand on the rock of the word 'we' in a sea of whistles and indignation.

And if our lines still retain the dirty hallmarks of your 'common sense' and 'good taste', they will already have the first flickerings of the lightning of the New Future Beauty of the Self-valued (self-made) Word.

D. Burlyuk   V. Mayakovsky
Aleksandr Kruchenykh   Viktor Khlebnikov
Moscow. 1912 December.

Ibid pp. 50–1.

143   The Orthodox Church

The Orthodox Church was in need of reform but attempts to hold a Church Council (Sobor) were unsuccessful. As the official state church it was the target of radicals and revolutionaries.

(i) Suppport for the Regime: Special Message read in all Moscow Churches, 15 October 1905

What We Should Do in These Troubled Days

Your hearts will empty of blood when you see what is being done around us – already not the Poles, not foreign enemies, but our own Russian people, who have lost the fear of God and believe in traitors, hold our first capital, as it were, in siege. . . . At the order of hidden traitors, strikes are beginning everywhere, in factories and mills, in schools, and on the railroads. And now it has come to this, that the supply of necessities of life has stopped. . . .

Oh, if our unfortunate workers knew who they are who lead them, who control them, who send to them these trouble-makers and instigators, they would turn from them as from poisonous serpents, as from rabid animals! Here is the truth – these so-called 'Social Democrats' are revolutionaries who have long denied God by their acts; they have renounced, or perhaps never knew, the Christian faith; they attack its servants, its laws, and mock its holy things. Their chief nest is abroad; they dream of enslaving all the world; in their secret writings they call Christians cattle, to whom God gave, they say, the form of man in order that they, the chosen, might enjoy our services. . . . With satanic cunning they catch in their nets light-minded persons. . . .

Protect yourselves, beloved brethren, protect yourselves and your children from these deceivers; for the sake of God, for the sake of your own eternal salvation, protect yourselves! Woe to the world from deceit – says the Saviour – but still more, woe to him from whom cometh deceit.

What is to be done? We must recognize the danger. . . . And then – each one of us is a son of our native land, a true subject of his Tsar. Can a son be indifferent to the groans of his suffering mother? Yet now she, our native land, once holy, and now so sinful before God – she groans, tormented, rent by her children, our unfortunate brothers. What would you do, a loving son, if your younger brother began to strike, to torment, your mother, to abuse her and dishonour her? Oh, of course, nature itself would call upon you in the words of God's commandment: Honour, love, protect thy mother. . . .

But look! Her unfortunate, maddened children are tormenting your dear mother, your native Rus, they are trying to tear her to pieces, they wish to take away her hallowed treasure – the Orthodox faith. . . . They defame your Father-Tsar, they destroy His pictures, they disparage His Imperial decrees, and mock Him. Can your heart be calm before this, O *Russian* man? Does not your heart burn with rage, does not your whole being shake with indignation, righteous indignation? What should you do?

Again ask of your conscience. It will remind you of your truly loyal oath. It will say to you – be a loving servant of your Tsar. Perform the tasks which the Tsar's servants ask of you. Be prepared to die for the Tsar and for Rus. Remember how your forefathers untrembling died for him.

> J.S. Curtiss, *Church and State in Russia*. New York, 1940, pp. 259–60. Originally in *Moskovskie Vedomosti*, 16 October 1905.

(ii) Links with the Union of the Russian People

Telegram from the Metropolitan of Moscow to the All-Russian Congress of the Russian People, October 1906

Deeply touched by the attention of the Congress of Russian People. It would be sinful for a servant of the Church not to respond to the prayers of those in whose hearts God 'hath proclaimed the good tidings of His Church'. I earnestly pray to the All-Highest that He may help the Congress of Russian People to attain the blessed desires which inspire them.

> Vladimir, Metropolitan of Moscow

> Ibid p. 268, Originally in *Veche*, 10 October 1906.

144   The Orthodox Church: The Need for Reform

(i) Priests

Who does not know the type of the shabby, timid 'little father' of the village, who is eternally in fear of a visitation of the father district priest, of the constable, of the police sergeant; who, together with his psalmist, is eternally writing, by the light of a tiny lamp, tens of 'statements' and 'reports' which are needed by no one, in order to send them to be numbered and sealed by the consistory? Who does not know the type of 'farming' little father, who sows and reaps and journeys to the bazaars and markets in order to buy and sell horses, cattle, sheep and so on? Who does not know, moreover, the type of little father who is the terror of his parish and of the surrounding countryside, threatening, at the command of the consistory, 'traitors' in the person of teachers of zemstvo schools, and writing 'reports' to the provincial authorities?

Is this that prophet, pastor and teacher who can 'with his words set aflame the hearts of men' and can teach his parishioners Eternal Truth? Is this that fearless spiritual leader who openly accuses Pilate, who drives the money-changers from the temple, who encourages his flock in disaster, comforts them in sorrow, and for the sake of truth goes to the cross, as did He Whom he names as his Teacher? The answer is clear.

> Ibid p. 67. Originally in *Yuzhnoe Obozrenie*, 10 April 1905.

(ii) Seminaries

By chance I went as a mere observer to service in one of the largest seminaries. Before me stood a huge crowd of youths, jammed tightly in a not very roomy church. In that crowd I saw some talking, laughing, reading papers and booklets, but I did not see any praying; many students left the church and there in the vestibule smoked cigarettes; the proctors, doubtless, saw all this, but evidently they felt their complete powerlessness to deal with this huge crowd, undoubtedly infected with a frightful religious indifference by those numerous elements who entered only for the sake of a free education . . . and who remained entirely strange to the idea of serving the Church of Christ.

> Ibid pp. 190-1. Originally in Svateishii Sinod, *Zhurnaly i Protokoly zasedanii Vysochaishe uchrezhdennogo presobornogo prisutsviya*, vol. 2. St Petersburg, 1906, p. 547.

(iii) Report of the Budget Commission of the Duma, 1915

When we study the reports of the Most Holy Synod, our attention is drawn to the regularly recurring phenomenon that, even with the agreement of the legislative institutions, of the Pre-Sobor Conference, and in parts of the Most Holy Synod, on the necessity of certain reforms, these reforms have not been realized; the institutions remain as archaic as before, and the condition of things continues to be exceedingly unsatisfactory, even hopeless. . . .

But to live longer in this fashion is impossible. We must heal ourselves of this paralysis, we must become active, weakness and lack of purpose must be replaced by energy and strength. For this it will be necessary . . . with the united simultaneous efforts of the whole church, of all its members, to move it from that dead centre on which it has stood for many centuries.

> Ibid p. 318. Originally in Gosudarstvennaya Duma, *Doklady Byudzhetnoy Komissii*, IV Duma, Session IV, no. 4, pp. 8–10.

145   The Orthodox Church: Expenditure

(i)

Budget: General Expenditure

	Rubles
1908	29,739,152
1909	31,663,444
1910	34,195,217
1911	37,535,478
1912	40,129,979
1913	44,219,759
1914	53,093,225
1915	52,564,695
1916	62,920,835
1917*	66,796,000

* projected

> Ibid p. 346

(ii)

Budget: Expenditure on Church Schools

	Rubles
1905	10,091,916
1906	10,091,052
1907	0,433,145
1908	9,533,145
1909	10,683,145
1910	12,516,053
1911	15,151,365
1912	16,946,723
1913	20,233,219
1914	22,254,486
1915	c.22,000,000
1916	30,442,834
1917*	33,191,000

* projected

Ibid p. 350

146   The Old Believers: Pressure for Reform, 1908

Stolypin's government attempted to liberalize the position of the religious minorities. The Old Believers had separated from the Orthodox Church in the schism of the seventeenth century, and numbered about 10 million. Guchkov, the leader of the Octobrist Party, was a member of an Old Believer family, as were many other Moscow industrialists. Efforts to promote bills which would favour the Old Believers, however, came to nothing. The right wing of the State Council put an end to hopes of reform.

. . . The Chairman of the Duma commission on Old Believers, V.A. Karaulov, and A.I. Guchkov, a member of the commission, had been sent the proposals of the Eighth Old Believer Congress, and wanted to find out more about the bill dealing with the 'priestless' Old Believers, and so a meeting was arranged.

Before this took place, however, a meeting was held in St Petersburg between P.P. Ryabushinsky, deputy chairman of the Council of the Congress of Old Believers, M.I. Brilliantov, a Council member and . . . five members of the Duma commission. The discussion centred around the position of the Old Believers in general and measures which could be taken to improve the bill on Old Believer communities and would be most appropriate to the needs of all types of Old Believer parishes: neither the government nor the Duma intended to make separate laws for each division of the sect individually.

The problem therefore became more complicated. It was vital that substantial measures be taken to unite the different Old Believer groups, for otherwise there was a danger of delay in implementing a law to deal with Old Believer communities. . . .

. . .the good relations which were [established] between the various Old Believer groups were very successful in the preparation of a general set of proposals. The representatives of the different groups proceeded to discuss the individual clauses of the government bill in an amiable manner, and all were motivated by the aim of defending common interests and getting the bill enacted rapidly. . . .

The meeting [between the chairman of the Duma commission and Old Believers] took place in the offices of the Octobrist party. It included Karaulov, Guchkov, a professor from the Moscow ecclesiastical academy . . . the Octobrist party secretary and eight Old Believers. The aim of the meeting was mainly to allow the members of the Old Believer commission to discover the wishes of the Old Believers themselves. The bill was examined and various comments were made and it was suggested that the two groups should work together, so that by their joint efforts they could produce a bill which would satisfy Old Believers of all denominations and which would help the members of the Old Believer commission to put into law without affecting the interests of Christian life generally or the Manifesto on freedom of belief and conscience. . . .

A deputation from the various Old Believer groups, headed by the Chairman of the Council, D.V. Sirotkin, . . . visited the leaders of all the various political parties and the members of the Old Believer commission, and everywhere received a warm and sympathetic reception. . . .

Sirotkin and Brilliantov also had an interview with a deputy minister of Internal Affairs, S.E. Kryzhanovsky, and discussed the question of the enactment of the wishes of the Old Believers, which had been sent to the Ministry and now needed adapting to deal with the 'priestless' Old Believers. . . .

However, in view of the urgency of other matters and the pressure of work in the Duma, after April 1908 the Old Believer commission was unable to devote any more time to discussion of the Old Believer question and put off any final decisions until the autumn session of the Duma. The Old Believer commission will begin its work again then, and then will come the time for a solution to the centuries-old Old

Believer question. . . .

The Council of the Congress feels itself able to hope that now this bill has been revised it will be more appropriate to the life of the Old Believers, and will give them the freedom to breathe more easily after the past 250 years in which they have suffered so much misfortune and persecution.

> *Trudy devyatogo vserossiyskogo sezda staroobryadtsev.* Moscow, 1909 pp. 69–73

147   Vekhi (Landmarks)

The Russian intelligentsia viewed revolution as good *per se*. The state and society born of revolution would, by definition, be superior to the existing. The first group to question this assumption was the *Vekhi* or Landmarks group. Several of them had been Marxists but had converted to Christianity and had joined the Orthodox Church. After the appearance of their slim volume in 1909 they were showered with abuse and accused of siding with reaction. Few in the intelligentsia were willing to rethink the whole concept of revolution.

(i)

. . .As a result of its historical situation, the Russian intelligentsia has suffered a misfortune; love for egalitarian justice, love for the social good, and love for the welfare of the people have paralysed the love for truth and have almost destroyed any interest in truth. . . . The Russian intelligentsia has been unable to approach philosophy objectively, because it has treated truth itself subjectively, and has demanded from truth that it become a weapon of the social revolution, of the well-being of the people, of human happiness. . . . The fundamental moral opinion of the intelligentsia is summed up in the formula: let truth perish if this will improve the life of the people, if happiness will be increased, down with truth if it stands in the way of the sacred cry 'down with autocracy'.

> N.A. Berdyaev, 'Filoso-fskaya Istina i Intelligent-skaya Pravda' in *Vekhi. Sbornik Statey o Russkoy Intelligentsii.* Moscow, 1909, p. 8.

(ii)

. . .Spiritual habits, inculcated by the church, explain some of the best features of the Russian intelligentsia. . . . A certain puritanism, strict morals, an individual asceticism, in general, a strictness in their personal lives. . . . Christian features, sometimes quite without an individual's knowledge or desire, come from a person's surroundings, his family, his nanny, from a spiritual atmosphere pervaded by religiosity. This is seen in the spiritual makeup of the best and most significant of the makers of the Russian revolution. . . .

Our intelligentsia has rejected Christianity and the norms which it sets out for life, and together with atheism or, better to say, instead of atheism, they have taken up the dogma of the religion of 'man as God'. . . . The fundamental component of this faith is a belief in the natural perfectability of man, and in limitless progress, achievable through man's own efforts.

> S.N. Bulgakov, 'Geroizm i Podvizhnichestvo' in ibid pp. 29–36.

(iii)

. . .Now the intelligentsia confronts the great and important task of reviewing old values and the creative acquisition of new ones. This revolution might indeed turn out to be so decisive that the intelligentsia will cease to be an intelligentsia in the old Russian sense of the word. But this is all to the good. In place of the old intelligentsia will come a new 'intelligentsia' which will cleanse the name of the accumulated sins of centuries, whilst retaining inviolable the noble side of its meaning. . . . From an unproductive, anti-cultural nihilist moralism, we ought to move to a creative religious humanism, on which culture can be built.

> S.L. Frank, 'Etika Nigilizma' in ibid p. 210.

VII   Nationalities

148   The Situation of the Jews after 1905

The Jewish population of Russia numbered about five million at this time. Jews were restricted as to their place of residence: most had to live in the Pale of Settlement in the south and west. They were also unable to take advantage of educational and employment opportunities on the same terms as others citizens of the Russian Empire. One of the by-products of this was that the proportion of Jews in radical political parties was very high. The Jews had their own Social Democratic organization, the Bund. Jews were prominent in the leadership of both the Bolshevik and Menshevik wings of the Russian Social Democratic movement.

A wave of pogroms began in 1905.

The counter-revolution fired its first volleys into the heart of the Jewish people. During the pogroms between October 1905 and October 1906, 1,002 Jews were killed, 1,918 were wounded . . . and 201,000 suffered losses to their property. . . .

Unfortunately, due to the nature of the Duma electoral law, and even more so after the changes of 3 June 1907, not one representative of the Jewish proletariat was elected to the Duma, and therefore the activity of the Jewish deputies was often marked by indecisiveness. . . . In the First Duma the Jewish deputies formed a group which acted as an advisory body in the struggle to achieve full rights for Jews. Deputy Vinarev made a vigorous protest against the fact that the government declaration made no mention of Jewish civil equality. No less forceful were the attacks made by the Jewish deputies, in conjunction with their Russian colleagues, against the policy of the bureaucracy in connection with the Belostok pogrom.

. . .At the sixth congress of the Bund in December 1905, the party developed its policy on the nationalities question in general and on the Jewish question in particular. . . .

The congress called for (1) complete civil and political equality for

Jews; (2) legal guarantees that the Jewish population could use its native language in its dealings with the courts, government bodies and the institutions of local and regional self-government; (3) the removal from the competence of central government and local and regional self-government of cultural questions (education etc.) and their transfer to national groups, in the form of institutions elected by all their members on the basis of a universal, direct, equal and secret ballot.

. . .In this period the Jewish national movement manifested itself most strongly in the development of language, journalism, creative and scientific literature and drama. . . . The Jewish periodical press also achieved a wide circulation; its significant growth demonstrates the cultural and political development of the Jewish masses and the growth of the language. Many new literary faces came to the fore . . . and many old writers, who had previously written in Russian and Hebrew, now began to write in the vernacular.

> L. Martov, P. Maslov and
> A. Potresov (eds.), *Obshches-*
> *tvennoe Dvizhenie v Rossii v*
> *nachale XX-ogo veka*, vol. 4,
> part 2. St Petersburg, 1912,
> pp. 217–18.

149   Witness to a Pogrom

This extract is from the memoirs of Nikita Sergeevich Khrushchev (1894–1971) who was First Secretary of the Communist Party of the Soviet Union (1953–64) and Soviet Prime Minister (1958–64). The year is probably 1909. The Black Hundreds were an extreme organization, in receipt of Okhrana (secret police) funds, whose objective was to terrorize radicals and revolutionaries as well as Jews. The most violent of these organizations, and responsible for the worst pogroms, was the Union of the Russian People.

In my childhood in the Donbass [in the Ukraine], I once witnessed a pogrom with my own eyes. I went to school four versts [about two and a half miles] from the mine where my father worked. One day I was coming home from school. It was a lovely, sunny, autumn day, with spiderwebs flying about in the air like snow. We were barefoot that day, like every day from spring until late autumn. Every villager dreamed of owning a pair of boots. . . . My schoolmates and I met a man driving a wagon. When he saw us he stopped and started to weep.

'Children', he said, 'if only you knew what they're doing in Yuzovka!' We started to walk faster. As soon as I arrived home I threw down my school bag and ran all the way to Yuzovka. When I approached the town I saw a huge crowd lined up on top of the heaps of iron ore that were being stored next to the railway tracks. . . . I saw that the Cossacks had already arrived. A bugle started to blow. I had never seen soldiers before. We had no soldiers in Yuzovka. So it was all an exciting novelty for me. . . . A volley of rifle fire rang out. Someone shouted that they were shooting into the air. Someone else shouted that they were shooting with blanks and that only one or two soldiers were shooting with live bullets, just to scare the Jews a little. . . . The crowd dispersed late in the evening. The workers from our mine were bragging the next day about how many boots and other trophies they'd picked up during the looting. One man said he had made off with ten pairs of boots. Some of the miners were telling about how the 'yids' marched around calling the Russians abusive names, carrying banners, and bearing their 'yid tsar' on their shoulders. When the Russians attacked them with clubs, he hid in a leather factory. The Russians set this factory on fire, and the 'yid tsar' was burned alive inside.

The day after the pogrom started I ran straight from school to Yuzovka to see what was going on there. There was still a lot of looting. I saw clock repair shops which had been broken into, and feathers were flying along the streets where the looters were ripping open mattresses and shaking the feathers out of the windows of Jewish homes.

Then a rumor started that there had been a decree that for three days you could do whatever you wanted to the Jews. For three days there was no check on the looting. After the three days were up, the police, who along with the Black Hundreds had taken advantage of the workers' primitive mentality to incite the pogrom in the first place, started to restore order. But nothing was done about all the looting and rampage. The powers who had decreed the pogrom kept their word: three days had been put at the disposal of the Black Hundreds, and all the pillage and murder went unpunished. I heard that many of the Jews who had been beaten were in the factory infirmary. I decided to go there and have a look with one of my friends, another little boy. We found a horrible scene. The corpses of Jews who had been beaten to death were lying in rows on the floor.

Khrushchev Remembers With an Introduction, Commentary and Notes by Edward Crankshaw, translated by Strobe Talbott. London, 1971, pp. 234–5.

150   Finland

Finland was acquired by the Russian Empire in 1809 but had retained a substantial degree of autonomy. The Imperial government became more concerned about the nationality question after the 1897 census had revealed that only 44.3 per cent of the population was Russian. In 1905 the Finns reasserted their autonomy by rescinding many of the Imperial government's measures tightening the links between Finland and Russia. Under Stolypin, the Russian government embarked on a policy of irrevocably subordinating Finland to the Imperial government in St Petersburg. These extracts are from a government bill in 1910.

. . .Russia possesses the rights of a sovereign power in relation to Finland, and because of this all questions which concern both Finland and other parts of the Empire should be decided according to Russian laws; local Finnish legislation can concern exclusively internal Finnish matters.

This self-evident and theoretically indisputable situation has long been obscured in Russo-Finnish relations by sharp fluctuations in legislative practice. For almost a century, laws on subjects of general imperial significance have been promulgated in Finland sometimes using the general Imperial procedure, and sometimes the local Finnish legislature, depending on chance circumstances. As a result of this, the supremacy of the former procedure over the latter has not been assured. Local Finnish legislation has often encroached on areas which should normally have been decided by general Imperial Russian laws, especially since the 1860s when the Finnish Diet became active. For example, the Diet has (a) implemented a monetary reform, destroying the former unified currency system in the Empire and Finland; (b) resolved (in 1878) the question of military service in Finland and created a body of special Finnish troops; (c) established a series of burdensome restrictions on Russians living in Finland in relation to the civil service, trade, industry and political and civil rights. . . .

The growth of Finnish separatism, which threatens not only the dignity, rights and interests of Russia, but also its very unity, has naturally evoked a response from the Russian side. A wave of Russian self-consciousness and national feeling has grown up, albeit slowly, against the bellicose separatism of the Finns. The organization and development of general Imperial legislation must be seen as one of the most important measures in the defence of the rights of Russia.

. . .the fundamental provisions of this bill . . . are:

1 Since Finland is an indivisible part of a united Russian empire it enjoys regional self-government only in respect of its internal affairs, the basis and extent of which are defined by the general legislation of the Empire.

2 The Fundamental Laws of the Empire carry as much force in Finland as in other parts of the state. . . .

3 The internal affairs of Finland are defined as those matters which do not concern other parts of the Empire . . . and it is only in these matters that Finland is governed by special rules on the basis of a separate legislature.

All other matters which concern Finland will henceforth, as at present, be decided through the general Imperial legislative procedure. Should the opinion of the Finnish Diet be asked on such matters, its views shall be no more than advisory.

4 For the greater benefit of Finland, and for better acquaintance with its needs, the State Duma and State Council will contain representatives of the population of Finland.

5 Laws promulgated by the general Imperial legislative procedure may abrogate or amend those laws promulgated by the separate Finnish procedure, but not vice-versa.

> *Obyasnitelnaya zapiska k proektu Predsedatelyu Soveta Ministrov o poryadke izdaniya kasayushchikhsya Finlyandii zakonov i postanovleniy obshchegosudarstvennogo znacheniya.* St Petersburg, 1911, pp. 11–12, 17–18.

151   The German Population of Russia, 1914

Although the German population was relatively small, it enjoyed an influence out of all proportion to its size. Many senior civil servants and high ranking military officers came from German, especially Baltic German, families.

German Russians.[1]	1,471,000
Volga region	600,000
Black Sea, Crimea/Ukraine	520,000
Asiatic Russia and Siberia	102,000
North Caucasus	100,000
Transcaucasia	21,000
St Petersburg	22,000
Town dwellers[2]	106,000
	1,471,000
Ethnic Germans.[3]	
Volhynia	200,000
Baltic provinces	165,000
Poland	500,000
Bessarabia	80,000
	945,000
Total German population	2,416,000

Notes
1 'German Russians' refers to the descendants of colonists and settlers brought to Russia by Catherine II and Alexander I.
2 Includes town dwellers and other Germans scattered in European Russia.
3 'Ethnic Germans' refers to population of German nationality living in territories annexed by the Russian Empire, but who were not related to the German Russians.

A. Giesinger, *From Catherine to Khrushchev: The Story of Russia's Germans*. Winnipeg, Man., 1974, *passim*.

152   The 1916 Uprising in Central Asia

There were about ten million Muslims in the Russian Empire, concentrated in Central Asia. Many of them had only come under Russian rule in the second half of the nineteenth century. They retained their cultural and religious cohesiveness: this was evident in the Muslim communities' reaction to the possible imposition of conscription in 1916. The Russian Army wished to recruit Muslims for support work in the rear not as front line troops.

Report of the deputy Military Procurator, V.E. Ignatovich, to A.N. Kuropatkin, commander of the Turkestan military district, on the nature of the uprising . . . 31 December 1916

. . .I examined the question of the disturbances which arose in connection with the implementation of the regulation of 25 June 1916 dealing with the call-up of the non-Russian population for reserve work for the army.

. . .The edict of 25 June was received in Tashkent on 9 July. Prior to this the regional governor-general had been instructed to prepare the local population for the measure. . . . Even before this, however, news about the impending conscription had percolated through to the local population, partly from rumours and partly from the press, which meant that the first information which the population got about the call-up was that it was to be universal for all males aged between nineteen and forty-three. News of such conscription, which would have immediately deprived the local population of its entire work-force, leaving only old men and women – both incapable of working, the first group because of their age and second because of the rules of the harem – caused serious unrest. At the same time absurd rumours about the call-up spread amongst the mass of the population. Most importantly, a significant section of the population did not believe that the conscription was only for reserve work and was convinced that their menfolk were going to be made into soldiers. . . . Becoming a soldier meant dying somewhere amongst unbelievers and this was contrary to the religious teachings of some groups, whilst in general the population believed that freedom from military service had been granted to them when the region was conquered. . . . In general it was believed that the local administrative officials had sold the population for large sums of money and it was only because of this that this new burden was being imposed. . . .

These local officials who, in the eyes of the mob, were guilty, were subjected to the most cruel and violent punishment, leaving them as shapeless corpses; their homes were destroyed, their belongings looted, and the local administrative offices were wrecked.

Report of the Governor-General of Turkestan, A.N. Kuropatkin, to D.S. Shuvaev, Minister of War, on the results of the conscription for reserve work, the popular uprising and its causes, and the punitive measures taken by the authorities, 4 January 1917

. . .on 16 July 1916 General Erofeev submitted an application for the entire Turkestan region to be declared to be under martial law, and this was done on the following day. After this announcement and the dispatch of troops throughout the area, the disturbances came to a halt everywhere.

. . .In putting down the unrest the following losses were sustained: . . . 3,256 Russians were killed or wounded and 53 native officials.

. . .the numbers of local inhabitants killed by their fellow-countrymen is not known as the local population buried its dead secretly and carried off the wounded with them.

> *Vostanie 1916-ogo goda v Sredney Azii i Kazakhstane.* Moscow, 1960, p. 68.

(There appears to be no published casualty figures for the Muslim community in the 1916 uprising, but it is estimated that between 1914 and 1918 the population of Turkestan dropped by 1.23 million. G. Wheeler, *The Modern History of Soviet Central Asia*. London, 1964, p. 94.)

Further reading

Bater, J.H., *St Petersburg: Industrialization and Change*, London, 1976.

Browder, R.P. and Kerensky, A.F., eds., *The Russian Provisional Government: Documents*, 3 vols., Stanford, 1961.

Crisp, O., *Studies in the Russian Economy before 1914*, London, 1976. 'Labour and Industrialisation in Russia', in P. Mathias and M.M. Postan, eds., *Cambridge Economic History of Europe*, vol. VII, pt. 2, Cambridge, 1978.

Edelman, R., *Gentry Politics on the Eve of the Russian Revolution*, New Brunswick, NJ, 1980.

Emmons, T. & Vucinich, W.S., eds., *The Zemstvo in Russia*, Cambridge, 1981.

Florinsky, M., *The End of the Russian Empire*, New Haven, Conn., 1931.

Galai, S., *The Liberation Movement in Russia 1900–1905*, Cambridge, 1973.

Golder, F.A., ed., *Documents of Russian History 1914–1917*, New York, 1927.

Haimson, L.H., ed., *The Politics of Rural Russia, 1905–1914*, Bloomington Ind. 1979.

Harcave, S., *First Blood: the Russian Revolution of 1905*, London, 1965.

Harding, N., *Lenin's Political Thought*, 2 vols., London, 1977 and 1981.

Hasegawa, T., *The February Revolution: Petrograd 1917*, Seattle, 1981.

Hosking, G.A., *The Russian Constitutional Experiment*, Cambridge, 1973.

Katkov, G., *Russia 1917*, London, 1967.

Katkov, G., *et al.*, eds., *Russia enters the Twentieth Century*, London, 1971.

Katkov, G., *The Kornilov Affair*, London, 1980.

Levin, A., *The Second Duma*, New Haven, Conn., 1940.

Levin, A., *The Third Duma*, Hamden, Conn., 1973.

Lieven. D., *Russia and the Origins of the First World War*, London, 1983.

Manning, R.T., *Gentry and Government*, Princeton, 1982.

Mehlinger, H.D. and Thompson, J.M., *Count Witte and the Tsarist Government in the 1905 Revolution*, Bloomington, Ind., 1972.

Pearson, R., *The Russian Moderates and the Crisis of Tsarism 1914–1917*, London, 1977.

Rabinowitch, A., *Prelude to Revolution*, Bloomington, Ind., 1968.

Rabinowitch, A., *The Bolsheviks Come to Power*, New York, 1976.

Read, C., *Religion, Revolution and the Russian Intelligentsia 1900–1912*, London, 1979.

Seton-Watson, G.H.N., *The Russian Empire, 1801–1917*, Oxford, 1967.

Shanin, T. *The Akward Class*, Oxford, 1972.

Stavrou, T.G., ed., *Russia under the Last Tsar*, Minneapolis Minn., 1969.

Stone, N., *The Eastern Front*, London, 1975.

Szeftel, M., *The Russian Constitution of 23 April 1906*, Brussels, 1976.

Troyat, H., *Daily Life in Russia under the Last Tsar*, London, 1961.

Ulam, A., *Lenin and the Bolsheviks*, London, 1966.

Wallace, D.M., *Russia*, London, 1912.

Weissman, N.B., *Reform in Tsarist Russia*, New Brunswick, NJ, 1981.

Yaney, G.L., *The Urge to Mobilize: Agrarian Reform in Russia 1861–1930*, Urbana, Ill., 1982.

Chronology

1905

3 Jan. Beginning of a strike in the Putilov Works, St Petersburg which quickly spreads

9 Jan. Bloody Sunday – a march on the Winter Palace by St Petersburg workers and their families, led by the priest Father Gapon, to deliver a petition to Tsar Nicholas II is broken up with considerable loss of life; a wave of protests follows and the situation becomes so serious that the Tsar eventually grants a Duma and other concessions

11 Jan. General D. F. Trepov is appointed governor general of St Petersburg; the office is a military and administrative one and had ceased to exist in 1880 but the exceptional circumstances led to its recreation; on 10 Nov. 1905 post again abolished

20 Jan. A. G. Bulygin succeeds Prince P. D. Svyatopolk-Mirsky, dismissed on 18 Jan., as Minister of the Interior

26 Jan. Lenin replies to August Bebel; Bebel had informed Lenin on 21 Jan. that the Executive Committee of the German SPD had decided to ask Lenin to appear before a tribunal, consisting of Bolsheviks and Mensheviks, so as to overcome the split in the RSDRP; Lenin states that only the III Party Congress can decide such matters

28 Jan. School strike and boycott begins in Russian Poland; it achieves the recognition of the use of Polish in education and administration

4 Feb. Lenin meets Father Gapon in Geneva; Grand Duke Sergei Aleksandrovich, uncle of the Tsar, governor general of Moscow since 1891, is murdered in the Kremlin by the social revolutionary I. P. Kalyaev

6–25 Feb. Russian forces suffer heavy defeat at Mukden

4 Mar. General N. P. Linevich replaces Kuropatkin as C in C of Russian troops in Far East

16 Mar. Finnish law on military service of 30 June 1901 revoked

12–27 Apr. III RSDRP Congress in Brussels and London, attended only by Bolsheviks; Mensheviks challenge its legality and arrange their own conference in Geneva; Lenin becomes the acknowledged leader of the Bolsheviks

17 Apr. Law on religious tolerance permits for the first time believers to leave the Orthodox Church (in effect recognizes the Old Believers) and join other churches or sects; decree affecting other confessions passed on 1 May

20–21 Apr. I Congress of the All-Russian Union of Railwaymen in Moscow; this union plays an important role in strike movement

23–26 Apr. Jewish pogrom in Zhitomir

1 May Polish and Lithuanian are again recognized as school languages in Western provinces of Russia; Poles may again buy land

8–9 May Founding and I Congress of Union of Unions in Moscow, a grouping of professional associations

12 May–22 Jul. Strike in textile centre Ivanovo-Voznesensk

13–15 May First soviet of workers deputies formed during strike in Ivanovo-Voznesensk

14 May. First issue of Bolshevik newspaper *Proletariy* appears in Geneva edited by Lenin. It appears until 12 Nov. (26 numbers).

14–15 May Japanese fleet under Admiral Togo destroys Russian navy commanded by Rear Admiral Z. P. Rozhdestvensky in the Tsushima Straits

6 June During a reception for a delegation of zemstvo deputies, led by Prince S. N. Trubetskoy, the Tsar announces his willingness to accept participation of elected representatives of people in government; Polish permitted in education and administration in Russian Poland

14–25 June Mutiny on the battleship Potemkin

16 June Decree improving position of Jews in Russia

22–23 June Jewish pogrom in Cherkassk

11 Jul. Tsar Nicholas II and Kaiser Wilhelm II meet on island of Björkö and agree on defensive alliance

27 Jul. Russo-Japanese peace negotiations begin in Portsmouth (New Hampshire); Russian delegation is headed by Witte

31 Jul. Founding congress of the first Russian peasant organization, the illegal All-Russian Peasant Union in Moscow; it demands nationalization of the land and a national assembly

25 Jul. Lenin's 'Two Tactics of Social Democracy in the Russian Revolution' is published in Geneva; in it Lenin develops Bolshevik tactics in the revolution of 1905–07; whereas the goal of the Mensheviks is to see the liberal bourgeoisie take power, Lenin proposes a 'democratic dictatorship of the proletariat and the peasantry'

6 Aug. Publication of draft decree of Bulygin on consultative Duma

23 Aug. Treaty of Portsmouth signed with aid of US President Roosevelt

24 Sep.–4 Oct. I Congress (illegal) of All-Russian Trades Unions in Moscow

7 Oct. Railwaymen's strike in Moscow leads to general political strike movement in Russia

12–18 Oct. Founding congress of Constitutional Democrats (Kadets) in St Petersburg; leaders are P. N. Milyukov and I. I. Petrunkevich

13 Oct. Election of St Petersburg soviet of workers' deputies; meets on 14 Oct.

15 Oct. General strike in Russian Poland; martial law declared

17 Oct. Tsar issues October Manifesto; Lenin prepares to return

18–25 Oct. Many Jewish pogroms in Kherson, Tauride, Poltava, Bessarabia and Chernigov provinces; 876 dead and many injured according to authorities

22 Oct. Finnish constitution re-established

8 Nov. Lenin arrives in St Petersburg

11-15 Nov. Uprising of sailors in Sebastopol led by Lieutenant P. P. Shmidt

16 Nov.-15 Dec. All-Russian strike of post and telegraph personnel; organizers arrested in Moscow on 21 Dec.

17 Nov. Union of Russian People founded; leaders include A. I. Dubrovin and V. M. Purishkevich; its militant wing is the Black Hundreds, involved in many pogroms

22 Nov. First meeting of Moscow soviet of workers deputies

26 Nov. Lenin takes part in a session of the St Petersburg soviet

3 Dec. St Petersburg soviet dissolved and members arrested

4 Dec. Union of 17 October (Octobrists) founded; liberal conservative party led by A. I. Guchkov and others

9-20 Dec. Armed uprising in Moscow; railwaymen do not succeed in preventing troop reinforcements from St Petersburg arriving by rail; army stays loyal

11 Dec. Franchise extended to workers, artisans and lower middle classes in towns

12-17 Dec. I Conference of Bolsheviks in Tammerfors, Finland; Bolsheviks decide to boycott elections to first Duma

31 Dec. I Congress of Social Revolutionary Party (PSR or SRs)

1906

5-11 Jan. II Kadet Congress accepts monarchy, opposes seizures of land by peasants and condemns revolutionary violence

13-23 Jan. II Muslim Congress in St Petersburg

24 Jan.-8 Feb. II (illegal) All-Russian Trades Union Congress in St Petersburg

11 Feb. Lenin addresses St Petersburg RSDRP city conference – Bolsheviks in majority – and his motion on boycott of Duma passed

23 Feb. Statutes of State Council in effect; becomes second legislative chamber

4 Mar. Temporary law on association legalizes political groupings and trade unions

8 Mar. Power of Duma to regulate budget considerably weakened

25 Mar. Russia participates in international Morocco conference; co-signatory of Algeciras act which resolves crisis

10-25 Apr. IV (Unification) Congress of RSDRP in Stockholm; unification only formal as Mensheviks dominate congress; Lenin remains leader of Bolsheviks

4 Apr. Kokovtsov, Finance Minister, secures a French loan worth 2,250 million francs

19 Apr. German, Estonian and Latvian permitted as languages of instruction in schools in Baltic provinces

23 Apr. Fundamental Laws promulgated

27 Apr–8 Jul. First Duma in session

13 May Motion of no confidence in Goremykin government by Duma; it demands government which enjoys its confidence

20 June Finnish parliament passes new Finnish constitution; receives royal assent on 7 July 1906

10 Jul. Vyborg Appeal signed by about 200 Duma deputies (Trudoviki, social democrats, Kadets); initiators tried 12–18 December 1907 and sentenced to three months imprisonment

17–20 Jul. Mutiny and armed uprising in Sveaborg, Kronstadt and Reval

12 Aug. Attempt to assassinate Stolypin

19 Aug. Field courts martial introduced

3–7 Nov. II RSDRP conference (also called I All-Russian conference) in Tammerfors; Lenin again in minority; he proposes local organization should decide on Duma boycott

1907

20 Feb.–2 June Second Duma in session

16–20 Apr. Conference of national (people's) socialist parties of Russia and Finland; no agreement on socialist nationality programme

30 Apr.–19 May V RSDRP Congress in London; Bolsheviks in majority; no reconciliation with Mensheviks

2–3 June Arrest of social democratic Duma deputies and leaders of SR party; accused of conspiracy against Tsar; electoral law changed

17 Jul. Russia and Japan agree on interest spheres; Japan receives Korea and southern Manchuria, Russia northern Manchuria and Outer Mongolia

21–23 Jul. III RSDRP conference in Kotka, Finland; Bolsheviks to take part in Duma elections but no pact with Kadets

18 Aug. Anglo-Russian agreement signed in St Petersburg on Persia, Afghanistan and Tibet; northern Persia Russian zone of influence, central Persia joint zone and southern Persia Russian zone; Afghanistan British zone, neither to intervene in Tibetan internal affairs

16 Oct. Secret German-Russian agreement on Baltic Sea signed in St Petersburg; status quo confirmed

1 Nov.–9 June 1912 Third Duma in session

1908

Feb.–Oct. Lenin works on *Materialism and Empirio-Criticism*, a philosophical attack on A. A. Bogdanov, God-builders and other revisionists; socialism will not come through reform but through sudden change

10 Apr. Russia, Denmark, Germany and Sweden sign agreement on Baltic Sea to maintain status quo

27–28 May Nicholas II meets Edward VII in Reval

3 June Trans-Siberian railway to receive second track

1 Sep. University of Warsaw reopens; closed since 1905

2 Sep. Izvolsky, Foreign Minister meets Count von Aehrenthal, Foreign

Minister of Austria-Hungary in Buchlau (Moravia) to discuss possible agreement on Balkans

10–16 Dec. I All-Russian Women's Congress in St Petersburg

1909

21 Jan. Duma passes law on inviolability of person

March Vekhi (Landmarks) published; contributions by Gershenzon, S. N. Bulgakov, P. B. Struve, S. L. Frank and others; criticism of views on revolution of Russian intelligentsia

10 Mar. German ultimatum forces Russian government to accept annexation of Bosnia and Herzegovina by Austria-Hungary

25 Apr. With British agreement Russian troops occupy Tabris and put down revolt against Persian Shah

11 Oct. Nicholas II meets Victor Emanuel III in Racconigi; Italy agrees to opening of Straits to Russian warships

28 Dec. I All-Russian Congress to combat alcoholism in St Petersburg

1910

5 Mar. Russia and Austria-Hungary agree on maintenance of status quo in Balkans

29 May Duma passes legislation to introduce zemstva in six western provinces

14 June Tsar signs Duma agrarian law; concludes Stolypin's land reform

17 June Law ends Finnish autonomy; almost all important decisions on Finland now fall within competence of Russian Council of State

21 June Second Russo-Japanese agreement on spheres of influences; Korea in Japanese zone and Outer Mongolia in Russian confirmed

16 Aug. I All-Russian Zemstvo Congress on education; demand for obligatory schooling

10 Sep. Anglo-Russian agreement on Tibet

14 Sep. Izvolsky becomes Russian ambassador to Paris

7 Nov. Leo Tolstoy dies at Astapovo, north of Lipetsk

1911

11 Jan. University autonomy restricted – public and private meetings in universities forbidden; senate of Moscow University resigns on 28 Jan. in protest and many professors support action on 4 Feb.

24 Jan. Duma passes bill on primary education; 100 million ruble fund for primary schools agreed

26–29 Jan. Student strike during whole of semester called in St Petersburg and Moscow Universities

5–16 Feb. L. A. Kasso, Minister of Education, reacts by sending striking students down

11 Mar. Stolypin forces Tsar – by threatening to resign – to put law on introduction of zemstva in six western provinces into effect; Council of State had rejected it; Duma and Council of State suspended for three days to achieve this

6 Aug. German-Russian agreement signed in St Petersburg on railway building; Russia has exclusive rights in north Persia; Tehran to be joined to
Baghdad railway

1 Sep. Stolypin badly wounded in assassination attempt; dies 5 Sep.

5 Nov. Conflict between US and Russia over Jewish question leads to US
terminating Russo-American trade agreement (due to expire 5 Nov. 1912)

29 Nov. Russian ultimatum to Persia leads to American financier Morgan
Shuster, in Tehran since 13 May, being expelled

14 Dec. Intervention of Russian troops in Outer Mongolia after fall of Manchu
dynasty ensures autonomy for Outer Mongolia within Chinese empire

1912

5–17 Jan. Prague conference of RSDRP leads to final split between
Mensheviks and Bolsheviks on Lenin's initiative; Bolsheviks claim to be
'true' RSDRP; Stalin elected member of new Central Committee in
absentia

20 Jan. Russians obtain same rights as Finns in Finland

4 Apr. Lena gold mine massacre; over 200 strikers killed by authorities

22 Apr. Pravda appears legally in St Petersburg as Bolshevik newspaper; 636
numbers published by Jul. 1914 – from Jul. 1913 under various names

9 June Law introducing zemstva in Astrakhan, Orenburg and Stavropol provinces

15 June Reform of legal system in countryside; JP courts (abolished 12 Jul. 1889)
reintroduced

19 June Duma passes Admiralty's plan for naval building programme covering
years 1912–16 and involving expenditure of 430 million rubles

23 June Law on sickness and accident insurance for workers

25 June Russo-Japanese agreement on spheres of influence after Chinese revolution of 1911 and the autonomy of Outer Mongolia

3 Jul. Secret Franco-Russian naval agreement concluded in Paris which
foresees joint operations in all eventualities

21 Oct. Russo-Mongolian agreement signed in Ulan Bator guaranteeing autonomy of Outer Mongolia but in reality turning it into a Russian protectorate

15 Nov.–25 Feb. 1917 Fourth Duma in session

1913

Jan. Stalin writes his pamphlet *Marxism and the National Question* in Vienna

18 Mar. Conference on solving the Balkan question opens in St
Petersburg – takes place after first Balkan war

23 Oct. Sino-Russian declaration on autonomy of Outer Mongolia under Chinese suzerainty

28 Oct. Mendel Beilis acquitted by Kiev court of ritual Jewish murder after two
and a half years under arrest; so ends Beilis affair

1914

26 Jan. Russo-Turkish agreement on reforms in Turkish Armenia concluded in Istanbul

12 Mar. Law on separation of spouses

June-July Strikes in Baku and St Petersburg

12 Jul. Russia decides to support Serbia

15 Jul. Austria-Hungary declares war on Serbia after murder of Crown Prince Ferdinand and his wife in Sarajevo

16 Jul. Russia partially mobilizes

18 Jul. General mobilization by Russia; German ultimatum demands demobilization within 12 hours

19 Jul. Germany declares war on Russia; Grand Duke Nikolai Nikolaevich named C in C Russian troops

24 Jul. Austria-Hungary declares war on Russia

4 Aug. General von Rennenkampf, commander of the Vilna military district with 1 Russian army crosses the border into East Prussia and begins hostilities

5 Aug.-8 Sep. On the Galician front Russian troops of the 3, 4, 5 and 8 armies drive Austro-Hungarian troops out of east Galicia and the Bukovina

7 Aug. After the battle of Gumbinnen German troops withdraw to Vistula

11 Aug. France, Great Britain and Russia agree not to conclude separate peace with Germany and her allies; Japan also agrees on 27 Aug.

13-17 Aug. Battle of Tannenberg; Russian 2 army defeated by German 8 army under von Hindenburg

18 Aug. St Petersburg renamed Petrograd

21 Aug. Russian troops take Lvov

24 Aug.-2 Sep. Battle of Masurian lakes; 1 Russian army forced out of East Prussia

26 Aug. Russian troops occupy east Galicia

16 Oct. Without formal declaration of war Turkish fleet attacks Russian fleet and ports on Black Sea

20 Oct. Russia declares war on Turkey

5 Nov. Bolshevik deputies in fourth Duma arrested in Petrograd, tried on 10-13 Feb. 1915 and banished to Siberia

1915

25 Jan.-13 Feb. In another battle of Masurian lakes, battered 10 Russian army forced to evacuate East Prussia completely

3 Feb. Property of citizens of states at war with Russia confiscated

19 Feb. Sazonov, Foreign Minister, sends official note to British and French ambassadors claiming the Straits and Istanbul for Russia; accepted by Great Britain 27 Feb. and France 28 Mar.

9 Mar. Fortress of Przemysl falls to Russian troops; Austro-Hungarians besieged since 26 Oct. 1914

14-26 Apr. Lithuania and Courland fall to German troops

19 Apr. Germans under von Mackensen break through 3 Russian army in

Galicia and force Russians to retreat on wide front

9 June Russian troops forced to abandon Lvov

July I Congress of War Industries Committee; over 200 local committees founded

9 Aug. Progressive Bloc formed in Fourth Duma

17 Aug. Tsar approves creation of four special commissions with special powers on defence, fuel, food and transport

23 Aug. Nicholas II replaces Grand Duke Nikolai Nikolaevich as Supreme C in C

23–26 Aug. First international socialist conference at Zimmerwald with Lenin and Zinoviev representing Bolsheviks; Lenin's proposal to transform imperialist war into civil war not accepted

2–7 Oct. Bulgaria joins war on German side and declares war on Great Britain, Russia, France and Italy

28 Dec.–18 Feb. 1916 Russian army under Yudenich launches successful offensive against Turkish troops in Caucasus; Turks withdraw 4 Jan. 1916; Russians take fortress of Erzerum 3 Feb.

1916

20 Jan. Boris Sturmer replaces Goremykin as Chairman of Council of Ministers

11–17 Apr. Second international socialist conference at Kienthal; Lenin, Zinoviev and Ines Armand represent Bolsheviks but Lenin's views fail to convince majority

22 May–31 Jul. Brusilov offensive on Russian south-west front breaks through German-Austrian front in Volhynia and the Bukovina; Romania joins Allied side and declares war on Central Powers; Russians suffer considerable losses which gradually demoralize army; second Brusilov offensive Sep.–Oct. and third Brusilov offensive Oct.–Dec. fail

17 Oct. Political strikes in Petrograd

23 Oct. Central Powers create Kingdom of Poland

10 Nov. Sturmer dismissed as Chairman of Council of Ministers; successor is A. F. Trepov

17 Dec. Rasputin murdered by Prince F. F. Yusupov

27 Dec. Trepov goes and Prince N. D. Golytsin becomes last Chairman of Council of Ministers under monarchy

1917

31 Jan. Strikes and unrest among industrial workers in Petrograd

5 Feb. Petrograd military district separated from northern front and placed under command of General Khabalov who is to maintain order

10 Feb. Last report of Duma president to Tsar; points out need for a new government enjoying public confidence

18 Feb. Beginning of strike of workers of Putilov works in Petrograd

22 Feb. First lock-outs in Petrograd

23 Feb. International Women's Day demonstration; striking Putilov workers join in

25 Feb. Strike movement spreads to whole of Petrograd; troops obey orders and fire on demonstrators

26 Feb. Duma members reject Tsar's decree to dissolve Duma

26–27 Feb. Troops change sides and guarantee success of February Revolution

27 Feb. Provisional Duma committee formed under chairmanship of Rodzyanko, president of Duma; first session of Petrograd soviet of workers deputies in Tauride palace

28 Feb. Provisional Duma committee sets up military commission to supervise troops; *Izvestiya*, organ of Petrograd soviet, appears; elections to Moscow soviet

1 Mar. British and French ambassadors in Petrograd recognize de facto provisional Duma committee; Order no 1 drawn up by Petrograd soviet

2 Mar. Provisional Duma committee announces formation of Provisional Government with Prince G. E. Lvov as Prime Minister; Nicholas II abdicates in favour of his son, then his brother Mikhail

3 Mar. Provisional Government announces programme – civil rights to be guaranteed and Constituent Assembly to be called

8 Mar. Nicholas II and family arrested and interned in Tsarskoe Selo

9 Mar. US first government to recognize new Russian government; followed by France, Great Britain and Italy on 11 Mar.

12 Mar. Death penalty abolished by Provisional Government; Stalin, Kamenev and other Bolsheviks return to Petrograd

25 Mar. Grain monopoly introduced by government

3 Apr. Lenin returns to Petrograd and reads his 'April Theses' to Petrograd soviet 4 Apr.

20 Apr. Workers and soldiers demonstrate in Petrograd against Milyukov note of 18 Apr. on continuation of war and claim for indemnities and annexations; Milyukov resigns and brings down government

25 May–4 June During III PSR Congress, group known as Left SRs form; they support Bolsheviks

3–24 June I All-Russian Congress of soviets of workers and soldiers deputies in Petrograd; dominated by Mensheviks and SRs

18 June Kerensky offensive begins on south-west front under Brusilov; failure leads to demonstrations in Petrograd in which Bolshevik slogans in majority for first time

2 Jul. Trotsky's Mezhraiontsy, founded in Nov. 1913, as mediators between Bolsheviks and Mensheviks, merges with Bolsheviks

19 Jul. Brusilov replaced by Kornilov as Supreme C in C

25–30 Aug. Kornilov Affair; Kerensky declares Kornilov rebel

10 Oct. Bolsheviks in majority in Petrograd and Moscow soviets; decide on armed uprising; Zinoviev and Kamenev oppose this in *Novaya Zhizn* on 11 Oct.

25 Oct. October Revolution; Bolsheviks take power